AF446321

R. Gupta's®

Banking
AWARENESS

BANKING APTITUDE TEST

> *Useful for*
> IBPS (CWE)–PO/MT, SBI & Associate Banks–PO/Clerk,
> Regional Rural Banks, Specialist Officer,
> Jammu & Kashmir Bank etc.

by
RPH Editorial Board

RAMESH PUBLISHING HOUSE, New Delhi

Published by:

O.P. Gupta *for* Ramesh Publishing House

Admin. Office:

12-H, New Daryaganj Road, Opp. Officers' Mess,
New Delhi-110002 ① 23261567, 23275224, 23275124

E-mail: info@rameshpublishinghouse.com
Website: www.rameshpublishinghouse.com

Showroom:

• Balaji Market, Nai Sarak, Delhi-6 ① 23253720, 23282525
• 4457, Nai Sarak, Delhi-6, ① 23918938

Book Code: R-1465

11th Edition: 1703

ISBN: 978-93-5012-770-4

CONTENTS

✭✭✭✭✭✭

Banking General Awareness

CHAPTER 1

Bank Terminology

AAA : AAA is a term or a grade that is used to rate a particular bond. It is the highest rated bond that gives maximum returns at the time of maturity. Usually the grade AAA is given to the best debt obligation or a security, by a credit rating agency.

ABA Routing Number : A series of numbers located at the bottom of an account holder's checks or deposit slips. These number identify a particular address for a specific banking institution, - a routing address, which the RBF uses when funds transactions move within the banking system.

ABA Transit Number : The ABA transit number is assigned by the American Bankers Association. It is a numeric coding that indicates and facilitates the amount of check payments, balances and dues that are to be cleared among different banks at the clearing house.

ABO : ABO is an abbreviation for the term 'Accumulated Benefit Obligation'. It is basically the measure of the liability of the pension plan of an organization and is calculated when the pension plan is to be terminated.

Absorption : Absorption is a term related to real estate, banking and finance fields. The word 'absorption' means the process of renting a real estate property that is newly built or is recently renovated.

Absorption Time : The term 'absorption time' is used to define the time period that is required to complete the process of absorption.

Abstract of title : The 'abstract of title' is a written report that defines, records and identifies the history and ownerships of a particular asset, usually a real estate.

Accelerated Depreciation : A method of depreciation of fixed assets, where the early deductions are greater in monetary terms and later ones are smaller.

Acceleration : Acceleration is the process, where the lender demands a full and final payment of the debt or loan, before the allotted time period for repayment. A clause in the document of the debt usually empowers the lender to accelerate the time period.

Acceleration Clause : A clause in the debt document that empowers the lender to accelerate the payment, (i.e. or that is) the lender can demand the full amount of loan before the date of maturity.

Acceptance : Acceptance which is also known as the banker's acceptance is a signed instrument of acknowledgment that indicates the approval and acceptance of all terms and conditions of any agreement on behalf of the banker. It is a very wide term that is used in context with financial agreements and contracts.

Accepting House : An accepting house is a banking or finance organization that specializes in the service of acceptance and guarantee of bills of exchange. This organization specializes in two prominent functions, that is facilitating the different negotiable instruments and merchant banking.

Accepting Party: The party (either an individual or a group of individuals or organizations) that accept the terms and conditions of a proposed agreement or contract put forth by another party.

Accommodation Maker : A person who signs the note of application and renders his credit history during the process of application of a loan is called accommodation maker. The accommodation maker, usually receives no direct financial benefit from the loan. The term is also used in the concept of 'accommodation bills', when two or more people help each other by rendering liquidity of a negotiable instrument.

Account : An account is a record of all financial transactions that are related to an asset, individual, transaction or any organization. It is a major term in the field of accountancy and is conventionally denoted by the A/c. It can also be defined as a transaction between a buyer and a seller about payments and dues which develop creditor-debtor relations.

Account Aggregation : An online facility that is made available by some banks or financial organizations, in which all the transactions related to the bank account, credit facilities, debts and investments can be handled and operated with the help of a single interface or account. Account aggregation is a form of Internet banking, provided for ease of transaction.

Account Analysis : The term 'account analysis' is used in basically two contexts. First, it is used to define the study and conclusion of a single account. Second, it is also a procedure, where the profitability of a single demand account or many demand accounts is projected and analyzed.

Account Control Agreement : An account control agreement is an agreement that perfects the interests of the creditor in a securities account.

Account Debtor : An account debtor is a person or an organization that is in debt and is obliged to pay either on an account or chattel paper or contract right. Account debtors are, sometimes, simply referred to as debtors.

Account Reconciliation : Account reconciliation is a process with the help of which the account balance can be easily verified. Account reconciliation is usually done at the end of a week, month, financial year or at the end of any financial period. It is usually done with the help of receipts, ATM notes, bank statements etc.

Account Reconciliation Services : Account reconciliation services are basically services that specialize in the compilation of reconciliation documents and statements. Reconciliation services cater to the demands of individuals and huge organizations that have a large number of transactions taking place everyday.

Account Value : An account value is the total value of any account, applicable when a person has many accounts and transactions in the same bank or financial institution. The account value is a total value that is expressed in monetary terms.

Accreting Swap : Accreting swap is a swap of interest which has an increasing notional amount.

Accretion : Accretion, is a process, where increments and periodic increases are made in the book value or the balance sheet value of an asset. In the field of banking and finance, accretion is the process where the price of a bond that has been bought at a discount is changed to the par value of the bond. It is also defined as a change in the price of a bond that has been bought at a discount to the par value of the bond.

Accretion Bond : An accretion bond is basically a bond that has been purchased at a discount and whose book value is incremented to the par value or the face value.

Accrual Basis : Accrual is the process of accumulation of interest or money. Accrual basis, which is also known as accrual convention, is the method by which, investors, economists and businessmen count the number of days in a month or a year(s). Of the most common examples of accrual basis is the 30/360 convention, wherein the accrual basis is calculated by assuming that every month has 30 days. Accrual basis is often used as the common parameter for the calculation of interests and returns.

Accrual Bond : An accrual bond is also known as range bond. An accrual bond is a bond that has a tendency to pay the investors, an above the market rate. Sometimes, an accrual rate is also defined as a security that does not have a period payment for the rate of interest. The interest is accrued and then added later on at the time of maturity.

Accrual Convention : It is the method of calculating the time period on a specific investment by the investors. Accrual convention is many a times calculated with the help of different interest calculation mechanisms. Accrual convention is also known as accrual basis.

Accrued Interest : Accrued Interest is the interest, accumulated on an investment but is not yet paid. Often, accrued interest is also termed as interest receivable. Some banking books prefer to call it as the interest that is earned, but not yet paid.

Accrued Interest : Interest earned but not yet received.

Accumulated Depreciation : Accumulated depreciation is the total all the periodic reductions from the book value of fixed assets. It is also termed as an allowance for depreciation.

Accumulator : Accumulator is also known as capital appreciation bond. The accumulator is a type of security that is related to capital and is issued on face value, but the interest is not paid to the investor on the basis of the time period. Instead, the total amount of accrued interest is paid along with the face value upon the maturity of the security.

ACH : ACH is the abbreviation of the banking term automated clearing house. The automated clearing house operates on a national level and helps banks and financial institutions in the clearance of balances and negotiable instruments that are used at a personalized as well as a mercantile modes of transactions.

Acquisition : Purchase of controlling interest in a firm, generally through tender offer for the target shares.

Active Tranche : Active tranche basically stands for REMIC or Real Estate Mortgage Investment Conduit. The REMIC tranche is basically a bond that is backed up by a large set of mortgages. The principal and interest that are paid by the borrowers, are transferred to the people who hold tranche (tranche refers to a portion or money) in REMIC.

Actual Delay Days : Actual delay days are also simply known as 'delay days'. The actual delay days are the actual days of the lag times. The lag time is the time period that starts after the expiry of the last date of repayment.

Actuary : Insurance company official, responsible for estimating future claims and disbursement and for calculating necessary fund and premium levels.

Adjustable Rate Mortgage (ARM) : Adjustable rate mortgage or ARM is basically a type of loan, where the rate of interest is calculated on the basis of the previously selected index rate. Due to this, the rate of interest that is charged differs periodically, usually in every month. Hence, the rate of interest and the total interest remain variable through out the term/time period.

Administered Rates : Administered rates are the rates of interest which can be changed contractually by lender. In some cases, these rates can also be changed by the depositor and also the payee. The laws and provisions that monitor the concept of administered rates differ in each jurisdiction.

ADS : Authorized Dealers

Advising Bank : A Bank usually located in the country of residence of an Exporter, used by an Importer's bank to authenticate a Letter of Credit before it is passed on to the Exporter.

AEZs : Agricultural Export Zones

Affidavit : A written statement, sworn to be true by the person signing it, before someone authorized by court of law.

Agent Bank : A participating bank in a syndicated loan that handles all the operations and deals with the borrower on behalf of the members of the syndicate.

AIDB : All India Development Bank

AIFI : All India Financial Institution

ALCO : Asset-Liability Management Committee

ALM : Asset/ liability management involves a set of techniques to create value and manage risks in a bank.

AMC : Asset Management Committee

American Depository Receipt (ADR) : A certificate registered in the holder's name or as a bearer security giving title to a specified number of shares in a non-US-based company deposited in a bank outside the USA. These certificates are traded on US stock exchanges.

American option : An option that can be exercised on or any time before the date of expiry.

Amortization : Process of full payment of debt in installments of principal and earned interest over a definite time.

Amortizing Swap : Amortizing swap is a swap in the rate of interest that has a declining notional principal.

Amount at risk : Balance of the sum payable not covered by reserves, potentially falling on the net worth (net assets) of the company.

Annuity : Fixed amount of cash to be received every year for a specified period of time.

Anticipated Income Doctrine of Liquidity : The anticipated income doctrine of liquidity is basically an explanation of bank liquidity development in which the net cash flow of the borrowers is considered as the source of loan repayment instead of usual subsequent new borrowings.

APEDA : Agricultural and Processed Food Products Exports Development Authority.

Appraisal : An appraisal is basically a statement, document or an estimated rise or drastic climb in the price of a particular real estate. The term 'appraisal' is also used in connection to raising the book value of a real estate.

Arbitrage : Simultaneous purchase and sale of identical or equivalent financial instruments or commodity futures so as to benefit from difference in their price relationship.

Arbitrageur : An arbitrageur is an independent and individual broker who deals in arbitrage.

ARF : Automatic Refinance Facility

ASB : Accounting Standards Board

Ascending Rate Bond : Security with which has a coupon rate that increases in previously defined increments at scheduled intervals, is termed as an ascending rate bond.

As-extracted Collateral : As extracted collateral are extracted or non-extracted minerals created by a debtor having an interest in minerals, and are subject to security interest, either before or after extraction. In short, mined or non-mined minerals can also be used as collaterals.

Asset Backed Security (ABS) : A security that is backed with the help of some kind of valuable assets, is known as an asset backed security. Sometimes, ABS is also referred to as the monthly rate of repayment of a secured loan.

Asset/Liability Risk : A risk that current obligations/ liabilities cannot be met with current assets. A fundamental risk in all organizations, which should manage the risk and maintain liquidity or become insolvent.

Assets : Things that one owns which have value in financial terms.

Assignee : Assignee is an individual or an organization or party to whom an assignment is made and commitment taken.

Assignment : In the field of banking and finance, an assignment is the transfer of any contractual agreement between two or more parties. The party that assigns the contract is the assignor and the party who receives the assignment is the assignee.

Assumable : Assumable is a very different type of mortgage loan application, where the new buyers of a real estate that has already been pledged as collateral, assumes the liability of a loan and also the ownership of the real estate.

Audit Risk : The risk of giving an incorrect audit opinion.

Automated Banking Machines (ABMs) : Terminals that allow bank customers to perform many everyday banking tasks, e.g., deposits, withdrawals, bill payments and transfers between accounts.

Automated Clearing House (ACH) : An automatic clearing house is a nation wide electronic clearing house that monitors and administers the process of check and fund clearance between banks. The ACH is an electronic system and thus minimizes the human work in the process of clearance. It distributes credit and debit balances automatically.

Automated Teller Machines (ATMs) : A computerized machine used for banking transactions, e.g. depositing or withdrawing money, making balance/ transaction inquiries and transfers; operated through magnetic plastic cards with the held of personal identification numbers (PINs).

Automatic Stay : The automatic stay is an injunction that automatically becomes effective, after any person or organization files for bankruptcy. The automatic stay basically precludes the creditors from taking the debtor or the property of the debtor.

Available Balance : The portion of a customer's account balance having no restrictions from the bank and available for immediate withdrawals.

Average life : Weighted average of the maturities of various loans or bonds after taking into account agreed amortization's.

Back-end value : Amount paid to the remaining shareholders in the second stage of a two-tier or partial tender offer.

Balance of Payment : Statement showing the country's trade and financial transactions (all economic transactions), in terms of net outstanding receivable or payable from other countries, with the rest of the world for a period of time.

Balance Sheet : Statement of assets and liabilities of a company at any particular time. The assets on a balance sheet will always equal the liabilities plus the owner's equity.

Balance Transfer : A balance transfer is the repayment of a credit debt with the help of another source of credit. In some cases, balance transfer also refers to transfer of funds from one account to another.

Balloon Payment : The final lump-sum payment that is made at the maturity date of a loan. A large payment that may be charged at the end of a loan or lease.

Bancassurance : It is the term used to describe the partnership or relationship between a bank and an insurance company whereby the insurance company uses the bank sales channel in order to sell insurance products.

Bank : A bank is an establishment that helps individuals and organizations, in the issuing, lending, borrowing and safeguarding functions of money.

Bank Account : A bank account is an account held by a person with a bank, with the help of which the account holder can deposit, safeguard his money, earn interest and also make check payments.

Bank Credit : Includes Term Loans, Cash Credit, Overdrafts, Bills purchased & discounted, Bank Guarantees, Letters of Guarantee, Letters of credit.

Bank Debits : The sum of the value of all cheques and other instruments charged against the deposited funds of a bank's customer.

Bank Debt : A bank debt is basically any debt that is owed to a bank, by any kind of consumer, organization or corporation. The debt may be anything from a bank loan to a credit card debt or an overdraft that has been used.

Bank Rate : Interest rate paid by major banks if they borrow from RBI, the Central Bank of the country. The Bank Rate influences the rates of interest major banks/ financial institutions charge and pay their customers.

Bank Statement : A periodic record of a customer's account that is issued at regular intervals, showing all transactions recorded for the period in question.

Banker's Acceptance : Negotiable time drafts, or bills of exchange, that have been accepted by a bank which, by accepting, assumes the obligation to pay the holder of the draft the face value of the instrument on the specified maturity date. Bankers' Acceptances are generally used to finance export, import, shipment, or storage of goods.

Banking Ombudsmen Scheme : The Banking Ombudsman Scheme enables an expeditious and inexpensive forum to bank customers for resolution of complaints relating to certain services rendered by banks. The Banking Ombudsman is a senior official appointed by the Reserve Bank of India to redress customer complaints against deficiency in certain banking services. The Banking Ombudsman Scheme was first introduced in India in 1995, and was revised in 2002. The current scheme became operative from the 1 January 2006, and replaced and superseded the banking Ombudsman Scheme 2002.

Bankruptcy : A condition in which a firm (or individual) is unable to meet its (his) obligations and, hence, its (his) assets are surrendered to a court for administration.

Basis Point : One-hundredth of one percentage point (i.e. 0.01%), normally used for indicating spreads or cost of finance.

Bear : Someone who believes the market will decline.

Bear Markets : Unfavorable markets associated with falling prices and investor pessimism.

Bearer bond : A bond that does not have the owner's name registered on the books of the issuer. Interest and principal, when due, are payable to the holder.

Bid and Asked : Often referred to as a quotation or quote. The bid is the highest price anyone wants to pay for a security at a given time, the asked is the lowest price anyone will take at the same time.

Bid/Bond Guarantee : A guarantee issued by a bank on behalf of a seller to a buyer to support the sellers' bid or tender for a contract. If the sellers' bid is accepted, the buyer can claim compensation under the guarantee.

Bid-ask Spread : The difference between a dealer's bid and ask price.

BIFR : Board for Industrial and Financial Reconstruction.

Bill Discounting : Receiving payment on a bill of exchange prior to the bill's maturity by surrendering the bill for the face value less applicable interest for the time remaining up to maturity.

Bill of Exchange : An order written by the seller of goods instructing the purchaser to pay the seller (or bearer of the bill) a specified amount on a specified future date.

Bill of Lading : A document which represents ownership of goods in transit.

Billing Cycle : A billing cycle is a time period that covers the credit statement, that usually lasts for 25 days.

Billing Statement : A billing statement is a summary of all transactions, payments, purchases, finance charges and fees, that take place through a credit account during a billing cycle.

Biometric : Refers to a method of identifying the holder of a device by measuring a unique physical characteristic of the holder, eg by fingerprint matching, voice recognition or retinal scan.

Blue Chips : Shares in leading quoted companies that can be easily bought and sold without influencing their price (liquidity) and are regarded as low-risk investments.

Bond : A bond is a certificate that represents an interest bearing debt, where the issuer is required to pay a sum of money periodically till the maturity, and then receive back the accumulated amount.

Book Value : The cost price of an asset less accumulated depreciation.

Book-entry system : an accounting system that permits the transfer of claims (eg electronic transfer of securities) without the physical movement of paper documents or certificates.

Bought financing : Short-term financing arranged by a bank for offering continuing source of funds pending receipt of loan/bond issue proceeds.

Bounced Check : A bounced check is nothing but an ordinary bank check that any bank can refuse to encash or pay because of the fact that there are no sufficient finances in the bank account of the originator or drawer of the check.

BR Act : Banking Regulation Act.

Brand name capital : A firm's reputation; the result of non-salvageable investment which provides customers with an implicit guarantee of product quality for which they are willing to pay a premium.

Breach : A violation of a loan covenant or promise.

Break-even point : Refers to the price at which a transaction produces neither a gain nor a loss.

Bridge Financing : Also know as gap financing, bridge financing is a loan where the time and cash flow between a short term loan and a long term loan is filled up. Bridge financing begins at the end of the time period of the first loan and ends with the start of the time period of the second loan, thereby bridging the gap between two loans. It is also known as gap financing.

Bridge Loan : Temporary finance provided to a project until long-term arrangements are made. The bridge loan also known as a swing loan, is basically a real estate loan or a home loan, where the current residence/real estate is pledged by the borrower as a collateral in order to purchase a new residence.

BSE : Bombay Stock Exchange

Bull : One who expects prices to rise.

Bull Markets : Favorable markets associated with rising prices and investor optimism.

Bullet redemption : Repayment of a debt in one lump sum at the end of the maturity period. A common practice in Euro markets in respect of bond issues.

Bundling : Provision of more than one product or service to a customer at an inclusive price e.g. 'free' life insurance with a loan.

Bust-up takeover : An acquisition followed by divestment of some or all of the operating units of the acquired firm which are presumably worth more in pieces than as a going concern.

Buy-back : A public company, which buys its own shares, by tender offer, in open market, or in a negotiated buy-back from a large block holder.

Buy-in : A purchase of securities in the open market by the lender, where the borrower is not able to deliver the securities to the lender in accordance with the terms of the transaction (eg on the settlement date). All costs are borne by the borrower in this case.

Call Date : Date on which a bond may be redeemed before maturity at an option of the issuer.

Call Money : Loaned funds that are repayable upon the request of either party.

Call Option: The right to buy the underlying securities at a specified exercise price on or before a specified expiration date.

Call Provision : A feature of a bond that entitles the issuer to retire the bond before maturity

Callable : A bond issue, all or part of which may be redeemed by the issuing corporation under specified conditions before maturity. The term also applies to preferred shares that may be redeemed by the issuing corporation.

Callable Bonds : Bonds that give the issuer the right to redeem the bonds before their stated maturity.

Cap : A ceiling on the interest rate on a floating-rate note.

Capital : Funds invested in a firm by the owners for use in conducting the business.

Capital Account Convertibility(CAC) : It is the freedom to convert local financial assets into foreign financial assets and vice versa at market determined rates of exchange. This means that capital account convertibility allows anyone to freely move from local currency into foreign currency and back. The Reserve Bank of India has appointed a committee to set out the framework for fuller Capital Account Convertibility. Capital account convertibility is considered to be one of the major features of a developed economy. It helps attract foreign investment. capital account convertibility makes it easier for domestic companies to tap foreign markets.

Capital Adequacy Ratio (CAR) : A ratio of total capital divided by risk-weighted assets and risk-weighted off-balance sheet items. A bank is expected to meet a minimum capital ratio specifically prescribed by the Regulator.

Capital Asset or Improvement : Any structure or component considered as a permanent addition to real property that adds to its value and useful life.

Capital budget : The list of planned capital expenditures prepared usually annually

Capital Gain and Loss : Profit or loss from the sale of a capital asset. The difference between the price that is originally paid for a security and cash proceeds at the time of maturity (face value of bond) or at the time of sale (selling price of a bond or stock). When the difference is positive, it is a gain, but when it is negative, it is a loss.

Capital investments : Money used to purchase permanent fixed assets for a business, such as machinery, land or buildings as opposed to day-to-day operating expenses.

Capital Markets: The market in which long-term securities such as stocks and bonds are bought and sold.

Capital Structure : The composition of a firm's long-term financing consisting of equity, preference shares, and long-term debt.

Capitalization : Total amount of the various securities issued by a corporation. Capitalization may include bonds, debentures, preferred and common stock, and surplus. Bonds and debentures are usually carried on the books of the issuing company in terms of their par or face value. Preferred and common shares may be carried in terms of par or stated value. Stated value may be an arbitrary figure decided upon by the director or may represent the amount received by the company from the sale of the securities at the time of issuance.

Cardholder Agreement : The cardholder's agreement is a written statement that depicts all the terms and conditions of a credit card agreement. The cardholders agreement constitutes many elements, such as rate of service charges, billing dispute remedies and communications with the credit card companies or service providers.

Cash cows : Business segments, having a high market share in low growth product markets, which generate more cash flow than needed for reinvestment.

Cash Credit (CC) : An arrangement whereby the bank gives a short-term loan against the self-liquidating security.

Cash Discount : A discount given to buyers for cash rather than credit purchase.

Cash Flow : The cash flow is often defined as the liquid balance of cash as well as the bank balance that is available with an organization or a corporation. In some cases, the cash flow is also defined as the net amount of cash that is generated by the net income that has been generated by an organization or corporation in a particular time period.

Cash flow forecast : An estimate of when and how much money will be received and paid out of a business. It usually records cash flow on a month-by-month basis.

Cash Reserve : The cash reserve is the total amount of cash that is present in the bank account and can also be withdrawn immediately.

Cash sale : A transaction on the floor of the stock exchange that calls for delivery of the securities the same day. In "regular way" trade, the seller is to deliver on the third business day, except for bonds, which are the next day.

Cashier's Check : The cashier's check is drawn by a bank on it's own name to make payments other organizations, banks, corporations or even individuals.

Central Bank : A central bank is the governing authority of all the other banks in a country.

Certificate of Deposit (CD) : A negotiable instrument issued by a bank evidencing time deposit

Certified Check : A personal check drawn by an individual that is certified (guaranteed) to be good. The face of the check bears the words "certified" or "acccepted," and is signed by an official of the bank issuing the check. It signifies that sufficient funds are on deposit and earmarked for payment of the check.

Chain of Title : The history of all documents that transfer title of real property, -starting with the original or earliest existing document and ending with the most recent.

Charge-Off : The balance on a credit obligation that a lender no longer expects to be repaid and writes off as a bad debt.

Cheque : A check is a negotiable instrument that instructs the bank to pay a particular amount of money from the writer's bank, to the receiver of the cheque.

Chip card : Also known as an IC (integrated circuit) card. A card containing one or more computer chips or integrated circuits for identification, data storage or special purpose processing used to validate personal identification numbers (PINs), authorise purchases, verify account balances and store personal records. In some cases, the memory in the card is updated every time the card is used (eg an account balance is updated).

CIBIL : Credit Information Bureau of India Ltd.

CIF : Cost, Insurance and Freight

Ciphertext : the encrypted form of data.

CLB : Company Law Board

Clean-up merger : Also called Take-out merger. The consolidation of the acquired firm into the acquiring firm after the acquirer has obtained control.

Clearing House : The clearing house is a place where the representatives of the different banks meet for confirming and clearing all the checks and balances with each other. The clearing house, in most countries across the world, is managed by the central bank.

Clearing member : A member of a clearing house. All trades must be settled through a clearing member. A direct clearing member is able to settle only its own obligations. A general clearing member is able to settle its own obligations as well as those of clients. Variations of these two types of clearing member may also exist.

Closed network : Telecommunications network used for a specific purpose, such as a payment system, and to which access is restricted.

Closed-end (Mutual) Fund: A fund with a fixed number of shares issued, and all trading is done between investors in the open market. The share prices are determined by market prices instead of their net asset value.

Closeout : The process of offsetting existing contracts. Closeout may be used by the clearing house to prevent further losses from positions carried by an entity that has defaulted.

Closing : Closing of an account is the final stage of any transaction where both the parties receive almost equal consideration from each other. The term 'closing' from ledger books where the two accounts are 'closed down' i.e. both debit and credit sides become equal.

CMS : Cash Management Services.

Co-borrower : The co-borrower is a person who signs a promissory note as a guarantee that the loan would be repaid. Thus the co-borrower plays the role of a guarantor and is equally responsible for the loan.

Collateral : Property (real, personal or otherwise) pledged as security for a loan. Also, any supplementary promise of payment, such as a guarantee.

Collected Funds : Cash deposits or checks that have been presented for payment and for which payment has been received; funds are readily available. Ledger funds are deposits made to an account but for which funds have not actually been received as in the deposit of a check.

Collusion : A secret agreement between two or more persons to defraud another person of his or her right in order to achieve an unlawful objective.

Co-Maker : A person who signs a note to guarantee a loan made to another person and is jointly liable with the maker for repayment of the loan.

Commercial Credit Risk : The risk of loss from providing credit to corporate counter-parties. Extension of credit can take the form of direct loans and contingencies/guarantees.

Commercial Paper (CP) : Issue of short-term notes, without any underwriting, representing a promise to repay the amount at a specified future date.

Commitment fee : A fee charged by a bank in respect of an unused balance of a line of credit or sanction of loan designed to offset the bank's cost of keeping the funds available.

Compound Interest : Compound interest is the interest that is 'compounded' on a sum of money that is deposited for a long time. The compound interest, unlike simple interest, is calculated by taking into consideration, the principal amount and the accumulated interest.

Conglomerate : A corporation that has diversified its operations usually by acquiring enterprises in widely varied industries.

Consolidated balance sheet : A balance sheet showing the financial condition of a corporation and its subsidiaries.

Consumer Credit : Consumer credit is the credit and loan facility that is provided to the consumer for the purchase of goods, services and real estate property. Most consumer credit is unsecured with the help of a collateral

Consumer Price Index (CPI) : An index that measure movements in the average price of products and services.

Contactless cards : Cards that do not require physical contact between the card and the card reader or terminal.

Convertibility Clause : A provision in some loans that allows the borrower to hange the interest rate from fixed to variable or vice-versa.

Convertible Bond : A bond with an option, allowing the bondholder to exchange the bond for a specified number of shares of common stock in the firm. A conversion price is the specified value of the shares for which the bond may be exchanged. The conversion premium is the excess of the bond's value over the conversion price.

Convertible Security : Bond or preferred stock which is convertible into equity shares generally at the option of the holder

Corporate Banking : Banking services for large firms.

Corporate Bond : Long-term debt issued by private corporations.

Corporate Governance : A system by which organizations are directed and controlled. Board of directors are responsible for the governance of their organizations.

Corporate Tax : A tax on the profits of firms, as distinct from taxation of the incomes of their owners.

Correspondent banking : An arrangement under which one bank (correspondent) holds deposits owned by other banks (respondents) and provides payment and other services to those respondent banks. Such arrangements may also be known as agency relationships in some domestic contexts. In international banking, balances held for a foreign respondent bank may be used to settle foreign exchange transactions. Reciprocal correspondent banking relationships may involve the use of so-called nostro and vostro accounts to settle foreign exchange transactions.

Cost of Funds Index (COFI) : An index that is used to determine interest rates and/or changes of interest rate for certain types of loans. It represents the weighted average cost of funds from all sources, which a bank has access to: internal funds, other bank borrowings, the Federal Government/Federal Reserve Board.

Counterparty : The opposite party to a financial transaction such as a securities trade or swap agreement.

Coupon Rate : The stated interest rate on a bond.

Covenant : A clause in loan agreements that promises or obligates and/or restricts that borrower. If violated, a breach has occurred, which may cause the loan to become immediately due.

CRAR : Capital to Risk-Weighted Assets Ratio.

CRAs : Credit Rating Agencies.

Credit Card Debt Consolidation Loan : Credit card debt consolidation loan is availed from a bank in order to pay off all credit card debts.

Credit Counseling : Credit counseling is a consultancy session where the credit counselor suggests debt relief solutions and debt management solutions to the clients.

Credit Crunch : Refers to a situation where supply of credit falls even though there is sufficient demand for it.

Credit History : A record of how a person or company has borrowed and repaid debts.

Credit limit : Limit on the credit exposure a payment system participant incurs vis-à-vis another participant (bilateral credit limit) or vis-à-vis all other participants (multilateral credit limit) as a result of receiving payments that have not yet been settled.

Credit Rating : An assessment of the likelihood of an individual or business being able to meet its financial obligations. Credit ratings are provided by credit agencies or rating agencies to verify the financial strength of the issuer for investors.

Credit Risk : The risk of loss from failure of the counterparty to perform as agreed (contracted). The risk that a counterparty will not settle an obligation for full value, either when due or at any time thereafter. In exchange-forvalue systems, the risk is generally defined to include replacement cost risk and principal risk.

Credit Scoring : This is the process of assessing an individual's credit-worthiness. The process involves taking information from an individual on an application form (for example when applying for a store card) and weighting the answers given. Certain responses will attract higher scores than others and the total score will determine whether or nor the organization wants to do business with the individual, or if they represent too high a credit risk.

Credit Scoring System : A statistical system used to determine whether or not to grant credit by assigning numerical scores to various characteristics relating to creditworthiness.

Credit-worthiness : A creditor's measure of a consumer's or company's past and future ability and willingness to repay debts.

CRISIL : Credit Rating and Investment Services of India Limited.

Cross default : Two loan agreements connected by a clause that allows one lender to recall the loan if the borrower defaults with another, and vice versa.

Cryptanalysis : Area of cryptography dedicated to studying and developing methods by which, without prior knowledge of the cryptographic key, plaintext may be deduced from ciphertext.

Cumulative Dividends : A feature of preferred stock that requires all past dividends on preferred stock to be paid before any equity dividends are paid.

Currency basket : Arrangements whereby two or more currencies are clubbed together with defined weights, and whose exchange rate/ interest rate is determined by computing weighted average market rates.

Currency Market Risk : The risk of loss from having positions in any of the currency markets. The risk can be from outright positions. It can also reside in the balance sheet or in the income flows of a company.

Current Account Convertibility : It defines at one can import and export goods or receive or make payments for services rendered. However, investments and borrowings are restricted.

Current assets : Short-term assets, constantly changing in value, such as stocks, debtors and bank balances.

Current liabilities : Short-term liabilities, due to be paid in less than one year, such as bank overdrafts, money owed to suppliers and employees.

Current Yield : The yield on a security resulting from dividing the interest payment or dividend on it by its current market price.

Custodian : an entity, often a bank, that safekeeps and administers securities for its customers and that may provide various other services, including clearance and settlement, cash management, foreign exchange and securities lending.

Custody of Securities : Registration of securities in the name of the person to whom a bank is accountable, or in the name of the bank's nominee; plus deposition of securities in a designated account with the bank's bankers or with any other institution providing custodial services.

D/A (documents against acceptance) : Refer to shipping documents presented to a bank on a collection basis to be passed to the buyer when he or she accepts a bill of exchange. The bank holds the bill of exchange until it ends (maturity) when they ask the buyer to pay the seller.

D/P (documents against payment) : Refer to shipping documents presented to a bank on a collection basis to be passed to the buyer (drawee) when payment is made.

Day of value : Day on which a payment is due to be credited to the receiving participant in the payment system. The day of value for the receiving participant's customer (that is, the day on which the receiving participant credits the customer in its books) may or may not be the same day, depending on specific arrangements or local practice.

Day order : An order to buy or sell that, if not executed, expires at the end of trading day on which it was entered.

Daylight credit : Credit extended for a period of less than one business day; in a credit transfer system with end-of-day final settlement, daylight credit is tacitly extended by a receiving institution if it accepts and acts on a payment order even though it will not receive final funds until the end of the business day. Also called daylight overdraft, daylight exposure and intraday credit.

DCF : Discounted Cash Flow.

Debentures : Debentures are long term corporate bonds that are unsecured in nature. It must be noted that debenture holders are not protected by any collateral and tend to be treated like ordinary creditors

Debit : Debit is a banking term that indicates the amount of money that is owed by a borrower. It also indicates the amount that is payable, or the amount that has been deducted from an account. The origin of the term is from the concept of debit side of a ledger account.

Debit Card : A debit card is an instrument that was developed with digital cash technology, and is used when a consumer makes that payment first to the credit card company and then swipes the card. The debit card operates in the exact opposite manner of the credit card.

Debt : A debt is any amount that is owed by an individual, organization or corporation to a bank.

Debt Consolidation Loan : A debt consolidation loan is a type of loan, where the bank or the lending institution provides the borrower with a loan that helps the borrower to pay off all his previous debts.

Debt Management : Debt management is a process of managing debts and repaying creditors. Debt management is a very broad concept covering almost anything related to debts and their repayment.

Debt Recovery : Debt recovery is the process that is initiated by the banks and lending institutions, by various procedures like debt settlement or selling of collaterals.

Debt Repayment : Debt repayment is the total process repayment of a debt along with the interest. Sometimes, the consolidation that is provided is also included in debt repayment.

Debt Settlement : Debt settlement is a procedure wherein a person in debt negotiates the price with the lender of a loan, in order to reduce the installments and the rate of repayment, and ensure a fast and guaranteed repayment.

Debt/equity ratio : A comparative ratio of debt and equity used to measure the gearing/ health of a business.

Deed : A deed is a very important document that indicates the ownership of an asset, especially a real estate. The deed is also used to convey the property from the seller to the buyer. The legal document that conveys or transfers title of property.

Deed of Trust : The legal document (in some states) that conveys title of real property to a trustee on behalf of the owner.

Default : A default is a scenario where the debtors of a bank are unable to repay the debt or the loan.

Default Risk : The risk that a borrower may not repay principal and/or interest as originally agreed.

Default Risk Premium : The component of a required interest rate that is based on the lenders' perceived risk of default.

Defaulter pays : A loss-sharing arrangement where each participant is required to collateralise any exposures it creates for other participants. As a result, losses from a party's default are borne by the defaulting party.

Deferred : An action that has been postponed until a future date.

Delayed debit card : Card issued by banks indicating that the holder may charge his account up to an authorised limit. It enables him to make purchases but does not offer extended credit, the full amount of the debt incurred having to be settled at the end of a specified period. The holder is usually charged an annual fee.

Dematerialization : The elimination of physical certificates or documents of title which represent ownership of securities so that securities exist only as accounting records.

Deposit Slip : A deposit slip is a bill of itemized nature and depicts the amount of paper money, coins and the cheque numbers that are being deposited into a bank account.

Depositor : The person who deposits money into a bank account is called a depositor.

Depreciation : An annual deduction of a part of the cost of an asset. In general, it means a decline in market value.

Derivative : A financial contract the value of which depends on the value of one or more underlying reference assets, rates or indices. For analytical purposes, all derivatives contracts can be divided into basic building blocks of forward contracts, options or combinations thereof.

DFI : Development Financial Institution.

Direct Debit : An amount of money taken from a bank account, set up by the recipient and can vary in amount and exact time that it is taken from an account. Mortgages are usually direct debits.

Direct Financing : Provision of funds for investment to the ultimate user of funds.

Direct taxes : Taxes which affect the consumer directly, such as income tax, corporate tax, capital gains tax etc.

Discount : The amount by which a bond or preferred stock sells below its par or face value. In foreign exchange market, it is the amount by which

forward price is less than the spot price. In general, it means an extent of reduction in the price / value of the asset/ product which is given when it is sold.

Discretionary account : An account in which the customer gives the broker or someone else discretion to buy and sell securities or commodities, including selection, timing, amount, and price to be paid or received.

Diversification : Spreading investments among different types of securities and various companies in different fields.

Dividend : A dividend is a part of the profit that is earned by a corporation or joint stock companies, and is distributed amongst the shareholders.

Documentary Credit : Written undertaking by a bank on behalf of an importer authorizing an exporter to draw drafts on the bank up to a specified amount under specific terms and conditions. They are used to facilitate international trade. Also called Letter of Credit (LC).

Dow theory : A theory of market analysis based upon the performance of the Dow Jones Industrial Average and transportation stock price averages. The theory says that the market is in a basic upward trend if one of these averages advances above a previous important high, accompanied or followed by a similar advance in the other. When both averages dip below previous important lows, this is regarded as confirmation of a downward trend. The Dow Jones is one type of market index.

Draft : A written order from one party (the drawer) to another (the drawee) to pay a party identified on the order (payee) or to the bearer a specified sum, either on demand (sight draft) or on a specified date (time draft).

DRT : Debt Recovery Tribunal.

Due diligence : While finalizing documentation, the lead manager and the legal counsel conduct a thorough review of the borrowing entity with reference to the financials, legality, and all such matters relevant in a public offering of securities.

Early Withdrawal Penalty : An early withdrawal penalty is basically a penalty that is levied by a bank because of an early withdrawal of a fixed investment by any investor. There can be several types of early withdrawal penalties, like forfeiting the promised interest.

Earnest Money : a deposit made by a potential buyer to show that they are serious about buying an asset.

Earnest Money Deposit : An earnest money deposit is made by the buyer to the potential seller of a real estate, in the initial stages of negotiation of purchase.

Earning Assets : Earning assets generate returns, either in the form of returns or in the form of interest or cash. One must note that in the case of earning assets, the owner does not have to take any daily efforts to achieve returns.

Earning Yield : The ratio of earning per share to market price of the share.

Earnings: The total profits of a company after taxation and interest.

E-Cash : Also known as electronic cash and digital cash, e-cash is a technology where the banking organizations resort to the use of electronics, computers and other networks to execute transactions and transfer funds.

ECBs : External Commercial Borrowings.

ECGC : Export Credit Guarantee Corporation.

Education Loan : An education loan, also known as student's loan, is specifically meant to provide forthe borrower's expenditure towards education. In the majority of countries, educational loans tend to have a low rate of interest. The period of repayment also starts after the completion period of the loan.

Effective rate of interest : The percentage rate of return on an annual basis, reflecting the effect of intra-year compounding.

Electronic Filing : Electronic filing is the method of filing of tax returns and tax forms on the Internet.

Electronic Funds Transfers (EFT) : EFT allows entities to transfer funds from an account electronically. It can be used by creditors to pull funds from a customer automatically. EFT's are efficient, immediate, and easy.

Electronic purse : A reloadable multipurpose prepaid card which may be used for small retail or other payments instead of coins.

Encryption : Encryption is a process that is used to ensure the privacy and security of a person's confidential financial information. The actual process involves scrambling of the data of the person, in such a manner, so that only the person himself can see the data.

Endorsement : Endorsement is basically the handing over of rights of a financial/legal document or a negotiable instrument to another person. The person who hands over his/her rights is known as the endorser, and the person to whom the rights have been transferred is known as the endorsee.

Endowment Mortgage : Interest only is paid over the term of this sort of mortgage and the capital is repaid at the end of the term by using the monies from an endowment policy.

Entrepreneur : A person who conceives, starts and manages a business.

EOUs : Export-Oriented Units.

Equitable mortgage : A type of mortgage under which one still owns the property which is security for the mortgage. The owner can occupy or live in the property.

Equity : The value of a business after all debts and other claims are settled. Also, the amount of cash a business owner invests in a business and/ or the difference between the price for which a property could be sold and the total debts registered against it.

Equity swap : A swap which involves an exchange of return on a recognized stock index or a specified basket of individual stocks for a fixed or floating rate of interest.

Escrow Account : An account for which a bank acts as an uninterested third party (custodian / depository) to ensure compliance with the terms of the deal between two parties only upon the fulfillment of some stated conditions. The account becomes operative on the occurrence of the stated event. Banks hold such accounts in which funds accumulate to pay taxes, insurance on mortgage property, etc.

Exchange Rate : The rate at which one currency may be exchanged for another.

Exchange Rate Risk : The risk that changes in currency exchange rates may have an unfavourable impact on costs or revenues of economic units.

Excise duties : Duties levied on items manufactured within the country and paid by the manufacturer.

Ex-dividend : A synonym for "without dividend." The buyer of a stock selling ex-dividend does not receive the recently declared dividend. When stocks go ex-dividend, the stock tables include the symbol "x" following the name.

Expiration Date : This term indicates the invalidity of a financial document or instrument, after a specified period of time.

Exports : Products and services sold to other countries.

Ex-rights : Without the rights. Corporations raising additional money may do so by offering their stockholders the right to subscribe to new or additional stock, usually at a discount from the prevailing market price. The buyer of a stock selling ex-rights is not entitled to the rights.

Face Value : Face value is the original value of any security or negotiable instrument.

Face-to-face payment : Payment carried out by the exchange of instruments between the payer and the payee in the same physical location.

Factoring : This is when a business sells its invoices to a specialist company or bank which chases payment and pays a percentage of the invoice back to the original business. The business can then continue with its work and problems from cash-flow are reduced by having money from unpaid invoices up-front.

Fair Market Value (FMV) : The highest price that a buyer, willing but not complelled to buy, and the lowest a seller, willing but not compelled to sell, would accept.

FCCB : A Foreign Currency Convertible Bond (FCCB) is a type of convertible bond issued in a currency different than the issuer's domestic currency. In other words, the money being raised by the issuing company is in the form of a foreign currency. A company may issue an FCCB if it intends to make a large investment in a country using that foreign currency.

Fiduciary : Undertaking to act as executor, administrator, guardian, conservator, or trustee for a family trust, authorised trust, or testamentary trust, or receiver or trustee in a bankruptcy.

Field Audits : Field audits are basically the audits that are conducted by bank officials, on the site itself, in order to assess the status and condition of the collateral. Many a times, field audits are also conducted in order to assess the financial situation of debtors, especially corporations, who have availed huge loans.

Final Maturity : A final maturity is the date of maturity when a last, single loan matures from a pool of loans. The final maturity indicates the total and final payment of the pool of mortgage loans.

Financial Instrument : A financial instrument is anything that ranges from cash, deed, negotiable instrument, or for that matter any written and authenticated evidence, that shows the existence of a transaction or agreement.

Financial Intermediary : A financial intermediary is basically a party or person who acts as a link between a provider who provides securities and the user, who purchases the securities. Share broker, and almost all the banks, are the best examples of financial intermediaries.

Financial Statement : A financial statement is a record of historical financial figures, reports and a record of assets, liabilities, capital, income and expenditure.

Fixed assets : Assets such as land, buildings, machinery or property used in operating a business that will not be consumed or converted into cash during the current accounting period.

Fixed Rate : A predetermined rate of interest applied to the principal of a loan or credit agreement.

Fixed Rate Mortgage : A fixed rate mortgage is a home loan, for which the interest rate remains constant and fixed throughout the lifetime of loan.

Fixtures : The term 'fixture' is used in the context of a real estate property, when assets like furniture are attached to the real estate and are also included in its book value. Banks, in many a cases, are known to include fixtures in the value, if the real estate property has been pledged as a collateral.

Fleckless : From the German "fleckenlos", which means spotless; a device (card) or a system is said to be fleckless when it can provide evidence that it has not been tampered with.

Float : The amount of uncollected funds represented by checks in the possession of one bank but drawn on other banks or the time that elapses between the day a check is deposited and the day it is presented for payment to the financial institution on which it is drawn.

Floor : The huge trading area - about the size of a football field - where stocks, bonds and options are bought and sold on the Stock Exchange.

Floor broker : A member of the stock exchange who executes orders on the floor of the Exchange to buy or sell any listed securities.

Forbearance Agreement : A forbearance agreement is an authenticated agreement between a debtor and a creditor, and is utilized by the creditor, when the debtor initiates a debt settlement or the loan is defaulted, or the former becomes bankrupt.

Foreclosure : A foreclosure is a standardized procedure where creditors like banks, are authorized to obtain the title of the real estate property that has been pledged as a collateral.

Foreign Currency Surcharge : The foreign currency surcharge is is levied by some banks and credit card companies, when a credit card or an ATM is used in a foreign country.

Foreign Exchange : Various instruments used to settle payments for transactions between individuals or organizations using different currencies (e.g. notes, cheques, etc.)

Foreign Exchange Rate : The value of a nation's currency in terms of another nation's currency.

Foreign Trade : The exchange of goods between two nations.

Forfaiting : A form of export finance in which the forfaiter accepts, at a discount from the exporter, a bill of exchange or promissory note (note) from the exporter's customer; the forfaiter in due course collects payment of the debt. Such notes are normally guaranteed by the customer's bank. Maturities are normally up to three years.

Forward Contract : A contract in which one party agrees to buy, and the other to sell, a specified product at a specified price on a specified date in the future.

Forward Cover : Forward purchase or sale of foreign currency to offset an anticipated future cash flow.

Forward rate agreement : A forward contract on interest rates in which the rate to be paid or received on a specific obligation for a set period of time, beginning at some time in the future, is determined at contract initiation.

Free Cash Flow : A free cash flow is basically is a total of financially liquid assets that does not include capital expenditures and dividends.

FRNs : Floating Rate Notes.

Funded debt : Generally, a short-term debt that has been converted into long-term debt funding.

Futures : Contracts to buy something in the future at a price agreed upon in advance. First developed in the agriculture commodity markets but often involve foreign exchange, and Government bonds.

General collateral : Securities that satisfy the general requirements of a lender of cash to collateralise its cash lending. General collateral comprises securities which are not in particular demand in the market; categories of general collateral are usually defined by market convention.

Global custodian : A custodian that provides its customers with custody services in respect of securities traded and settled not only in the country in which the custodian is located but also in numerous other countries throughout the world.

Going-concern value : The value of the firm as a whole over and above the sum of the values of each of its parts; the value of an organization's learning and reputation.

Goodwill : The excess of the purchase price paid for a firm over the book value received. Recorded on the acquirers' balance sheet.

Government Bonds : A government bond, which is also known as a government security, is basically any security that is held with the government and has the highest possible rate of interest.

Grace Period : A grace period is an interest-free period that is to be given by a creditor to a debtor after the period of the loan gets over, before initiating the process of loss recovery. The grace period depends on the amount of the loan and also the credit score of the borrower.

Grant : A grant is any type of financial aid that is given by the government.

Gridlock : A situation that can arise in a funds or securities transfer system in which the failure of some transfer instructions to be executed (because the necessary funds or securities balances are unavailable) prevents a substantial number of other instructions from other participants from being executed.

Gross Dividends : Gross dividends are basically the total amount of dividends that are earned by an individual, or corporation in a single accounting and tax year. It must be noted that capital gains are also included in gross dividends.

Gross Domestic Product (GDP) : The total of market value of the finished goods and services produced in a country in a given year. Comprising three sectors viz. Agriculture, Industry & Services.

Gross Income : Gross income is the total income of a person, organization or corporation in one financial year, before making any deductions.

Gross Income Test : A gross income test, is a kind of test, where one can prove to any government authority that a person is one's dependent.

Gross National Product (GNP) : The total market value of finished goods and services produced in the country in a given year, plus the income of domestic residents from investments made abroad, minus the income earned by foreigners abroad from the domestic market.

Gross Profit margin : The difference between the sales a business generates and the costs it pays out for goods.

Ground Rent : Ground rent is the amount of rent that a leaseholder pays periodically to the owner for using a piece of land.

Guarantor : A party who agrees to be responsible for the payment of another party's debts should that party default.

Guaranty : The undertaking of responsibility by one party for another party's debt or obligation to perform some specific act or duty. Although the original debtor is responsible for the debt, the guarantor becomes liable in the event of a default.

Haircut : The difference between the market value of a security and its collateral value. Haircuts are taken by a lender of funds in order to protect the lender, should the need arise to liquidate the collateral, from losses owing to declines in the market value of the security.

Hedge : Hedge is a strategy that is used to minimize the risk of a particular investment and maximize the returns of an investment. A 'hedge' strategy is, most of the times, implemented with the help of a hedge fund. This terms has been written from the banker's point of view and may be interpreted differently in the field of finance.

Hedge fund : 'Hedge' means to reduce financial risk. A hedge fund is an investment fund open to a limited range of investors and requires a very large initial minimum investment. It is important to note that hedging is actually the practice of attempting to reduce risk, but the goal of most hedge funds is to maximize return on investment.

Hire Purchase : When an item of large capital value is bought over time by paying a deposit and fixing a period over which the loan will run (usually between 12 and 60 months) and then paying fixed and equal repayments over this period.

Holding company : A company which controls another company, usually by owing more than half of its shares.

Holding Period : The holding period is the time duration during which a capital asset is held/owned by an individual or corporation. The holding period is taken into consideration, while pledging the asset as a collateral.

Home banking : Banking services which a retail customer of a financial institution can access using a telephone, television set, terminal or personal computer as a telecommunications link to the institution's computer centre.

Home Equity Debt : A home equity debt is a debt, where the borrower's house is pledged as a collateral.

Household Income : Household income is the income of all the members of one household put together. One must note that the income earned through the family business, is also counted in the household income.

ICD : Inter-Corporate Deposit.

Identity Theft : This is when criminals use an innocent person's details to open or use an account to carry out financial transactions. It is very easy to do with an individual's personal details, which is why shredding confidential information is so important.

IFSC Code : The Indian Financial System Code (IFSC) is being used as the addressing code in user-to-user message transmission. The Payment System Applications such as RTGS, CFMS and NEFT developed by the Reserve Bank of India (RBI) use these codes. The code consists of 11 characters - first 4 characters represent the entity; fifth position has been defaulted with a '0' (Zero) for future use; and the last 6 characters denote the branch identity.

Imports : Goods and services that a country buys from other countries.

Indemnification : An agreement to compensate for damage or loss. Custodians sometimes offer it to lending customers in a variety of forms.

Indemnity : If someone promises to compensate someone else for loss or damage, it is called an indemnity.

Indirect financing : The process by which deficit spending units obtain funds from financial intermediaries who, in turn, them from ultimate surplus spending units.

Indirect market participant : A market participant that uses an intermediary for the execution of trades on its behalf. Generally, institutional and cross-border clients are indirect market participants.

Indirect taxes : Taxes, which are charged on goods produced, imported or exported: Excise and Customs duties.

Industry life cycle : A conceptual model of the different stages of an industry's development.

1. Development stage: New product, high investment needs, losses;
2. Growth stage: Consumer acceptance, expanding sales, high profitability, ease of entry;
3. Maturity stage: Sales growth slows, excess capacity, prices and profits decline - key period for merger strategy;
4. Decline stage: Substitute products emerge, sales growth declines, pressure for mergers to survive.

Inflation : A percentage rate of change in the price level.

Inflation Premium : A premium for anticipated inflation that investors require in addition to the pure rate of interest.

Initial Public Offering (IPO) : An event where a company sells its shares to the public for the first time. The company can be referred to as an IPO for a period of time after the event." Insider Trading: The illegal use of non-public information about a company to make profitable securities transactions.

Insolvent : The condition when one is unable to pay one's debt obligations when due.

Installment Contract : An installment contract is a contract where the borrower, who is also the purchaser, pays a series of installments that includes the interest of the principal amount.

Installment Credit : Installment credit is a debt or loan that is to be returned to the lender in a set of periodic installments. Auto loans, home loans and other types of loans are included in installment credit.

Insufficient Funds : When an account balance is inadequate to cover a cheque that has been written and presented for payment.

Insurance : A contract whereby one party agrees to pay a sum to another party for a fee (premium) in the event that the latter suffers a particular loss. The person or firm that undertakes the risk is the insurer. The party desiring to be protected from loss is the insured party.

Intangible assets : Assets that cannot be touched. Examples are goodwill and patent rights.

Interest : Interest is a charge that is paid by any borrower or debtor for the use of money, which is calculated on the basis of the rate of interest, time period of the debt and the principal amount that was borrowed. Interest is, sometimes, also titled as the 'cost of credit'.

Interest Accrual Rate : The interest accrual rate is a percentage of interest that is calculated on the basis of the rate of interest and is expressed in terms of annual percentage rate or APR.

Interest Rate : Interest rate is the percentage of principal amount that is paid as an interest for the use of money. Usually, the interest rate is decided by a country's central bank, on the basis of the economic conditions.

Internal Rate of Return (IRR) : The rate of discount at which the net present value of an investment is zero.

Internet Banking : Internet banking is a system wherein customers can conduct their transactions through the Internet. This kind of banking is also known as e-banking or online banking.

Intraday liquidity : Funds which can be accessed during the business day, usually to enable financial institutions to make payments in real time.

Investment banker : Also known as an underwriter. The middleman between the corporation issuing new securities and the public. The usual practice is for one or more investment bankers to buy outright from a corporation a new issue of stocks or bonds. The group forms a syndicate to sell the securities to individuals and institutions. Investment bankers also distribute very large blocks of stocks or bonds - perhaps held by an estate.

IRA : Individual retirement account. A pension plan with tax advantages. IRAs permit investment through intermediaries like mutual funds, insurance companies and banks, or directly in stocks and bonds through stockbrokers.

ISAs : This stands for Individual Savings Accounts. These are available to all UK residents over 18 (mini ISAs are available to 16 and 17-year-olds). Investment limits apply to the total contributions made in any tax year, not to the total in the ISA itself. ISAs can be cash, stocks and shares or life insurance.

Judgment Clause : This relates to a provision regarding bank notes of hand or guarantees, and includes the authorization of the borrowers or sureties given to the bank, to create a judgment lien, at any time after the completion of the legal instruments.

Judicial Lien : It pertains to an interest in the holdings ,which are gained from judicial or court orders.

Jump Z-Tranche : A Z-tranche is a real estate mortgage investment conduit (REMIC), which is countenanced to obtain principal sums, before prior tranches are no longer active.

Junior Creditor : A creditor who possesses junior debt.

Junior Debt : The responsibilities of an issuing entity, for which quittance has contractually been considered, as a priority of miscellaneous liabilities of the same debtor.

Junk Bonds : This is a recognized term for high-yield sureties with quality standings below investment grade.

Kappa : This is a Greek term utilized in the banking sector that relates to the sensitiveness of an option's rate to alterations in the unpredictability cost.

Key Rate Duration : This pertains to a measure of duration, which computes efficient or empirical duration by altering the market price for a particular maturity date on the yield curve, while keeping all other variables constant.

Kiting : Writing a check in an amount that will overdraw the account, but making up the deficiency by depositing another check on another bank.

Knot Points : It relates to the points that are on the yield curve for which there are discernible rates for traded instruments.

L/C : Letter of credit

Land Contract : Otherwise known as an article of agreement, a land contract denotes a form of contract, wherein the buyer makes periodic installment payments to the seller, in order to buy a real estate. But, the title to the property is not transferred to the buyer, until he makes the final payment.

Land Flip : A colloquial expression used to denote a real estate fraud, wherein the prices of undeveloped property is artificially increased to high amounts, which are above the fair market value. This is often accomplished by a group of colluding buyers, who purchase and resell the same property, among its members, several times, each time increasing the price. When the price becomes unrealistically high, they sell the property or raise a loan for its development.

Lease : A contract, through which, the owner (lessor) of a certain property, allows another (lessee) to use the same for a specified period, in exchange for a value called the rent.

Lessee : One who takes property on lease.

Lessor : A person, Corporation, or other legal entity that leases property to a lessee.

Letter of Credit (LC) : A formal document issued by a bank on behalf of a customer, stating the conditions under which the bank will honour the commitments of the customer.

Leverage : The effect on a company when the company has bonds, preferred stock, or both outstanding. Example: If the earnings of a company with 1,000,000 common shares increases from $1,000,000 to $1,500,000, earnings per share would go up from $1 to $1.50, or an increase of 50%. But if earnings of a company that had to pay $500,000 in bond interest increased that much, earnings per common share would jump from $.50 to $1 a share, or 100%.

LIBOR : Libor stands for London Inter-Bank Offered Rate. This is a favourable interest rate offered for U.S. dollar or Eurodollar deposits between groups of London banks. It is an internationl interest rate that foillows world economic conditions and is defined by the maturity of its deposit term (i.e. 30-day LIBOR, 60-day LIBOR). This market allows banks with liquidity requirements to borrow quickly form other banks with surpluses. The LIBOR is officially fixed once a day by a group of large London banks, but the rate changes throughout the day. The difficulty with some LIBOR based loans is that the terms can be based upon set dollar amounts to draw-down or repay at specific dates.

Lien : An encumbrance against property form money due, either voluntary or involuntary.

Life Cap : The upper and lower limit for changes in the borrower's interest rate over the term of his/her loan.

Lifeline Account : A bank account meant for customers with low incomes. These accounts are characterized by little or no monthly fees and there is no strict rule regarding the minimum balance.

Line of Crdit : A pre-approved loan authorization with a specific borrowing limit based on creditworthiness. A line of credit allows borrowers to obtain a number of loans without re-applying each time as long as the total amount of funds does not exceed the credit limit. A pre-approved credit facility (usually for one year) enabling a bank customer to borrow up to the specified maximum amount at any time during the relevant period of time.

Liquidated Damages : A clause, which is commonly found in contracts, wherein the parties agree to pay a fixed amount, in case of any breach of the contractual provisions. The party, who violates the provisions has to pay the amount to the aggrieved party.

Liquidation : The process of converting securities or other property into cash. The dissolution of a company, with cash remaining after sale of its assets and payment of all indebtedness being distributed to the shareholders.

Liquidity : The extent to which or the ease with which an asset may quickly be converted into cash with the least administrative and other costs.

Liquidity Adjustment Facility(LAF) : A tool used in monetary policy that allows banks to borrow money through repurchase agreements. This arrangement allows banks to respond to liquidity pressures and is used by governments to assure basic stability in the financial markets.

Load : The portion of the offering price of shares of open-end investment companies in excess of the value of the underlying assets. Covers sales commissions and all other costs of distribution. The load is usually incurred only on purchase, there being, in most cases, no charge when the shares are sold (redeemed).

Loan Document : A business contract by which a borrower and lender enter into an agreement. Loans are classified according to the lender or borrower involved, whether or not collateral is required, the time of maturity, conditions of repayment, and other variables.

Loan Risk : This is the risk of loss from loaning money and having the borrower fail to repay, either due to genuine reasons or willfully.

Loan to Value (LTV) : The unpaid principal balance of a loan on property divided by the asset's appraised value. Generally, the lower the LTV the move favourable the term and interest rate of the loan. For example, on a $100,000 building, with a note due of $80,000, the LTV ratio would be 80%.

Locked in : Investors are said to be locked in when they have profit on a security they own but do not sell because their profit would immediately become subject to the capital gains tax.

Lock-in Period : A guarantee given by the lender that there will be no change in the quoted mortgage rates for a specified period of time, which is called the lock-in period.

Long Term Debt : An amount owed for a period exceeding one year, from the date of last balance sheet/accounting year. Otherwise known as funded debts, long term debts refers to those loans, which become due, after one year from the last balance sheet/accounting year. Such debts can be a bank loan, bonds, mortgage, debenture, or other obligations.

Long-term Liabilities : Money that one owes over a period longer than 12 months, such as mortgages, bank loans and other obligations.

Loss Given Default (LGD) : A term used to denote the actual loss incurred by a bank, in case of default by a debtor to pay off the loan. If there is any collateral pledged by the debtor, the value of such assets will be reduced from the loan amount.

MAC : Message authentication code: a hash algorithm parameterized with a key to generate a number which is attached to the message and is used to authenticate it and to guarantee the integrity of the data transmitted.

Magnetic ink character recognition (MICR) : A technique, using special MICR machine-readable characters, by which documents (ie cheques, credit transfers, direct debits) are read by machines for electronic processing.

Manipulation : An illegal operation. Buying or selling a security for the purpose of creating false or misleading appearance of active trading or for the purpose of raising or depressing the price to induce purchase or sale by others.

Manufactured payment : An equivalent payment made by the borrower of securities to the lender in lieu of actual dividends or other income earned on the securities (net of any applicable taxes), which the lender would have received if it had not lent the securities.

Margin : The amount paid by the customer when using a broker's credit to buy or sell a security.

Margin call : A demand for additional funds or collateral, following the marking to market of a securities lending transaction, if the market value of underlying collateral falls below a certain level relative to the loaned asset. Similarly, if the value of the underlying collateral assets, following their revaluation, were to exceed the agreed margin, the return of collateral might be required.

Margin call : A demand upon a customer to put up money or securities with the broker. The call is made when a purchase is made; also if a customer's account declines below a minimum standard set by the exchange or by the firm.

Market Capitalization : The total value, at market prices, of the securities at issue for a company or a stock market or sector of the stock market. Calculated by multiplying the number of shares issued by the market price per shares.

Master agreement : An agreement that sets forth the standard terms and conditions applicable to all or a defined subset of transactions that the parties may enter into from time to time, including the terms and conditions for closeout netting.

Matched book : Portfolio of assets and portfolio of liabilities having equal maturities. The term is used most often in reference to money market instruments and money market liabilities. In reference to securities lending, this entails borrowing securities and then relending the same securities for an equivalent period for the purpose of borrowing and lending money at a locked-in rate. In contrast, an unmatched book refers to borrowing and lending of the same securities for different maturities to take a short or long interest rate position.

Maturity : The date on which the principal balance of a loan becomes due and payable.

MICR Code : Magnetic Ink Character Recognition, or MICR, is a character recognition technology used primarily by the banking industry to facilitate the processing of cheques. The technology allows computers to read information (such as account numbers) off of printed documents. Unlike barcodes or similar technologies, however, MICR codes can be easily read by humans.The use of magnetic printing allows the characters to be read reliably even if they have been overprinted or obscured by other marks, such as cancellation stamps. Almost all Indian, US, Canadian and UK checks use the E-13B font.

Micro Credit : It is a term used to extend small loans to very poor people for self-employment projects that generate income, allowing them to care for themselves and their families.

Money Laundering : This is when money gained from crime is put into a bank so that it can be accessed safely by the criminals and terrorists. It makes the proceeds of illegal activities easier to get to.

Money market fund : A mutual fund whose investments are in high-yield money market instruments such as federal securities, CDs and commercial paper. Its intent is to make such instruments, normally purchased in large denominations by institutions, available indirectly to individuals. An open ended mutual fund that invest in short-term debts and monetary instruments such a Treasury bills and pays money market rates of interest.

Money Market : Market in which short-term securities are bought and sold.

Money order : An instrument used to remit money to the named payee, often used by persons who do not have a chequing account relationship with a financial institution, to pay bills or to transfer money to another person or to a company. There are three parties to a money order: the remitter (payer), the payee and the drawee. Drawees are usually financial institutions or post offices. Payees can either cash their money orders or present them to their bank for collection.

Money Transfer : This is the movement of money from one account to another.

Money Transfer Abroad : This is the movement of money from one account to another, the second being in a different country from the first.

Multilateral netting : An arrangement among three or more parties to net their obligations. The obligations covered by the arrangement may arise from financial contracts, transfers or both. The multilateral netting of payment obligations normally takes place in the context of a multilateral net settlement system.

Mutual Fund : A company that invests in and professionally manages a diversified portfolio of securities and sells shares of the portfolio to investors.

National Electronic Fund Transfer (NEFT) : It is an online system for transferring funds of Indian financial institution . This facility is used mainly to transfer funds below Rs. 1,00,000.The key difference between RTGS and NEFT is that while RTGS is on gross settlement basis, NEFT is on net settlement basis.

NBFC : Non-Banking Finance Companies.

NCD : Non-Convertible Debenture.

Negative Amortization : Negative amortization occurs when a loan payment is less than the loan's accuring interest. This causes the loan to grow instead of reduce or amortize. Also known as deferred interest.

Net Income : The amount that is left after paying the taxes is called the net income.

Net Operating Loss : A total loss that is calculated for a tax year and is attributed to business or casualty losses.

Net Present Value : Capital budgeting criterion, which compares the present value of cash inflows of a project discounted at the risk-adjusted cost of capital to the present value of investment outlays discounted at the risk-adjusted cost of capital.

Net Worth : Book value of a company's common stock, surplus, and retained earnings.

Netting : An agreed offsetting of positions or obligations by trading partners or participants. The netting reduces a large number of individual positions or obligations to a smaller number of obligations or positions. Netting may take several forms which have varying degrees of legal enforceability in the event of default of one of the parties.

No Cash Out Refinance : A home loan, which is at a lower interest, an amount which does not go over the closing costs and the outstanding principal of the original mortgage.

No Documentation Loan : When the applicant furnishes minimum information, giving, only name, address, contact information for the employer and social security number, for the application of the loan, it is called a no-documentation loan.

Nominee : A person or entity named by another to act on his behalf. A nominee is commonly used in a securities transaction to obtain registration and legal ownership of a security.

Non Performing Assets (NPA) : When due payments in credit facilities remain overdue above a specified period, then such credit facilities are classified as NPA.

Non Recourse Loan : A loan which is secured by collateral and for which the borrower is not personally liable, is called a non recourse loan.

Non-cash clearing : A method for clearing futures contracts in which positions are periodically marked to market and resulting obligations are collateralised.

Non-Liquid Asset : A possession or asset which cannot be changed into cash very easily is called non liquid asset.

Non-Recourse Discounting : Purchase from the seller of accepted term Bills of Exchange at a discount to allow for funding of the advance from the discount date until the maturity date of the bills. When the discount is provided on a non-recourse basis the financing bank has no recourse to the seller in the event of non-payment by the buyer or the buyers' bank.

Non-Recurring Closing Costs : A lumpsum fees paid at a real estate set up, which includes appraisal, origination, title insurance, credit report and points, is referred to as non-recurring closing costs.

Nonrepudiability : The ability to prevent denial or repudiation by the sender or receiver of a payment message.

Note-based system : An electronic money system in which the electronic funds are represented by records (electronic notes) that are uniquely identified by a serial number and are associated with a fixed, unchangeable denomination.

NSE : National Stock exchange of India Limited.

Obligation : The responsibility to perform some act or pay a sum of money when due.

OCR : Optical character recognition.

OD : Overdraft

Off-Balance Sheet : Includes all banking transactions that do not appear on the balance sheet of a bank as an asset or as a debt. Includes all commitments for which a cash flow arises conditional on a specific event. For instance, a loan guarantee will create an obligation only if there is a default. Derivatives are a form of off-balance sheet transactions.

Off-board : This term may refer to transactions over-the-counter in unlisted securities or to transactions of listed shares that are not executed on a national securities exchange.

Offer : The price at which a person is ready to sell. Opposed to bid, the price at which one is ready to buy.

Offline Debit Card : This refers to a card which is issued by a bank and has a VISA or Mastercard logo on it. It can be issued, either instead of or along with a ATM card.

Offsetting : This is when the credit balances in a current and savings account are netted off against the account holders borrowings (typically a mortgage) so that the rate paid on the borrowing is reduced as a result of the credit held in other accounts, which reduces the amount that is being borrowed.

Omnibus account : A single account for the commingled funds or positions of multiple parties. A clearing member will often maintain an omnibus account at the clearing house for all of the clearing member's clients. In this case, the clearing member is responsible for maintaining account records for individual clients.

On-Line : A computer system where input data are processed as received and output data are transmitted as soon as they become available to the point where they are required.

Online Banking : The accessing of bank information, accounts and transactions with the help of a computer through the financial institution's website on the Internet, is called online banking. It is also called Internet banking or e-banking

Open End Credit : Open end credit means a line of credit that can be used a number of times, up to a certain limit. Another name for this type of credit is charge account or revolving credit.

Open Market Operations(OMO) : The buying and selling of government securities in the open market in order to expand or contract the amount of money in the banking system by RBI. Open market operations are the principal tools of monetary policy.

Open Outcry Trading : Trading that is conducted on the floor of an exchange without any electronic intermediation.

Open-End Credit : Commonly referred to as a Line of Credit. May be used repeatedly up to a certain limit; also called a Charge Account or Revolving Credit.

Open-End Lease : Often, referred to as a finance lease. A lease that may involve a balloon payment based on the value of the property when it is returned.

Operating Cycle : The length of time taken by a firm to produce its final product, sell it to customers, and collect proceeds of the sale in cash.

Operating Lease : Short-term, cancelable lease.

Operating synergy : Combining two or more entities results in gains in revenues or cost reductions because of complementarities or economies of scale or scope.

Operational Risk : Includes all risks not included in market risks and credit risks, such as losses arising from fraud, failure in computer systems and data entry errors.

Opportunity Cost : The rate of return that can be earned on the best alternative investment. In general, the gain or return on the next best investment opportunity or the next best use of resources, which is forgone by putting the resources to a given use.

Optical Character Recognition (OCR) : A technique, using special OCR machine-readable characters, by which documents (eg cheques, credit transfers, direct debits) are read by machines for electronic processing.

Optimization routine : Routine processes in a payment system to determine the order in which payments are accepted for settlement. Optimisation routines are used to improve system liquidity and increase settlement efficiency.

Option : A formal contract which grants the holder of the option the right to buy or sell a certain quantity of an underlying interest or asset at a stipulated price within a specific period of time.

Option Contract : A contract that gives the buyer the right, but not the obligation, to buy or sell an underlying asset by (or on) a specific date for a specific price. For this right the purchaser pays a premium.

Ordinary Dividends : Dividends, which are a distribution of the profits of a company, are called ordinary dividends.

Ordinary Income : Income, not qualifying as a capital gain, is called ordinary income.

Original Principal Balance : The amount borrowed by any borrower is called the original principal balance.

Origination Fee : The charges a lender or creditor levies for processing a loan. It includes cost of loan document preparation, verification of the credit history of the borrower and conducting an overall appraisal.

Over the counter : A method of trading that does not involve an exchange. In overthe- counter markets, participants trade directly with each other, typically through telephone or computer links.

Overbought : An opinion as to price levels. May refer to a security that has had a sharp rise or to the market as a whole after a period of vigorous buying which, it may be argued, has left prices "too high."

Overdraft : When the amount of money withdrawn from a bank account is greater that the amount actually available in the account, the excess is known as an overdraft, and the account is said to be overdrawn.

Overdraft Protection : A service which permits a verification account to be connected to other savings or line of credit for facilitation of protection against overdrafts is called overdraft protection.

Overdraft System : The system in which the borrower is allowed to overdraw on his current account with the banker upto a certain specified limit during a given period.

Overnight money : A loan with a maturity of one business day. Also called day-to-day money.

Oversight : A public policy activity principally intended to promote the safety and efficiency of payment and securities settlement systems and in particular to reduce systemic risk.

Oversight of payment systems : A central bank task, principally intended to promote the smooth functioning of payment systems and to protect the financial system from possible "domino effects" which may occur when one or more participants in the payment system incur credit or liquidity problems. Payment systems oversight aims at a given system (eg a funds transfer system) rather than individual participants.

Oversold : The reverse of overbought. A single security or a market which, it is believed, has declined to an unreasonable level.

Over-the-counter : A market for securities made up of securities dealers who may or may not be members of a securities exchange. The over-the-counter market is conducted over the telephone and deals mainly with stocks of companies without sufficient shares, stockholders or earnings to warrant listing on an exchange. Over-the-counter dealers may act either as principals or as brokers for customers. The over-the-counter market is the principal market for bonds of all types.

Owner Financing : When the seller loans the whole sum or a part of it to a buyer, it is called owner financing.

Paperless credit transfers : Credit transfers that do not involve the exchange of paper documents between banks. Other credit transfers are referred to as being paper-based.

Par Value : The value of a security when it is issued. For bonds and preferred stock, par value is equivalent to face value.

Partial Shipment : A load sent in more than one consignment. In a Letter of Credit, the buyer can say whether this is allowed or not allowed.

Partnerships : Shared ownership among two or more individuals, some of whom may, but do not necessarily, have limited liability with respect to obligations of the group. There is a written agreement among partners detailing the terms and conditions of participation in a business ownership arrangement.

Pass Through Certificates : Debt instruments backed by a portfolio of assets.

Payback period : Length of time required for an asset to generate cash flows just enough to cover the initial outlay.

Payee : Payee is the person to whom the money is to be paid by the payer.

Payer : Payer is the person who pays the money to the payee.

Payment lag : The time lag between the initiation of the payment order and its final settlement.

PCMCIA card : Personal computer media control interface adapter: a device that is attached externally to a PC and can perform various functions such as memory storage and modem communications. PCMCIA cards can be designed in such a way as to provide a certain level of tamper-resistance.

Penny stocks : Low-priced issues, often highly speculative, selling at less than $1 a share. Frequently used as a term of disparagement, although some penny stocks have developed into investment-caliber issues.

Personal Identification Number (PIN) : Personal identification number or PIN is a secret code of numbers and alphabets given to customers to perform transactions through an automatic teller machine or an ATM.

Phishing : This is when a criminal uses the internet to try to fraudulently obtain details of peoples accounts so that they can use these accounts themselves, usually to take money out of.

Plain vanilla transactions : The most common and generally the simplest types of derivatives transaction. Plain vanilla is a relative concept, and no precise list of plain vanilla transactions exists. Transactions that have unusual or less common features are often called exotic or structured.

Pledge : If someone pledges goods, they let a second person take possession of the goods, but the person pledging the goods still owns them. It is often done as security for money owed or to make sure that something is done as promised.

Point of Sale (POS) : Point of sale a terminal is where cash registers are replaced by computerized systems. This term refers to the use of payment cards at a retail location (point of sale). The payment information is captured either by paper vouchers or by electronic terminals, which in some cases are designed also to transmit the information. Where this is so, the arrangement may be referred to as "electronic funds transfer at the point of sale" (EFTPOS).

Posting Date : Posting date is the date on which outdoor advertisements hit the markets. Usually these dates are in multiples of five.

Power of Attorney : A power of attorney is a document, which gives power to the person appointed by it to act for the person who signed the document. A written instrument, which authorizes one person to act as another's agent or attorney. The power of attorney may be for a definite, specific act, or it may be general in nature. The terms of the written power of attorney may specify when it will expire. If not, the power of attorney usually expires when the person granting it dies.

Preference Shares: A corporate security that pays a fixed dividend each period. It is senior to ordinary shares but junior to bonds in its claims on corporate income and assets in case of bankruptcy.

Prefunding : The requirement that funds be available in accounts at the settlement institution before institutions use these accounts to extinguish their settlement obligations.

Prepayment : Payment of the principal amount of a loan ahead of the scheduled date.

Pre-Qualification : A preliminary stage prior to bidding process, where the applicant is verified of whether he has the resources and the ability to do a given job.

Present Value : The discounted value of a payment or stream of payments to be received in future, taking into consideration a specific interest or discount rate. Present Value represents a series of future cash flows expressed in today's value.

Previous Balance : Previous balance is an outstanding amount which appears on the credit card statement on date when it is generated.

Prime Lending Rate (PLR) : The rate of interest charged on loans by banks to their most creditworthy customers.

Prime rate : The lowest interest rate charged by commercial banks to their most creditworthy customers; other interest rates, such as personal, automobile, commercial and financing loans are often pegged to the prime.

Principal : Amount of debt that must be repaid. Also means a person who deals in securities on his own account and not as a broker.

Product Differentiation : Development of a variety of product configurations to appeal to a variety of consumer tastes.

Product Life Cycle : A conceptual model of the stages through which products or lines of businesses pass. Includes development, growth, maturity, and decline. Each stage presents its own threats and opportunities.

Product Mix : The composite of products offered for sale by an organization.

Productivity : The amount of physical output for each unit of productive unit.

Promissory Note : A signed undertaking from one party containing a promise to pay a stated sum to a specified person or a company at a specified future date.

Prospectus : A detailed report published by the Initial Public Offering company, which includes all terms and conditions, application procedures, IPO prices etc, for the IPO

PSB : Public Sector Bank

PSE : Public Sector Enterprise

PSU : Public Sector Undertaking

Purchasing Power Parity (PPP) : The concept that homogeneous goods cannot have more than one price measured in any one currency. If the price increases domestically, the domestic currency will depreciate so that the price denominated in foreign currency remains the same.

Pure Conglomerate Merger : A combination of firms in non-related business activities that is neither a product-extension nor a geographic-extension merger.

Put Option : The right to sell the underlying securities at a specified exercise price on of before a specified expiration date.

PVP : Payment versus payment.

Qualified Opinion : An auditor's opinion mentioned in his report which holds some reservations regarding the process of audit is called as a qualified opinion.

Quality Spread : The difference between the yields of Treasury securities and non-Treasury securities, as a result of different ratings or quality, is termed as quality spread.

Queuing : A risk management arrangement whereby transfer orders are held pending by the originator/ deliverer or by the system until sufficient cover is available in the originator's/deliverer's clearing account or under the limits set against the payer; in some cases, cover may include unused credit lines or available collateral.

Quick Ratio : Quick ratio is also called as the acid-test ratio. It measures the company's liabilities and determines its position to pay off its

Range Bonds : Bonds which cease the payments because the reference rate of the bond increases or decreases, as compared to predetermined rate on a given index.

Rate Risk : Rate risk is the rate of return determined to attract capital on a given investment.

Rate Sensitive : Rate sensitive pertains to deposit account or security investment. If any changes are made to the related interest rate that causes variations in its demand and supply.

Rating : Refers to the credit quality of a counterparty. External ratings are given by rating agencies (ranging from AAA very safe asset to C). Internal ratings are granted by the bank itself.

Ratio : Comparison of two figures used to evaluate business performances, such as debt/equity ratio return on investment, etc.

Real Time Gross Settlement system (RTGS) : The Reserve Bank of India (India's Central Bank) maintains this payment network, which is available on weekdays only from 10 am to 1:30 pm. Fees for RTGS vary from bank to bank. Both the remitting and receiving must have Core banking in place to enter into RTGS transactions. RTGS is a large value (minimum value of transaction should be Rs. 1,00,000) funds transfer system whereby financial intermediaries can settle interbank transfers for their own account as well as for their customers.

Reconciliation : Checking all bank account papers to make sure that the bank's records and customer's records are in sync.

Reconveyance : In banking terms, reconveyance is transfer of property to its real owner, once the loan or the mortgage is paid off.

Record Date : A date set by the issuer, on which an individual must own the shares, so as to be eligible to receive the dividend.

Recourse : In the context of a sale of a loan by a bank to investors, they have the right to call the guarantee from the bank should the borrower be unable to meet its obligations

Redemption : Redemption means paying off all the money borrowed under an agreement.

Redemption Fee : A commission or fee paid, when an agent or an individual sells an investment, such as mutual funds or annuity.

Redemption price : The price at which a bond may be redeemed before maturity, at the option of the issuing company. Redemption value also applies to the price the company must pay to call in certain types of preferred stock.

Reference Asset : An asset such as debt instrument which has a credit derivative is called as a reference asset.

Reference Rate : The basis of floating rate security is called as the reference rate.

Refinance : Refinance means clearing the current loan with the proceeds of a new one and using the same property for collateral.

Refunding : The act of paying back the amount or returning the funds is called as refunding.

Reinvestment Risk : The risk that arises from the fact that dividends or any yields may not be eligible for investment to earn the rate of interest is called as the reinvestment risk.

Relative Value : The liquidity, risk and return of one instrument in relation to another financial instrument is the relative value.

Repossession : Taking back of property by a seller or a lender from the buyer or the borrower due to default of payment.

Repricing : Repricing means a change in the rate of interest.

Reservable deposits : Bank deposits subject to reserve requirements.

Reserve Account : An account which is maintained by depositing undistributed parts of profit for future needs is called as a reserve account.

Reserve Requirement : The obligation for banks to maintain balances (bank reserves) at the central bank in respect of certain types of liabilities repo rate: the return earned on a repo transaction expressed as an interest rate on the cash side of the transaction. Cash money or liquidity that member banks need to hold with the Federal Reserve System.

Residual Value : The anticipated value that a company calculates, to sell its asset at the end of its full life.

Resistance Level : A price at which sellers consistently outnumber buyers, preventing further price rises.

Resolution : A formal document expressing the intention of a board of directors of a corporation.

Reverse repo : A contract with a counterparty to buy and subsequently resell securities at a specified date and price, the mirror image of a repo.

Revolver : A credit agreement that allows a customer to borrow against a preapproved credit line. Usually used for working capital needs, the borrower is only billed for the amount that is actually borrowed plus any interest due. Collateral may be based upon accounts receivable and inventory.

Revolving Letter of Credit : A Letter of Credit in which the value of the Letter of Credit is automatically reinstated upon utilization. A Letter of Credit may revolve by value, time or both.

Revolving Line of Credit : Revolving line of credit is a rule followed by the lender, which binds him to allow a certain credit to the borrower.

Rights : When a company wants to raise more funds by issuing additional securities, it may give its stockholders the opportunity, ahead of others, to buy the new securities in proportion to the number of shares each owns. The piece of paper evidencing this privilege is called a right. Because the additional stock is usually offered to stockholders below the current market price, rights ordinarily have a market value of their own and are actively traded. In most cases they must be exercised within a relatively short period. Failure to exercise or sell rights may result in monetary loss to the holder.

Rights Issue: An offer by way of rights to current holders of securities that allows them to subscribe for securities in proportion to their existing holdings.

Risk Assessment : A process used to identify and evaluate risks and their potential effect.

RTGS System : The acronym 'RTGS' stands for Real Time Gross Settlement. RTGS system is a funds transfer mechanism where transfer of money takes place from one bank to another on a 'real time' and on 'gross' basis. This is the fastest possible money transfer system through the banking channel. Settlement in 'real time' means payment transaction is not subjected to any waiting period. The transactions are settled as soon as they are processed. 'Gross settlement' means the transaction is settled on one to one basis without bunching with any other transaction.

Safekeeping : An arrangement for holding and protecting a customer's assets, like valuables, documents, etc. Such arrangements are commonly provided by banks and some financial institutions, usually for a fee. The customer is issued a safekeeping receipt, which indicates that the assets do not belong to the bank and they have to be returned to the customer, upon his request.

Sale : Transfer of ownership of some type of property from one person to another, for some consideration.

Sale Leaseback : A sale of property, wherein the title is transferred to the buyer, on condition that the property will be leased to the seller on a long-term basis, after the sale.

Salvage : The attempt to get repayment of some portion of a loan obligation which has already been written off the bank's books.

Same Day Funds : This banking term refers to the funds or money balances, which can be transferred or withdrawn on the same day of presenting and collection. In short, a transfer of money, which can be used by the recipient on the same day of transfer and this provision is subject to the net settlement of accounts between the bank, through which the money is sent and the receiving bank. This term is also used to refer to the transfer of federal funds from one bank to another over Fedwire and the transfers through the Clearing House Interbank Payments System (CHIPS) in New York.

Scale Economies : The reduction in per-unit costs achievable by spreading fixed costs over a higher level of production.

SEBI : Securities and Exchange Board of India.

SEBs : State Electricity Boards.

Second Mortgage : Otherwise known as 'second trust', a second mortgage is a mortgage which is taken out on property, which has been pledged as security to ensure payment (collateral) of an original or first mortgage. A first mortgage has priority in settlement of claims, before all other subsequent mortgages. Unlike a first mortgage, a second mortgage has a shorter repayment term, with higher interest rates.

Secured Loan : A loan which is backed by a pledging of real or personal property (collateral) by the borrower to the lender. Unlike unsecured loans, which is backed by a mere promise by the borrower that he will repay the loan, in case of a secured loan, the lender can initiate legal action against the borrower to reclaim and sell the collateral (pledged property).

Securitization : The process of transformation of a bank loan into tradable securities. It often involves the creation of a separate corporate entity, the Special Purpose Vehicle (SPV), which buys the loans financing itself with securities that are sold to investors.

Security : Property or assets, which are pledged to the lender by the borrower, as a guarantee to the repayment of a loan.

Segregation : A method of protecting client assets and positions by holding or accounting for them separately from those of the carrying firm or broker.

Selective Credit Control (SCC) : Control of credit flow to borrowers dealing in some essential commodities to discourage hoarding and black-marketing.

Seller Carryback : A form of financing, wherein the seller of a property finances the buyer, who finds it difficult to procure a loan or falls short of the amount needed to buy the property. In short, it is a part of the purchase amount, which the seller offers to finance. This term is also known as carryback loan or seller's second.

Seller's Market : A market, which has more buyers, as compared to the number of sellers. This condition leads to a rise in the prices, which is favorable for sellers.

Senior Debt : Debt which, in the event of bankruptcy, must be repaid before subordinated debt receives any payment.

Serial Bonds : Bonds that mature at specified intervals.

Series Bond : Bond which may be issued in several series under the same indenture.

Service Charge : A fee paid for using a service.

Service Provider : The organization which provides the outsourced service.

Set off : A method of cancelling or offsetting reciprocal obligations and claims (or the discharge of reciprocal obligations up to the amount of the smaller obligations). Set off can operate by force of law or pursuant to a contract.

SEZ : Specific Economic Zone.

SFC : State Financial Corporation.

Short-term Loan : Loan to a business for less than one year, usually for operating needs.

SICA : Sick Industrial Companies (Special Provisions) Act.

Sinking Fund : A fund to which a firm makes a periodic contribution to facilitate retirement of debt.

Smart Cards : Unlike debit and credit cards (with magnetic stripes), smart cards possess a computer chip, which is used for data storage, processing and identification.

Sort Code : A sort code is a specific number, which is assigned to a particular branch of a bank for internal purposes. Each branch is assigned with a sort code, which makes it easier to designate that particular branch of bank, than writing down the whole address.

Special Purpose Vehicle : A legal corporate entity created to buy loans from banks. It finances itself with securities issued to investors.

Spin off : The separation of a subsidiary or division of a corporation from its parent company by issuing shares in a new corporate entity. Shareowners in the parent company receive shares in the new company in proportion to their original holding and the total value remains approximately the same.

Split : The division of the outstanding shares of a corporation into a larger number of shares. A 3-for-1 split by a company with 1 million shares outstanding results in 3 million shares outstanding. Each holder of 100 shares before the 3-for-1 split would have 300 shares, although the proportionate equity in the company would remain the same; 100 parts of 1 million are the equivalent of 300 parts of 3 million. Ordinarily, splits must be voted by directors and approved by shareholders.

Stakeholder : In a payment system, stakeholders are those parties whose interests are affected by the operation of the system.

Standard Payment Calculation : A method used to calculate the monthly payment required to repay a loan, based on the loan balance, term of the loan and the current interest rate.

Standby Letter of Credit : A guarantee issued by a bank, on behalf of a buyer that protects the seller against non-payment for goods shipped to the buyer. The buyer pays the seller directly for the goods and only if the buyer fails to pay does the seller claim under the Standby Letter of Credit.

Standing Order : A regular payment made out of a current account which is of a set amount and is originated by the account holder.

Statement : All transactions in a bank account for a period of time. Statements are usually given once a month.

Statutory Audit : By law, certain companies need to have their accounts audited by suitably qualified accountants. This is called a statutory audit.

Sterilization : The use by a central bank of operations (such as open market sales) to reduce bank reserves (liquidity) which it has created through some other financial transactions such as the purchase of foreign currency.

Stocks : Traded on a stock exchange, these are shares in a company. Essentially, one purchases shares in an exchange for owning a part of a company.

Stop Payment : An order not to pay a check that has been issued buy not yet cashed. If requested soon enough, the check will not be debited from the payer's account.

Stress testing : The estimation of credit and liquidity exposures that would result from the realisation of extreme price and implied volatility scenarios.

Subsidy : A subsidy is a form of financial assistance paid to a business or economic sector. Most subsidies are made by the government to producers or distributors in an industry to prevent the decline of that industry or an increase in the prices of its products or to encourage it to hire more labor.

Swap : An agreement for an exchange of payments between two counterparties at some point(s) in the future and according to a specified formula.

Swapping : Selling one security and buying a similar one almost at the same time to take a loss, usually for tax purposes.

SWOT : Acronym for Strengths, Weakness, Opportunities and Threats; an approach to formulating firm strategy via assessment of a firm's capabilities in relation to the business environment.

Syndicate : Group of banks and financial institutions, which together contribute the necessary financing for a transaction.

Syndicated Loans : Loans to a company backed by a group of banks in order to share the risk in a large transaction among several financial institutions. There is usually a lead bank and several participating banks.

Synergy : The "2 + 2 = 5" effect. The output of a combination of two entities is greater than the sum of their individual outputs.

Systematic Risk : The risk that the failure of one participant in a payment or settlement system, or in financial markets generally, to meet its required obligations when due will cause other participants or financial institutions to be unable to meet their obligations (including settlement obligations in a payment and settlement system) when due.

Takeout Commitments : This term relates to a written promise by a loaner to make a long-term financial arrangement to substitute or replace a short-run loan.

Take-out Merger : The second-step transaction which merges the acquired firm into the acquirer and thus takes out the remaining target shares which were not purchased in the initial (partial) tender offer.

Tangible Assets : Physical assets such as plant, machinery, factories, and offices.

Tax Avoidance : Lawful agreement or re-arrangement of the affairs of an individual or company intended to avoid liability to tax.

Tax Evasion : Fraudulent or illegal arrangements made with the intention of evading tax, e.g. by failure to make full disclosure to the revenue authorities.

Tax Haven : An international banking and financial centre providing privacy and tax benefits.

Tax Incentives : Tax benefits. Most tax incentive measures fall into one or more of the following categories: tax exemption (tax holiday); deduction from the taxable base; reduction in the rate of tax; tax deferment, etc.

Tender offer : A public offer to buy shares from existing stockholders of one public corporation by another public corporation under specified terms good for a certain time period. Stockholders are asked to "tender" (surrender) their holdings for stated value, usually at a premium above current market price, subject to the tendering of a minimum and maximum number of shares.

Term Insurance : It is the insurance for a certain time period which provides for no defrayal to the insured individual, excluding losses during the period, and that becomes null upon its expiration.

Term Loan : A loan intended for medium-term or long-term financing to supply cash to purchase fixed assets such as machinery, land or buildings or to renovate business premises.

Term Note : A legal notice offered by a particular organization to investors through a dealer.

Term Structure of Interest Rates : This phrase relates to the relationship between interest rates on bonds of different due dates, generally described in the form of a chart, often known as a 'yield curve'.

Third market : Trading of stock exchange-listed securities in the over-the-counter market by non-exchange member brokers.

Ticker : A telegraphic system that continuously provides the last sale prices and volume of securities transactions on exchanges. Information is either printed or displayed on a moving tape after each trade.

Tier 1 Capital : Refers to core capital consisting of Capital, Statutory Reserves, Revenue and other reserves, Capital Reserves (excluding Revaluation Reserves) and unallocated surplus/ profit but excluding accumulated losses, investments in subsidiaries and other intangible assets

Tier 2 Capital : Comprises Property Revaluation Reserves, Undisclosed Reserves, Hybrid Capital, Subordinated Term Debt and General Provisions. This is Supplementary Capital.

Time Deposit : A kind of bank deposit which the investor is not able to withdraw, before a time fixed when making the deposit.

Time Draft : This term relates to a draft that is collectible at a particular future date.

Time Note : A 'time note' is a financial instrument, like a 'note of hand', which stipulates dates or a date of defrayal.

Time Value : This is the sum of money that an option's premium surpasses its intrinsic worth, and is also called as 'time premium'.

Title : The evidence one has of right to possession of land.

Title Deeds : Documents which prove who owns a property and under what terms.

Title Insurance : insurance against the loss of ownership of property resulting from a defect of title to the described parcel of real property.

Title Insurance : It is the insurance for the purpose of protecting a loaner or owner against loss, if there is any kind of a property ownership conflict.

Title Insurance Commitment : This term is concerned with the commitment which is brought out by a title insurance firm, and comprises the stipulations under which a title insurance policy will be made out.

Title Search : An investigation into the history of ownership of a property to check for liens, unpaid claims, or other problems, to prove that a seller can transfer free and clear ownership.

Total Return Swap : It is a kind of switch wherein an entity pays another entity according to the fixed rate in return for defrayals based on the return of a given asset.

Trade Credit : It is the credit which a company gives to another organization for the purpose of buying products or services.

Trade Creditors : Organisations, which are owed money for goods and services supplied.

Trade Date : The day on which the actual transaction takes place; one to five days before the settlement period, according to the kind of transaction.

Trade Debtors : Organisations, which owe money for goods and services supplied.

Trade Deficit : The amount by which merchandise imports exceed merchandise exports.

Trade Letter of Credit : This refers to a legal document that a customer asks for from his bank for the purpose of assuring that the defrayal for products would be transferred to the vendor.

Transaction : Action in a bank account. Could be a deposit, withdrawal, debit card payment, service charge or interest payment.

Treasury Bills : Treasury Bills (T-Bills) are short term, Rupee denominated obligations issued by the Reserve Bank of India (RBI) on behalf of the Government of India. They are thus useful in managing short-term liquidity. At present, the Government of India issues three types of treasury bills through auctions, namely, 91-day, 182-day and 364-day. There are no treasury bills issued by State Governments.

Tri-party repo : Repo in which bonds and cash are delivered by the trading counterparty to an independent custodian bank, clearing house or securities depository that is responsible for ensuring the maintenance of adequate collateral value during the life of the transaction.

Truncation : A procedure in which the physical movement of paper payment instruments (eg paid cheques or credit transfers) within a bank, between banks or between a bank and its customer is curtailed or eliminated, being replaced, in whole or in part, by electronic records of their content for further processing and transmission.

Trust : An entity created for the purpose of protecting and conserving assets for the benefit of a third party, the beneficiary- A contract affecting three parties, the settlor, the trustee and the beneficiary.

Trust Deed (Settlement Deed, Declaration of Trust or Trust Instrument) : Document that lays down the foundations of how the trustees are to administer and manage the trust assets and how they are to distribute and dispose of trust assets during the lifetime of the trust.

Trustee : Trustees have a fiduciary duty to act in accordance with a trust deed and for the benefit of the beneficiary (ies).

UCPDC : 'Uniform Customs and Practice for Documentary Credit' developed by the International Chamber of Commerce as the rules that govern the operation of Letter of Credit transactions worldwide. ICC publication No.500 contains details of the rules currently in use.

Unadvised Line : A line of credit which is sanctioned by the bank but not revealed to the borrower till the time of some particular occasion.

Uncertificated : This is a legal word that is utilized as an adjective to depict stocks, bonds, miscellaneous investments and deposit certificates, which are held in immaterial form as electronic computer records.

Uncollected Funds : A portion of a deposit balance that has not yet been collected by the depository bank.

Uncovered : It is the condition of an option bearer who doesn't even possess an offsetting position in the underlying instrument.

Undervaluation : When a firm's securities sell for less than their intrinsic, or potential, or long-run value for one or more reasons.

Underwriter : Any investment or commercial financial firm or a securities house that works with an issuing entity for the purpose of selling a new issue.

Underwriting : The arrangement in which investment bankers undertake to ensure the full success of the issue of securities.

Undivided Profits : This is a banking work for retained earnings.

Unexpected Loss or Unexpected Risk : The element or part of risk or loss which surpasses the anticipated amount.

Uniform Commercial Code : A set of statutes enacted by the various States to provide consistency amount the States' commercial laws. It includes negotiable instruments, sales, stock transfers, trust and warehous receipts, and bills of lading.

Universal Bank : A bank or a financial institution that has the legal authority to offer all financial services and may, thus, be engaged in securities dealing, insurance, underwriting, and the full range of more traditional banking services.

Universal Life Insurance : A type of life insurance which blends term insurance protection with a savings element.

Unlimited Guaranty : A guarantee understanding which doesn't consist of any provisos limiting the amount of debt guaranteed.

Unwind : A procedure followed in certain clearing and settlement systems in which transfers of securities and funds are settled on a net basis, at the end of the processing cycle, with all transfers provisional until all participants have discharged their settlement obligations. If a participant fails to settle, some or all of the provisional transfers involving that participant are deleted from the system and the settlement obligations from the remaining transfers are then recalculated. Such a procedure has the effect of allocating liquidity pressures and losses from the failure to settle to the counterparties of the participant that fails to settle. Unwinds can be distinguished from debits to securities accounts that do not imply the original transfer is rescinded (eg in cases where securities are discovered to be forged or stolen).

Unwinding : a procedure followed in certain clearing and settlement systems in which transfers of securities or funds are settled on a net basis, at the end of the processing cycle, with all transfers provisional until all participants have discharged their settlement obligations. If a participant fails to settle, some or all of the provisional transfers involving that participant are deleted from the system and the settlement obligations from the remaining transfers are then recalculated. Such a procedure has the effect of transferring liquidity pressures and possibly losses from the failure to settle to other participants, and may, in an extreme case, result in significant and unpredictable systemic risks. Also called settlement unwind.

Up tick : A term used to designate a transaction made at a price higher than the preceding transaction. Also called a "plus" tick. A "zero-plus" tick is a term used for a transaction at the same price as the preceding trade but higher than the preceding different price. Conversely, a down tick, or "minus" tick, is a term used to designate a transaction made at a price lower than the preceding trade.

Upstream Guaranty : A word that is utilized to give a description of a guarantee of a loan to a borrowing entity, when the borrowing party is an owning company or shareholder of the surety.

Usury : Charging an illegally high interest rate on a loan. Usuary rates are generally set by State law.

Usury Laws : The state and federal jurisprudences setting up uttermost permissible rates of interest that can be charged on certain types of credit extensions to particular kinds of borrowers.

Value At Risk (VAR) : The sum or portion of the value that is at stake of subject to loss from a variation in prevalent interest rates.

Value Based Management (VBM) : It is a structured approach to evaluate the performance of the company's unit managers or goods and services, in terms of the aggregate gains they render to stockholders.

Value Creation : The difference between the value of an investment and the amount of money invested by shareholders.

Variable Expenses : Costs of doing business that vary with the volume of business, such as advertising costs, manufacturing costs and bad debts.

Variable Life Insurance : This type of insurance is very similar to whole life insurance, wherein the cash worth is invested in equity or debt sureties.

Variable Rate : A variable rate loan or credit agreement, calls for an interest rate that may fluctuate over the life of the loan. The rate is often tied to an index that reflects changes in market rates of interest. A fluctuation in the rate causes changes in either the payments or the length of the term.

Variable Rate Mortgage : This is just another term used for Adjustable Rate Mortgage (ARM).

Variation margin : Funds that are paid to (or received from) a counterparty (clearing house or clearing member) to settle any losses (gains) that are implied by marking open positions to market.

VCF : Venture Capital Fund.

Vector Path : A series of the rate of paying finances in advance, in succession that is chosen to contemplate an assumed rate of interest scenario.

Venture Capital : Commonly refers to funds that are invested by a third party in a business either as equity or as a form of secondary debt.

Vertical Merger : A combination of firms, which operate at different levels or stages of the same industry manufacturer mergers with a type company (backward integration).

VRS : Voluntary Retirement Scheme

Waiver : In banking terms, a waiver is relinquishing the rights. Sometimes also considered to be the exemption or settlement of a part of debt.

Warehouse Lines of Credit : Warehouse line of credit is a facility provided to the borrower to get a warehouse mortgage portfolio for future security.

When-Issued (WI) : 'When issued' or WI is a conditional transaction made due to its authorized security or debt obligation.

White list : In a card-based system, a database containing the list of all authorised card numbers.

Whole Life Insurance : A whole life insurance is a contract between the insurer and the policy owner, that the insurer will pay the sum of money on the occurrence of the event mentioned in the policy to the insured. It's a concept wherein the insurer mitigates the loss caused to the insured on the basis of certain principles.

Wholesale Banking : Wholesale banking is a term used for banks which offer services to other corporate entities, large institutions and other financial institutions.

Winding up : Winding up of a company is done by paying the company's creditors, and then distributing monies left (if any) among the members.

Wire Transfers : Wire transfers is an Electronic medium used while transferring of funds.

With Recourse : A term used to signify that a seller or a drawer will be liable in case of non-performance of asset or non-payment of an instrument.

Withdrawals : Removing of funds from a bank account is called as making a withdrawal.

Withholding tax : A tax on income deducted at source, which a paying agent is legally obliged to deduct from its payments of interest on deposits, securities or similar financial instruments.

Without Recourse : A term which signifies that the buyer is responsible for non-performance of an asset or non-payment of an instrument, instead of the seller.

Working Capital : In banking terms, working capital is defined as the difference between current assets and current liabilities.

Wraparound Mortgage : An arrangement, wherein existing mortgage is refinanced with more money, with a rate of interest ranging between the old rates and current market rates.

Writer : A writer is an entity or a financial institution which promises to sell a certain number of shares or stocks at a price before a certain date.

Yield : (1) A measure of the income generated by a bond. The amount of interest paid on a bond divided by the price. (2) The rate of discount which makes the present value of the stream of future returns plus the terminal value of the asset equal to the current market price of the asset.

Yield Curve : Yield curve is a graph or a curve that shows the relationship between maturity dates and yield.

Yield Curve Risk : Yield curve risk is the huge risk involved in a fixed income instrument, due to major fluctuations in the market rates of interest.

Yield to Call (YTC) : The yield on a bond calculated on the supposition that the issuer will redeem the amount at the first call as stated on the bond's prospectus is called as yield to call.

Yield-to-Maturity (YTM) : The average annual yield that an investor receives because he holds it for life or till the maturity date is called as the yield to maturity.

Z score : Z score is a measure, used in the banking field, to determine the difference between a single data point and a normal data point.

Zero Balance Account : A bank account which does not require any minimum balance is termed as a zero balance account.

Zero Cost Collar : A type of arrangement, wherein, the borrower buys a cap from the bank and sells the floor. In this arrangement, the cost of the cap is recovered by sale proceeds of the floor or vice versa.

Zero Coupon Bond : A bond issued at a discount (i.e. below par value), earning no interest but redeemable at its par value, thus providing a guaranteed capital gain.

Zero Coupon Yield Curve : Zero coupon yield curve is also called as spot yield curve, and is used to determine discount factors.

Zero-Down-Payment Mortgage : Zero-down-payment mortgage is a type of mortgage given to a buyer who does not make any down payments while borrowing. The mortgage buyer borrows the amount at the entire purchase price.

Zero-Lot Line : Structure of a housing area such that every house has a designated plot. They may or may not have same walls.

Zoning : A government controlled area where only certain uses of the land are permitted is called zoning.

Zoning Variance : An exception made in the zoning rule by the local government is zoning variance.

Latest Facts Related to Banking and Insurance Sectors

- RBI replaces PLR system by Base Rate System since July, 2010. The Reserve Bank of India (RBI) has given complete freedom to banks to decide the methodology for calculating the base rate, which will be the new bench-mark to arrive at lending rates.

- The RBI set-up a committee to study issues and concerns in the micro-finance sectors (Chairmain : Shri Y.H. Malegam). Based on its recommendation, all Scheduled Commercial Banks (SCBs) have been advised by the RBI that bank credit to MFIs extended on, or after 1 April, 2011 for on-lending to individuals and also to members of SHGs/joint-liability groups (JLGs) will be eligible for categorization as priority sector advance.

- Industrial Development Bank of India (IDBI) has been the apex institution of industrial finance in the country. This bank has been given the status of a banking company w.e.f. September, 2004. IDBI, since October 1, 2004, started its business as a banking company.

★★★★★★

Banking : Meaning and Concepts

MEANING

Bank is a lawful organisation, which accepts deposits that can be withdrawn on demand. It also lends money to individuals and business houses that need it.

Banks are such places where people can deposit their savings with the assurance that they will be able to withdraw money from the deposits whenever required. People who wish to borrow money for business and other purposes can also get loans from the banks at reasonable rate of interest.

Banks also render many other useful services – like collection of bills, payment of foreign bills, safe-keeping of jewellery and other valuable items, certifying the credit-worthiness of business, and so on.

Banks accept deposits from the general public as well as from the business community. Any one who saves money for future can deposit his savings in a bank. Businessmen have income from sales out of which they have to make payment for expenses. They can keep their earnings from sales safely deposited in banks to meet their expenses from time to time. Banks give two assurances to the depositors :

(*a*) Safety of deposit, and

(*b*) Withdrawal of deposit, whenever needed

On deposits, banks give interest, which adds to the original amount of deposit. It is a great incentive to the depositor. It promotes saving habits among the public. On the basis of deposits banks also grant loans and advances to farmers, traders and businessmen for productive purposes. Thereby banks contribute to the economic development of the country and well being of the people in general. Banks also charge interest on loans. The rate of interest is generally higher than the rate of interest allowed on deposits. Banks also charge fees for the various other services, which they render to the business community and public in general. Interest received on loans and fees charged for services which exceed the interest allowed on deposits are the main sources of income for banks from which they meet their administrative expenses.

The activities carried on by banks are called banking activity. 'Banking' as an activity involves acceptance of deposits and lending or investment of money. It facilitates business activities by providing money and certain services that help in exchange of goods and services. Therefore, banking is an important auxiliary to trade. It not only provides money for the production of goods and services but also facilitates their exchange between the buyer and seller.

DIFFERENCES BETWEEN BANKS AND MONEYLENDERS

A bank is quite different from a moneylender. A bank performs two main functions. Firstly, it accepts deposits, and on that basis it lends money. The moneylenders, on the other hand, advance money out of their own private wealth and usually do not accept deposits from others. The following table shows the difference between a bank and moneylender.

Basis	Banks	Moneylenders
1. Entity	Bank are organised institutions.	Moneylenders are individuals.
2. Activity	Banking activities include acceptance of deposits as well as lending of money.	Activities of moneylender may not include acceptance of deposits.
3. Clients	Banks meet the needs of people in general and the business community in particular.	Moneylenders meet the needs of agriculturists and poor people.
4. Security	Banks accept tangible and personal security against loans.	Moneylenders generally accept gold, jewellery or land as security for giving loan.
5. Process of recovery of loans.	The process of recovery is flexible.	The process of recovery is rigid and strict.
6. Interest Rate	Interest charged by banks on loan is governed by RBI.	Rate of Interest is decided by the moneylender and is normally very high.

ROLE OF BANKING

Banks provide funds for business as well as personal needs of individuals. Let us know about the role of banking:

- ❑ It encourages savings habit amongst people and thereby makes funds available for productive use.
- ❑ It acts as an intermediary between people having surplus money and those requiring money for various business activities.
- ❑ It facilitates business transactions through receipts and payments by cheques instead of currency.
- ❑ It provides loans and advances to businessmen for short term and long-term purposes.
- ❑ It also facilitates import-export transactions.
- ❑ It helps in national development by providing credit to farmers, small-scale industries and self-employed people as well as to large business houses which lead to balanced economic development in the country.
- ❑ It helps in raising the standard of living of people in general by providing loans for purchase of consumer durable goods, houses, automobiles, etc.

TYPES OF BANKS

On the basis of functions, the banking institutions in India may be divided into the following types:

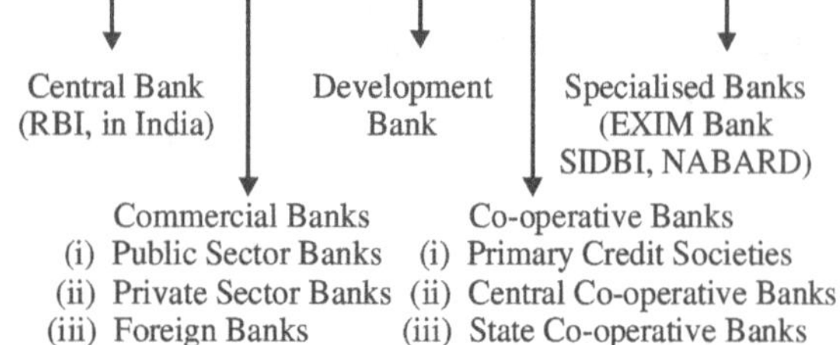

CENTRAL BANK

A bank which is entrusted with the functions of guiding and regulating the banking system of a country is known as its Central bank. Such a bank does not deal with the general public. It acts essentially as Government's banker, maintain deposit accounts of all other banks and advances money to other banks, when needed. The Central Bank provides guidance to other banks whenever they face any problem. It is therefore known as the banker's bank. The Reserve Bank of India is the central bank of our country.

The Central Bank maintains record of Government revenue and expenditure under various heads. It also advises the Government on monetary and credit policies and decides on the interest rates for bank deposits and bank loans. In addition, foreign exchange rates are also determined by the central bank.

Another important function of the Central Bank is the issuance of currency notes, regulating their circulation in the country by different methods. No other bank than the Central Bank can issue currency.

COMMERCIAL BANKS

Commercial Banks are banking institutions that accept deposits and grant short-term loans and advances to their customers. In addition to giving short-term loans, commercial banks also give medium-term and long-term loan to business enterprises. Now-a-days some of the commercial banks are also providing housing loan on a long-term basis to individuals.

Types of Commercial banks: Commercial banks are of **three** types i.e., Public sector banks, Private sector banks and Foreign banks.

(*i*) **Public Sector Banks:** These are banks where majority stake is held by the Government of India or Reserve Bank of India. Examples of public sector banks are: State Bank of India, Corporation Bank, Bank of Boroda and Dena Bank, etc. Public Sector Banks comprise 20 nationalised banks and State Bank of India and its 5 associate banks.

(*ii*) **Private Sectors Banks:** In case of private sector banks majority of share capital of the bank is held by private individuals. These banks are registered as companies with limited liability. For example: ICICI Bank, Times Bank, Yes Bank, HDFC Bank, Development Credit Bank, etc.

(*iii*) **Foreign Banks:** These banks are registered and have their headquarters in a foreign country but operate their branches in our country. Some of the foreign banks operating in our country are Hong Kong and Shanghai Banking Corporation (HSBC), Citibank, American Express Bank, Standard & Chartered Bank, ABN-Amro Bank, etc. The number of foreign banks operating in our country has increased since the financial sector reforms of 1991.

DEVELOPMENT BANKS

Business often requires medium and long-term capital for purchase of machinery and equipment, for using latest technology, or for expansion and modernization. Such financial assistance is provided by Development Banks. They also undertake other development measures like subscribing to the shares and debentures issued by companies, in case of under subscription of the issue by the public. Industrial Finance Corporation of India (IFCI) and State Financial Corporations (SFCs) are examples of development banks in India.

CO-OPERATIVE BANKS

Co-operative banks in India also perform fundamental banking activities but they are different from commercial banks. Commercial banks have been constituted by an Act passed by parliament while co-operative banks have been constituted by different States under various Acts related to co-operative societies of various states. **Co-operative bank organisation in India has three tier set up.** State Co-operative Bank is the apex co-operative institution in the state. Central or District Co-operative Bank works as district level. At the lowest level co-operative setup in Primary Credit Agency which works at village level.

Commercial banks have been constituted under unitary basis and every commercial bank has been given authority to seek refinance facility from RBI while only State Co-operative Bank has been provided this facility under co-operative banking structure.

Commercial bank can establish its branches in any district/state of the country while, contrary to it, co-operative bank can operate its activities only within limited area. For example, District Co-operative Bank can perform banking activities within the boundaries of the concerned district. Similarly,

Primary Credit Socieities can perform banking services within concerned villages. Co-operative banks cannot open their branches in foreign countries while commercial banks can do that.

Banking Regulation Act, 1949 is fully applicable to all commercial banks while it is partially applicable to co-operative banks. In other words, **RBI has partial control on co-operative banks.**

Co-operative banks work on principles of co-operative while commercial banks adopt pure commercial principles in their operation. That is the reason why Co-operative banks succeed in getting financial assistance from RBI on concessional rate.

Types of Co-operative Banks

There are **three** types of co-operative banks operating in our country. They are primary credit societies, central co-operative banks and state co-operative banks. These banks are organized at three levels, village or town level, district level and state level.

(i) **Primary Credit Societies:** These are formed at the village or town level with borrower and non-borrower members residing in one locality. The operations of each society are restricted to a small area so that the members know each other and are able to watch over the activities of all members to prevent frauds.

(ii) **Central Co-operative Banks:** These banks operate at the district level having some of the primary credit societies belonging to the same district as their members. These banks provide loans to their members (i.e., primary credit societies) and function as a link between the primary credit societies and state co-operative banks.

(iii) **State Co-operative Banks:** These are the apex (highest level) co-operative banks in all the states of the country. They mobilise funds and help in its proper channelisation among various sectors. The money reaches the individual borrowers from the state co-operative banks through the central co-operative banks and the primary credit societies.

SPECIALISED BANKS

There are some banks, which cater to the requirements and provide overall support for setting up business in specific areas of activity. EXIM Bank, SIDBI and NABARD are examples of such banks. They engage themselves in some specific area or activity and thus, are called specialised banks. Let us know about them.

(i) **Export Import Bank of India (EXIM Bank):** If you want to set up a business for exporting products abroad or importing products from foreign countries for sale in our country, EXIM bank can provide you the required support and assistance. The bank grants loans to exporters and importers and also provides information about the international market. It gives guidance about the opportunities for export or import, the risks involved in it and the competition to be faced, etc.

(ii) **Small Industries Development Bank of India (SIDBI):** If you want to establish a small-scale business unit or industry, loan on easy terms can be available through SIDBI. It also finances modernisation of small-scale industrial units, use of new technology and market activities. The aim and focus of SIDBI is to promote, finance and develop small-scale industries.

(iii) **National Bank for Agricultural and Rural Development (NABARD):** It is a central or apex institution for financing agricultural and rural sectors. If a person is engaged in agriculture or other activities like handloom weaving, fishing, etc. NABARD can provide credit, both short-term and long-term, through regional rural banks. It provides financial assistance, especially, to co-operative credit, in the field of agriculture, small-scale industries, cottage and village industries handicrafts and allied economic activities in rural areas.

Different Stages of the Development of Indian Banking

In order to make the Reserve Bank of India more powerful, the Indian Government nationalised it on January 1, 1949. With a view to have the co-ordinated regulation of Indian banking, the Indian Banking Act was passed in March 1949. According to this Act, the Reserve Bank of India was granted extended powers for the inspection of non-scheduled banks. For the development of the banking facilities in the rural areas the Imperial Bank of India was partially nationalised on 1 July, 1955 and it was named as the State Bank of India. Alongwith it other 8 (at present 5) banks were converted as its associate banks which form what is named as the State Bank Group. They are as follows:

1. The State Bank of Bikaner and Jaipur (In the beginning the State Bank of Bikaner and the State Bank of Jaipur were separate. But they were merged and named as the State Bank of Bikaner and Jaipur)
2. The State Bank of Hyderabad
3. The State Bank of Mysore
4. The State Bank of Patiala
5. The State Bank of Travancore.

In order to have more control over the banks, 14 large commercial banks whose reserves were more than ₹ 50 crore each were nationalised on 19th July, 1969. The nationalised banks are as follows:

1. The Central Bank of India
2. Bank of India
3. Punjab National Bank
4. Canara Bank
5. United Commercial Bank
6. Syndicate Bank
7. Bank of Baroda
8. United Bank of India
9. Union Bank of India
10. Dena Bank
11. Allahabad Bank
12. Indian Bank
13. Indian Overseas Bank
14. Bank of Maharashtra

After one decade, on April 15, 1980 those 6 private sector banks whose reserves we more than ₹ 200 crore each were nationalised. These banks are as:

1. Andhra Bank
2. Punjab and Sindh Bank
3. New Bank of India
4. Vijaya Bank
5. Corporation Bank
6. Oriental Bank of Commerce.

On 4th September, 1993 the Government merged the New Bank of India with Punjab National Bank and as a result of this the total number of nationalised bank got reduced from 20 to 19. IDBI Bank Ltd has become nationalised bank and the numbers now increased to 20.

DEPOSIT ACCOUNTS

Bank offers the facility of opening various types of accounts where a depositor can deposit money saved by him. Depending upon the nature of accounts deposit money can also be withdrawn to suit the convenience of the depositor.

Classification of Deposit Accounts

On the basis of purposes served, the deposit accounts can be classified as follows:

1. Saving Bank Account
2. Fixed Deposit Account
3. Current Account
4. Recurring Deposit Account

Saving Account

Saving bank account is primarily meant for people with limited means who want to save some money for future. In a saving bank account there are normally no restrictions on the amount to be withdrawn as well as on the frequency of withdrawal. The pass book issued to the saving bank account holder contains the rules regarding its operation. Saving bank account can be opened with a minimum amount of ₹ 500, if cheque book facility is not availed. In case cheque book facility is availed, then the minimum balance required to be maintained is ₹ 1000. The bank allows interest at the rate of about 4.0%. But the rate of interest keeps changing dependly upon the instructions of RBI.

Pay-in-slip

Pay-in-slips are printed forms with perforated counter foils used for depositing cash or cheque. It contains information in respect of the name of account holder, amount deposited, and the signature of the person depositing it.

Fixed Deposit Account

It is also known as term deposit account. Money deposited in fixed deposit account ranges for a period starting from 30 days to more than 3 years. At the end of the specified period, the depositor may either withdrawn the money or renew the deposit further for a specified period. Banks pay interest on fixed deposit dependly upon the period for which the deposit is kept with the bank.

Payment of Fixed Deposits Before the Date of Maturity

Fixed deposits are normally payable on maturity. In case the depositor requires the money before the due date, he or she makes a request to the bank for its payment. The bank may consider such a request and make payment of the fixed deposit. When the payment of fixed deposit is made before the date of maturity, the depositor loses interest.

Current Account

In current account, a customer can withdraw or deposit money any number of times he desires. Current account is suitable to those persons who either deposit or make payments freequently. It is thus suitable for business people and institutions which have frequent dealings with the bank. Bank permits overdraft facility on current account. In view of this facility, the banks do not pay any interest on current accounts. Some times, banks charge some amount from the current account holder as fees for the services extended.

Some features of the current accounts are:

1. It provides convenience of operation as certain facilities are associated with current account. The objective is not to mobilise saving through such account.

2. The current account has an operating cost. There are bank charges for the services provided to the holder of current accounts.

3. Banks do not pay any interest on such accounts.

Recurring Deposit Account

The procedure for opening a recurring deposit account is the same as in the case of saving bank account. Normally the withdrawal from such account is not permitted. However, the depositor can take loan from the bank against the security of recurring deposit account. The interest earned on recurring account is higher than on the saving account. It varies with the duration of deposit.

Distinction between Current Account and Saving Bank Account

S. No.	Basis of difference	Current acount	Saving acount
1.	Operation of accounts	Current account is mainly opened and operated by business firms and institutions.	Saving bank account is mainly opned by individuals and salaried people.
2.	Withdrawals	Deposits and withdrawals can be made frequently. There is no limit to its frequency.	Withdrawal are not permitted as frequent as in case of current account.
3.	Interest	No interest is paid by bank on such account.	Interest is paid on saving bank account though the rate of interest happens to be low.
4.	Overdraft	Overdraft facility is available.	No such facility is allowed.
5.	Service charges	Service charges are payable.	Service charges are not payable.

★★★★★★

Commercial Banks

At present 26 commercial banks in public sector are working in the country. Out of these 26 banks, 20 banks are nationalised banks and SBI group contains 6 banks.

CLASSIFICATION OF COMMERCIAL BANKS

The commercial banking institutions of the country can be divided into two groups:

A. **Secheduled Banks:** Those banks are scheduled banks which have been included in the Schedule (Second) of Reserve Bank Act, 1934. The banks included in this scheduled list should fulfil two conditions:

1. The paid up capital and collected funds of bank should not be less than ₹ 5 lakh.

2. Any activity of the bank with not adversely affect the interest of depositors.

Every scheduled bank enjoys following facilities:

1. Such bank becomes eligible for obtaining debts/loans on bank rate from RBI.

2. Such bank automatically acquires the membership of clearing house.

3. Such banks also get the facility of rediscount of first class exchange bills from RBI. This facility is provided by RBI only if the scheduled bank deposits an average daily cash fund with RBI which is decided by RBI itself and presents the recurring statements under the provisions of RBI Act, 1934 and Banking Regulation Act, 1949.

B. **Non-scheduled Banks:** The banks which are not included in the list of scheduled banks are called non-scheduled banks. The number of non-scheduled banks is continuously also have to follow CRR conditions. But such banks can have these funds with themselves as no compulsion has been made on non-scheduled banks to deposit CRR funds with RBI. These non-scheduled banks are not eligible for having loans from RBI for meeting their day-to-day general activities but under emergency condition these banks can be granted loans by RBI.

FUNCTIONS OF COMMERCIAL BANKS

The functions of commercial banks are of **two** types.

(A) Primary functions; and

(B) Secondary functions.

Let us discuss details about these functions.

PRIMARY FUNCTIONS

The primary functions of a commercial bank include:

(a) Accepting deposits; and

(b) Granting loans and advances.

Accepting deposits

The most important activity of a commercial bank is to mobilise deposits from the public. People who have surplus income and savings find it convenient to deposit the amounts with banks. Depending upon the nature of deposits, funds deposited with bank also earn interest. Thus, deposits with the bank grow along with the interest earned. If the rate of interest is higher, public are motivated to deposit more funds with the bank. There is also safety of funds deposited with the bank.

Grant of loans and advances

The second important function of a commercial bank is to grant loans and advances. Such loans and advances are given to members of the public and to the business community at a higher rate of interest than allowed by banks on various deposit accounts. The rate of interest charged on loans and advances varies according to the purpose and period of loan and also the mode of repayment.

(i) **Loans:** A loan is granted for a specific time period. Generally commercial banks provide short-term loans. But term loans, i.e., loans for more than a year may also be granted. The borrower may be given the entire amount in lump sum or in instalments. Loans are generally granted against the security of certain assets. A loan is normally repaid in instalments. However, it may also be repaid in lump sum.

(ii) **Advances:** An advance is a credit facility provided by the bank to its customers. It differs from loan in the sense that loans may be granted for longer period, but advances are normally granted for a short period of time. Further the purpose of granting advances is to meet the day-to-day requirements of business. The rate of interest charged on advances varies from bank to bank. Interest is charged only on the amount withdrawn and not on the sanctioned amount.

Types of Advances

Banks grant short-term financial assistance by way of cash credit, overdraft and bill discounting. Let us learn about these.

(a) **Cash Credit:** Cash credit is an arrangement whereby the bank allows the borrower to draw amount upto a specified limit. The amount is credited to the account of the customer. The customer can withdraw this amount as and when he requires. Interest is charged on the amount actually withdrawn. Cash Credit is granted as per terms and conditions agreed with the customers.

(b) **Overdraft:** Overdraft is also a credit facility granted by bank. A customer who has a current account with the bank is allowed to withdraw more than the amount of credit balance in his account. It is a temporary arrangement. Overdraft facility with a specified limit may be allowed either on the security of assets, or on personal security, or both.

(c) **Discounting of Bills:** Banks provide short-term finance by discounting bills, that is, making payment of the amount before the due date of the bills after deducting a certain rate of discount. The party gets the funds without waiting for the date of maturity of the bills. In case any bill is dishonoured on the due date, the bank can recover the amount from the customer.

SECONDARY FUNCTIONS

In addition to the primary functions of accepting deposits and lending money, banks perform a number of other functions, which are called secondary functions. These are as follows:

(a) Issuing letters of credit, travellers cheque, etc.

(b) Undertaking safe custody of valuables, important document and securities by providing safe deposit vaults or lockers.

(c) Providing customers with facilities of foreign exchange dealings.

(d) Transferring money from one account to another; and from one branch to another branch of the bank through cheque, pay order, demand draft.

(e) Standing guarantee on behalf of its customers, for making payment for purchase of goods, machinery, vehicles etc.

(f) Collecting and supplying business information.

(g) Providing reports on the credit worthiness of customers.

(i) Providing consumer finance for individuals by way of loans on easy terms for purchase of consumer durables like televisions, refrigerators, etc.

(j) Educational loans to students at reasonable rate of interest for higher studies, especially for professional courses.

STATE BANK OF INDIA AND ITS ASSOCIATE BANKS

On the recommendation of the Rural Credit Survey Committee the Imperial Bank of India was converted into the State Bank of India on July 1, 1955. Its 92 per cent shares were acquired by the RBI, and thus it has the distinction of becoming the first State owned commercial bank in the country. Among the factors which guided the establishmant of the State Banks of India the main consideration was that the country should have a big commercial bank committed to national purpose and should take banking to the countryside even if initially it was not a commercially viable proposition. In view of this necessity, the State Bank was required to function as a development agency basides performing the traditional functions of a commercial bank.

In 1959, the State Bank of India (Associate Banks) Act was passed and this paved the way for creating the State Bank Group. Now **State Bank of Hyderabad, State Bank of Bikaner and Jaipur, State Bank of Mysore, State Bank of Patiala and State Bank of Tranvancore** constitute the State Bank Group.

SBI LAUNCHED INDIA'S FIRST START-UP FOCUSSED BANK BRANCH SBI INCUBE

India's largest bank, State Bank of India (SBI), on January 14, 2016 launched and inaugurated India's first start-up focused bank branch called SBI In Cube in Bengaluru, Karnataka. The specialized branch aims to understand and address banking needs of a Start-up Business. The bank also launched the wealth management service SBI Exclusif, which is targeted at the fast-growing affluent segment in the country.

About SBI InCube

- The SBI InCube branch will work towards fulfilling the specific financial needs of the start-ups.
- The service will provide advisory services to the budding entrepreneurs under one roof.
- It will assist start-ups in cash management, regulations, taxation, mentoring, foreign exchange and remittances and other financial services.
- The branch, in its current form, will not fund start-ups *i.e.*, it will not provide loans. However, it will give them loans when they turn more mature.

CABINET APPROVES SBI MERGER WITH FIVE UNITS

The Cabinet on February 15, 2017 approved the proposed merger of State Bank of India (SBI) and five subsidiaries—a combination that will create the first Indian lender to rank among the world's top 50. State Bank of Bikaner and Jaipur (SBBJ), State Bank of Hyderabad (SBH), State Bank of Mysore (SBM), State Bank of Patiala (SBP) and State Bank of Travancore (SBT) will merge with the country's largest bank, widening the gap between SBI and the No. 2 lender, HDFC Bank Ltd. This merger will lead to far greater operational efficiency and synergy of operations. When the cost of operations comes down, the cost of funds will come down. SBI will become a very large bank but not merely from a domestic point of view. The proposed merger of SBI and its subsidiaries would create a banking behemoth with assets of nearly ₹ 30 lakh crore, more than three times the ₹ 8.28 lakh crore assets of HDFC Bank, the largest private sector bank by assets, as of December 31, 2016. The assets for the entity to be formed from SBI's merger with its subsidiaries takes into account the total assets as of 30 September. SBI was ranked 52 in the world in terms of assets in 2015, according to Bloomberg, and a merger will see it break into the top 50. All else remaining the same, the combined entity would be ranked 45th. The merger is likely to lead to savings of ₹ 1,000 crore annually.

OTHER NATIONALISED BANKS

A second category of public sector banks is of twenty commercial banks, of which fourteen were nationalised on July 19, 1969. Each one of these fourteen banks had deposits of Rs. 50 crore or more. This step, though not unprecedented in the history of Indian banking, had changed the very complexion of the banking structure in the country. The nationalisation was justified by the government on the ground that the major banks could not be any more allowed to remain captive organisation of the big business. Their policies should be inspired by the larger social purpose and be in accordance with the national priorities and objectives. Hence, a fundamental shift in their approach was witnessed in the post-nationalisation phase. The banking system in this period became an instrument of development. The Lead Bank Scheme formulated in December 1969 played a significant role in transforming these profit maximising institutions of yester years into catalysts of local development.

After nationalisation of 14 banks, there was rapid expansion of branch network. *On April 15, 1980 six more private owned commercial banks were nationalised.*

With the nationalisation of six more banks, the share of private sector in the entire banking declined to just 9 per cent. In 1993, New Bank of India has been merged with Punjab National Bank. At present, *the number of public sector banks other than the State Bank of India is twenty.*

NEW DEFINITION OF WEAK COMMERCIAL BANKS

- ❑ The Narasimham Committee (II) defined a weak bank as one whose accumulated losses and net NPAs exceed its net worth or whose operating profits less income on recapitalisation bonds was negative for three consecutive years.

- ❑ The Working Group on Restructuring Weak Public Sector Banks (Verma Committee) identified 7 parameters for identification of weak banks—CAR and Coverage Ratio under solvency; Return on Assets and Net Interest Margin under earning capacity; and three ratios under profitability, namely—(i) operating profit to average working funds, (ii) costs to income and (iii) staff cost to net interest income + all other income.

- ❑ Coverage Ratio is the ratio of the sum comprising equity capital + loan loss provisions—NPLs to total assets. This ratio allows simultaneous monitoring of NPA levels and equity capital.

REGIONAL RURAL BANKS (RRBs)

Regional Rural Banks (RRBs) were established in 1975 under the provisions of the RRB Act 1976 with a view to developing the rural economy as well as to creating an alternative channel to 'Co-operative Credit Structure' in order to ensure sufficient institutional credit for rural and agricultural sector. In other words, regional Rural Banks (RRBs) were established to take the banking services. These banks provide institutional credit to the weaker sections of the society at concessional rate of interest. These banks were also intended to mobilise rural savings and channelise for supporting the productive activities in the rural area. On October 2, 1975, initially 5 RRBs were established at Moradabad and Gorakhpur (UP), Bhiwani (Haryana), Jaipur (Rajasthan) and Malda (West Bengal). Later on RRBs were extended to other districts of the country.

Though RRBs were initially intended to support productive activities in the rural areas. With effect from April 1997 the concept of priority sector lending was made applicable to RRBs. Similarly, the interest rates on term deposits offered and interest rates on loans charged by RRBs have also been freed.

With a view to consolidating and strengthening RRBs the Government of India initiated, in September 2005, the process of amalgamation of RRBs, in a phased manner.

As a result of this amalgamation, the number of RRBs declined to 91 as on March, 31, 2008 (196 at end – March 2005) operating in 25 States across 586 districts. The number of RRBs declined further to 56 as on March 31, 2015.

National Rural Bank

Parliamentry Committee on agriculture finance and credit flow under the chairmanship of N. Janardan Reddy in its 55th report proposed the establishment of National Rural Bank. The committee put the view that all the farmers and crops should be covered within National Agriculture Insurance Scheme and at the same time Gram Panchayat should be approved as unit of insurance. Committee also recomended low insurance premium for Horticulture and Commercial Crops. Farmer's Forum Should be given participation in selecting projects of State Rural Basic Infrastructure Fund, the committee added. Besides, reduction in interest rate and making loan process more easier are another recommendations of the committee.

RRBs to Market Mutual Funds

RBI has allowed Regional Rural Banks to market mutual funds through their branches. RRBs may with approval of their boards of directors enter into agreements with mutual funds for marketing their units. As per the RBI notification, RRBs may enter into agreements with mutual funds for marketing the units subject to conditions:

- ❏ **The Bank** should not acquire the units from the secondary market.

- ❏ **The Bank** should not be buy back the units from its customers.

- ❏ **Retailing** of the units may be confined to select branches.

PARLIAMENT PASSES REGIONAL RURAL BANKS (AMENDMENT) BILL, 2014

Lok Sabha has passed the Regional Rural Banks (Amendment) Bill, 2014 on December 23, 2014, while the Rajya Sabha passed the bill on April 28, 2015. This bill amends Regional Rural Banks Act, 1976 and aims to strengthen the Regional Rural Banks and deepen their financial inclusion. Key facts of the Bill are the following.

Authorised Capital: The authorised capital of each Regional Rural Bank (RRB) increased from ₹ 5 crore to ₹ 2000 crore divided into 200 crore of fully paid share of ₹ 10 each. As per the parent Act the ₹ 5 crore share capital of RRBs is split into 5 lakh shares of ₹ 100 each.

Issued Capital: The authorised capital issued by any RRB's shall not be reduced below ₹ 1 crore and shares in all cases to be fully paid up shares of ₹ 10 each.

Shareholding: The bill allows RRBs to raise capital from sources other than the central and state governments, and sponsor banks. It will change the existing structure of ownership (the Centre has a 50 per cent share, the sponsor Bank 35 per cent and state government 15 per cent shareholding in the RRBs.)

Board of directors: Any person who is a director of an RRB is not eligible to be on the Board of Directors of another RRB. Directors will be elected by shareholders based on the total amount of equity share capital issued to such shareholders.

Tenure of directors: The bill raises the tenure of directors to 3 years from existing 2 years. No director can hold office for a total period exceeding six years.

Closure and balancing of books: The parent Act had provision which mentioned that the balance books of RRBs should be closed and balanced by 31st December every year. However this amendment bill changes this date to 31st March in order to bring RRB's balancing of books in uniformity with the financial year.

Establishment Years of Major Financial Institutions in India

❏ Imperial Bank of India	1921
❏ Reserve Bank of India (Nationalisation of RBI took place on January 1, 1949)	April 1, 1935
❏ Industrial Finance Corporation of India (IFCI)	1948
❏ State Bank of India (SBI)	July 1, 1955
❏ Unit Trust of India (UTI)	Feb. 1, 1964
❏ IDBI	July 1964
❏ NABARD	July 12, 1982
❏ IRBI (Now it has been renamed as IIBIL since March 6, 1997)	March 20, 1985
❏ SIDBI	1990
❏ EXIM Bank	January 1, 1982
❏ National Housing Bank (NHB)	July 1988
❏ Life Insurance Corporation (LIC)	September 1956
❏ General Insurance Corporation (GIC)	November 1972
❏ Regional Rural Banks (RRBs)	Oct. 2, 1975
❏ Risk Capital and Technology Finance Corporation Ltd.	March 1975
❏ Technology Development & Information Co. of India Ltd.	1989
❏ Infrastructure Leasing & Financial Services Ltd.	1988
❏ Housing Development Finance Corporation Ltd. (HDFC)	1977

BANDHAN BANK STARTED OPERATIONS

Bandhan Financial Services, a Micro Financial Institution (MFI), on August 23, 2015 started operations as a Scheduled Commercial Bank (SCB). Henceforth it has been named as Bandhan Bank. The banking services were inaugurated by the Union Finance Minister Arun Jaitley in Kolkata. On the inaugural day, the bank started operations with 501 branches in 24 states across the country with 1.43 crore accounts.

With this, Bandhan became the first micro finance company in the country to start operations as a full-fledged commercial bank. It is also the first commercial bank from Eastern India to get RBI clearance since independence. Bandhan started as a Non-Banking Finance Company in 2001 and focused on the lower strata of the especially unorganized sector workers. Another Private Sector Bank-IDFC Bank also started its operation on October 1, 2015. Basically IDFC was an infra-structure financier.

✮✮✮✮✮✮

Reserve Bank of India

Reserve Bank of India (RBI) is the Central Bank of the country. The reserve Bank of India was established in 1935 with a capital of Rs. 5 crore. In the begining the ownership of almost all the share capital was with the non- government shareholders. In order to prevent the centralisation of the equity shares in the hands of a few people, the Reserve Bank of India was nationalised on January 1, 1949.

FUNCTIONS OF RESERVE BANK

1. **Issue of Notes:** The Reserve Bank has the monopoly of note issue in the country. The Reserve Bank acts as the only source of legal tender money because the one rupee note issued by Ministry of Finance are also circulated through it. The Reserve Bank has adopted the **Minimum Reserve System** for the note issue. Since 1957, it maintains gold and foreign exchange reserves of Rs. 200 crore, of which atleast Rs. 115 crore should be in gold.

2. **Banker to the Government:** The second important function of the Reserve Bank is to act as the Banker, Agent and Adviser to the Government.

3. **Banker's Bank:** The Reserve Bank performs the same function for the other banks as the other banks ordinarily perform for their customers. It is not only a banker to the commercial banks, but it is the lender of the last resort.

4. **Controller of Credit:** The Reserve Bank undertakes the responsibility of controlling credit created by the commercial banks. To achieve this objective it makes extensive use of quantitative and qualitative techniques to control and regulate the credit effectively in the country.

5. **Custodian of Foreign Reserves:** For the purpose of keeping the foreign exchange rates stable the Reserve Bank buys and sells the foreign currencies and also protects the country's foreign exchange funds.

6. **Collection and publication of data:** The RBI has been entrusted with the task of collection and compilation of statistical information relating to banking and other financial sectors of the economy. Out of various publications of the RBI, two are relatively more important. The RBI Bulletin is a monthly publication. It presents not only statistical and other information in summary form, but also provides results of important studies and investigations conducted by the RBI. The Report on Currency and Finance is an annual publication. It provides a comprehensive review of various developments of economic and financial importance.

CONTROL OF CREDIT BY THE RESERVE BANK OF INDIA

In India, the legal framework of the RBI's control over the credit structure has been provided under the Reserve Bank of India Act, 1934 and the Banking Regulation Act, 1949. The RBI has been empowered to use almost all the traditional instruments of credit control under the former; the latter has given it additional powers to use some other direct methods of credit regulation. Like any other central bank, the RBI resorts to bank rate manipulations, open market operations, reserve requirement changes, direct action, rationing of credit and moral suasion. Apart from employing these traditional methods of credit control, it directly influences commercial banks' lending policy, rates of interest, form of securities against loans and portfolio distribution.

Bank Rate Policy

The bank rate or the central banks' rediscount rate is an important monetary instrument in modern economies. Its most useful role is to signal and/or clarify the central banks' monetary and interest rate stance to all participants in the financial sector and particularly to banks. If monetary policy is effective and credible, a change in the bank rate will result in a change in prime lending rate of banks and thus act an independent instrument of monetary control. However, the role of the bank rate as an instrument of monetary policy has been very limited in India because of these basic factors:

(a) The structure of interest rates is administered by RBI—they are not automatically linked to the bank rate;

(b) Commercial banks enjoy specific refinance facilities, and not necessarily rediscount their eligible securities with RBI at bank rate; and

(c) The bill market is under-developed and the different sub-markets of the money market are not influenced by the bank rate.

In other words, the bank rate in India is not the "pace setter" to the other market rates of interest and the money market rates do not automatically adjust themselves to changes in the bank rate. At the same time, the deposit rates and lending rates of banks (and of development finance institutions) are not related to the bank rate. The Government of India and RBI are reviewing the rules and procedures for general access to RBI rediscount facilities so as to make bank rate an active instrument of monetary policy as in other modern economies.

Open Market Operations

In economies with well-developed money markets, central banks use open market operations: i.e. buying and selling eligible securities by the central bank in the money market—to influence the volume of cash reserves with commercial banks and thus influence the volume of loans and advances they can make to the industrial and commercial sectors. RBI had not used this weapon for many years.

Since 1911, the enormous inflow of foreign funds into India created the problem of excess liquidity with the banking sector and RBI undertook large scale open market operations. When RBI sells Government securities in the market, it withdraws a part of the cash reserves of commercial banks and, thereby, reduces the ability of banks to lend to the industrial and commercial sectors. At any given time, the banks' capacity to create credit—i.e., to give fresh loans—depends upon their surplus cash, that is, the amount of cash reserves in excess of their statutory CRR. Once the surplus cash is eliminated and even part of the statutory CRR is reduced, the banks have to contract their credit supply so as to generate some cash reserves to meet their statutory CRR. As a result, the supply of bank credit which involves the creations of demand deposits, falls and money supply contracts.

The opposite will happen if RBI buys government securities from the market and pays for them. The commercial banks will find that they have surplus cash—they will create more credit and more bank deposits. The supply of money will expand. Such a policy of buying Government securities will be adopted to reverse economic recession in the country.

Cash Reserve Ratio (CRR)

The cash reserve ratio (CRR) is an effective instrument of credit control. Under the RBI (Amendement) Act 1962, the RBI is empowered to determine CRR for the commercial banks in the range of 3 per cent to 15 per cent for the aggregate demand and time liabilities.

Statutory Liquidity Ratio (SLR)

Every bank in India has to maintain at the close of business every day, a minimum proportion of their net demand and time liabilities as liquid assets in the form of cash, gold and un-encumbered approved securities. The ratio of liquid assets to demand and time liabilities is known as Statutory Liquidity Ratio (SLR).

In simple words, it is the percentage of total deposits banks have to invest in government bonds and other approved securities. An SLR bond also qualifies for the portfolio maintained by banks to meet the liquidity requirement.

What is the difference between SLR and CRR?

What SLR does is it restricts the banks leverage in pumping more money into the economy. On the other hand, CRR, or cash reserve ratio, is the portion of deposits that the banks have to maintain with the RBI. Higher the ratio, the lower is the amount that banks will be able to use for lending and investment.

The other difference is that to meet SLR, banks can use cash, gold or approved securities whereas with CRR it has to be only cash. CRR is maintained in cash form with RBI, whereas SLR is maintained in liquid form with banks themselves

What does a reduction in SLR mean?

A cut in SLR means that the home, car and commercial loan rates will go down. It also means that banks will now have the option of selling ₹ 40,000 crore of government securities that until now formed part of their statutory investments.

The RBI is empowered to increase this ratio up to 40%. An increase in SLR also restrict the bank's leverage position to pump more money into the economy.

SELECTIVE CREDIT CONTROL

Selective credit controls are generally meant to regulate credit for specific purposes. In a developing economy where frequent use of quantitative techniques of credit control may jeopardise development efforts, selective credit controls can be safely introduced to check misuse of borrowing facilities. The RBI, like many other central banks in various countries, has been empowered to use selective credit controls to regulate credit to specific branches of economic activities. Thus, it can prevent speculative hoarding of essential commodities and check undue rise in the prices.

Generally RBI uses three kinds of selective credit controls:

(a) minimum margins for lending against specific securities;

(b) ceiling on the amounts of credit for certain purposes; and

(c) discriminatory rate of interest charged on certain types of advances.

(d) Moral Suasion

(e) Publicity

RBI's Fresh Norms to Support Banks

In an attempt to improve the financial status of banks, the Reserve Bank of India has issued fresh norms on the treatment of provisions for restructure accounts, standard assets and non-performing assets (NPAs). The new norms are expected to improve capital adequacy and bring down the level of net NPAs. Under the revised norms, the banks can use the provisions made for decline in the fair value of restructured advances (standard assets and NPAs) for netting from relative assets.

The salient points under new norms are:

- The amount used for provisioning could be reduced from the outstanding advances.

- Banks have been allowed to restructure accounts which face temporary cash flow problems due to slowdown on the world horizon. It will mean lower risk weighted assets and lesser provision for loans.

- Floating provisions can be counted as part of Tier-II capital.

- Banks allowed to consider excess provisioning from the sale of NPAs for sharing up capital adequacy of Tier-II bonds.

These new norms on loan provisioning are expected to improve capital adequacy and bring down the level of NPAs which is an important indicator of financial health of banks.

RBI NOTIFIES FINAL GUIDELINES ON BAD LOANS FOR NBFCs

The Reserve Bank of India (RBI) has announced the final guidelines for the non-banking finance companies (NBFCs) with regard to the early detection and recovery of bad loans. The guidelines has become effective from April 1, 2014. In view of RBI, before a loan account turns into a non-performing asset, NBFCs will be required to identify incipient stress in the account by creating a sub-asset category 'special mention accounts' (SMA).

The RBI has set up three categories of SMAs:

SMA-0: principal or interest payment not overdue for more than 30 days, but account showing signs of incipient stress;

SMA-1: principal or interest payment overdue between 31–0 days; and

SMA-2: principal or interest payment overdue for 61-180 days.

The Central bank has warned that if NBFCs fail to report SMA status of the accounts to CRILC or resort to methods with the intent to conceal the actual status of the accounts or evergreen the account, they will be subjected to accelerated provisioning for these accounts and other supervisory actions.

RBI GIVES LICENCE FOR 11 PAYMENT BANKS

Opening the way for revolutionising cashless payments services in the country, the Reserve Bank of India has granted payment bank licences to 11 firms. These 11 applicants that have got 'in principle' approval for setting up payments banks will provide barebones facilities aimed at covering the vast population that has no access to financial services. They will take deposits, convey remittances and dispense payments to recipients, making them ideal for migrant workers who need to send money home, for instance. These 11 licence obtaining firms include telecom companies Vodafone and Airtel; non-banking financial company Cholamandalam Distribution Services Ltd; large conglomerates Reliance Industries and Aditya Birla Nuvo; and individuals Vijay Shekhar Sharma, founder of Paytm, and Dilip Shanghvi, Managing Director of Sun Pharmaceuticals. The Department of Posts, FinoPaytech, Tech Mahindra and National Securities Depository Ltd also got place in the list.

Payments banks differ from conventional banks as they are not allowed to lend to customers or issue credit cards. They can, however, accept deposits of up to 1 lakh and can offer current and savings account deposits. They can also issue debit cards and offer internet banking.

BANKING OMBUDSMAN

In order to address the complaints and grievances of customers against banks, a forum has been formed known as the Banking Ombudsman. The concept of Banking Ombudsman was introduced in India in the year 1995. It was revised thereafter in the years 2002 and 2006.

The Banking Ombudsman is appointed by Reserve Bank of India. He is a senior official appointed from the staff of the office of RBI. Unlike many other sectors where the senior authority is usually a retired official holding top positions in government institutions/banks, the banking ombudsman is an in-service official of RBI mostly a chief general manager/senior general manager.

Under the amendment in the year 2006, it was decided that the banking ombudsman should not be from any bank and should solely be from the staff of RBI so as to maintain the idea of impartial justice.

There are 15 offices of banking ombudsman in India presently. A customer has to file his complaint to the nearest office in his area. The office of Banking Ombudsman handles issues against all commercial banks, co-operative banks as well as Regional Rural Banks (RRBs).

It handles cases related to any kind of trouble faced by the customer in availing banking services which he has a right in. It also addresses to cases related to internet banking. It takes up cases having valuation less then ₹ 10 lakhs.

★★★★★★

Financial Market

MEANING

The financial markets act as a link between borrowers and lenders. It facilitates this function by acting as an intermediary between the borrowers and lenders of money. So, financial market may be defined as 'a transmission mechanism between investors (or lenders) and the borrowers (or users) through which transfer of funds is facilitated'. It consists of individual investors, financial institutions and other intermediaries who are linked by a formal trading rules and communication network for trading the various financial assets and credit instruments.

FUNCTIONS

The main functions of financial market are:

(a) It provides facilities for interaction between the investors and the borrowers.

(b) It provides pricing information resulting from the interaction between buyers and sellers in the market when they trade the financial assets.

(c) It provides security to dealings in financial assets.

(d) It ensures liquidity by providing a mechanism for an investor to sell the financial assets.

(e) It ensures low cost of transactions and information.

TYPES OF FINANCIAL MARKETS

A financial market consists of two major segments: (a) Money Market; and (b) Capital Market. While the money market deals in short-term credit, the capital market handles the medium term and long-term credit.

MONEY MARKET

The money market is a market for short-term funds, which deals in financial assets whose period of maturity is upto one year. It should be noted that money market does not deal in cash or money as such but simply provides a market for credit instruments such as bills of exchange, promissory notes, commercial paper, treasury bills, etc. These financial instruments are close substitute of money. These instruments help the business units, other organisations and the Government to borrow the funds to meet their short-term requirement.

The Indian money market consists of Reserve Bank of India, Commercial banks, Co-operative banks, and other specialised financial institutions. The Reserve Bank of India is the leader of the money market in India. Some Non-Banking Financial Companies (NBFCs) and financial institutions like LIC, GIC, UTI, etc. also operate in the Indian money market.

MONEY MARKET INSTRUMENTS

Following are some of the important money market instruments or securities.

(a) **Call Money:** Call money is mainly used by the banks to meet their temporary requirement of cash. They borrow and lend money from each other normally on a daily basis. It is repayable on demand and its maturity period varies in between one day to a fortnight. The rate of interest paid on call money loan is known as call rate.

(b) **Treasury Bill:** A treasury bill is a promissory note issued by the RBI to meet the short-term requirement of funds. Treasury bills are highly liquid instruments, that means, at any time the holder of treasury bills can transfer of or get it discounted from RBI. These bills are normally issued at a price less than their face value; and redeemed at face value. So the difference between the issue price and the face value of the treasury bill represents the interest on the investment. These bills are secured instruments and are issued for a period of not exceeding 364 days. Banks, Financial institutions and corporations normally play major role in the Treasury bill market.

(c) **Commercial Paper:** Commercial paper (CP) is a popular instrument for financing working capital requirements of companies. The CP is an unsecured instrument issued in the form of promissory note. This instrument was introduced in 1990 to enable the corporate borrowers to raise short-term funds. It can be issued for period ranging from 15 days to one year. Commercial papers are transferable by endorsement and delivery. The highly reputed companies (Blue Chip companies) are the major player of commercial paper market.

(d) **Certificate of Deposit:** Certificate of Deposit (CDs) are short-term instruments issued by Commercial Banks and Special Financial Institutions (SFIs), which are freely transferable from one party to another. The maturity period of CDs ranges from 91 days to one year. These can be issued to individuals, co-operatives and companies.

(e) **Trade Bill:** Normally the traders buy goods from the wholesalers or manufactures on credit. The sellers get payment after the end of the credit period. But if any seller does not want to wait or in immediate need of money he/she can draw a bill of exchange in favour of the buyer. When buyer accepts the bill it becomes a negotiable instrument and is termed as bill of exchange or trade bill. This trade bill can now be discounted with a bank before its maturity. On maturity the bank gets the payment from the drawee i.e., the buyer of goods. When trade bills are accepted by Commercial Banks it is known as Commercial Bills. So trade bill is an instrument, which enables the drawer of the bill to get funds for short period to meet the working capital needs.

CAPITAL MARKET

Capital Market may be defined as a market dealing in medium and long-term funds. It is an institutional arrangement for borrowing medium and long-term funds and which provides facilities for marketing and trading of securities. So it constitutes all long-term borrowings from banks and financial institutions, borrowings from foreign markets and raising of capital by issue various securities such as shares debentures, bonds, etc.

For trading of securities there are two different segments in capital market. One is primary market and the other is, secondary market. The primary market deals with new/fresh issue of securities and is, therefore, known as new issue market. The secondary market on the other hand, provides a place for purchase and sale of existing securities and is known as stock market or stock exchange.

The new issue market primarily consists of the arrangements, which facilitates the procurement of long-term finance by the companies in the form of shares, debentures and bonds. The companies usually issue those securities at the initial stages of their formation and so also later on for expansion and/or modernization of their activities. However, the selling of securities is not an easy task, as the companies have to fulfill various legal requirements and decide upon the appropriate timing and the method of issue. Hence, they seek assistance of various intermediaries such as merchant bankers, underwriters, stock brokers etc. to look after all these aspects. All these intermediaries form an integral part of the primary market.

The secondary market (stock exchange) is an association or organisation or a body of individuals established for the purpose of assisting, regulating and controlling the business of buying, selling and dealing in securities. It may noted that it is called a secondary market because only the securities already issued can be traded on the floor of the stock exchange. This market is open only to its members, most of whom are brokers acting as agents of the buyers and sellers of securities. The main functions of this market lie in providing liquidity (ready encashment) to securities and safety in dealings. It is because of the availability of such facilities that people are ready to invest in securities.

DISTINCTION BETWEEN CAPITAL MARKET AND MONEY MARKET

Capital Market differs from money market in many ways. Firstly, while money market is related to short-term funds, the capital market related to long term funds. Secondly, while money market deals in securities like treasury bills, commercial paper, trade bills, deposit certificates, etc., the capital market deals in shares, debentures, bonds and government securities. Thirdly, while the participants in money market are Reserve Bank of India, commercial banks, non-banking financial companies, etc., the participants in capital market are stockbrokers, underwriters, mutual funds, financial institutions, and individual investors. Fourthly, while the money market is regulated by Reserve Bank of India, the capital market is regulated by Securities Exchange Board of India (SEBI).

Distinction Between Capital Market & Money Market

	Point of Distinction	Capital Market	Money Market
1.	Time period / Term	Long term funds dealt with	Deals in short-term funds.
2.	Instrument Dealt In	Deals in shares, debenture, bonds and government securities.	Deals in securities like treasury bills, commercial paper, bills of exchange, certificate of deposits etc.
3.	Participants	Stock brokers, underwriters, mutual funds, financial institutions and individual investors.	Participants are commercial banks, non-banking finance companies, chit funds etc.
4.	Regulatory body	SEBI (Securities and Exchange Board of India.)	RBI (Reserve Bank of India)

✭✭✭✭✭

Institutional Financing

Soon after Independence, the Government of India set up a series of financial institutions to be of special help to the private sector industries in the matter of finance. IFCI was the first of these institutions (1948). It was followed by SFCs (set up by State Governments with cooperation of RBI and other banks) to provide long term finance to small and medium industrial units. ICICI (1955), IDBI (1964) and UTI (1964) followed soon after. LIC was set up in 1956 to mobilise individual savings and to invest part of the savings in the capital were set up and are commonly called public sector financial institutions.

CLASSIFICATION OF FINANCIAL INSTITUTIONS IN INDIA

The wide variety of financial institutions existing in India can be broadly classified into all-India financial institutions, State level institutions and other institutions. The financial institutions within these groups can be further categoriesed according to their main activities/functions into:

1. **All India Development Finance Institutions (DFIs):** Industrial Finance Corporation of India Ltd (IFCI), Small Industries Development Bank of India (SIDBI) and Industrial Investment Bank of India (IIBI). Industrial Credit and Investment Corporation of India Ltd. (ICICI Ltd) has ceased to be a development bank after its merger with ICICI Bank with effect from March 30, 2002.

2. **Specialised Financial Institutions:** Export-Import Bank (EXIM Bank), IFCI Venture Capital Funds (IVCF, formerly RCTC) Ltd., ICICI Venture Ltd. (formerly TDICI Ltd), Tourism Finance Corporation of India (TFCI) Ltd., and Infrastructure Development Finance Company (IDFC) Ltd.

3. **Investment Institutions:** Life Insurance Corporatiuon of India (LIC), Unit Trust of India (UTI), and General Insutrance Corporation of India (GIC) and its four erstwhile subsidiaries.

4. **Refinance Institutions:** National Housing Bank (NHB) and National Bank for Agriculture and Rural Development (NABARD).

5. **State Level Institutions:** State Financial Corporations (SFCs) and State Industrial Development Corporations (SIDCs).

6. **Other Financial Institutions:** Some other financial institutions are Export Credit and Guarantee Corporation of India Ltd. (ECGC) and Deposit Insurance and Crdit Guarantee Corporation (DICGC).

SPECIAL FINANCIAL INSTITUTIONS (SFI)

A number of special financial institutions have been set up by the central and state governments to provide long-term finance to the business organisations. They also offer support services in launching of the new enterprises and so also for expansion and modernisation of existing enterprises. Some of the important ones are Industrial Finance Corporation of India (IFCI), Industrial Investment Bank of India (IIBI), Industrial Credit and Investment Corporation of India (ICICI), Infrastructure Development Finance Company Ltd. (IDFC), Small Industries Development Bank of India (SIDBI), State Industrial Development Corporations (SIDCs), and State Financial Corporations (SFCs), etc. Since these institutions provide developmental finance, they are also known as Development Banks or Development Financial Institutions (DFI). Besides these development banks there are a few other financial institutions such as life Insurance Corporation of India (LIC), General Insurance Corporation of India (GIC) and Unit Trust of India (UTI) which provide long-term finance to companies and subscribe to their share and debentures. The main functions of these institutions are:

(i) to grant loans for a longer period to industrial establishment;

(ii) to help the establishment of business units that require large amount of funds and have long gestation period;

(iii) to provide support for the speedy development of the economy in general and backward regions in particular;

(iv) to offer specialized services operating in the areas of promotion, project assistance, technical assistance services and training and development of entrepreneurs;

(v) to provide technical and professional management services and help in identification, evaluation and execution of new projects.

Some of the Special Financial Institutions (SFI)

1. **Industrial Finance Corporation of India (IFCI):** It is the oldest SFI set up in 1948 with the primary objective of providing long-term and medium-term finance to large industrial enterprises. It provides financial assistance for setting up of new industrial enterprises and for expansion or diversification of activities. It also provides support to modernisation and renovation of plant and equipment in existing industrial units. It can grant loan or subscribe to debentures issued by companies repayable in not more than 25 years. It can also guarantee loans raised from other sources or debentures issued to the public, and take up underwriting of the public issue of shares and debentures by companies. For ensuring greater flexibility to meet the needs of the changing financial system IFCI now stands transformed to IFCI Ltd. with effect from 1 June, 1993.

2. **Industrial Credit and Investment Corporation of India (ICICI):** It was set up in 1955 for providing long-term loans to companies for a period upto 15 years and subscribe to their shares and debentures. However, the proprietary and partnership firms were also entitled to secure loans from ICICI. Like IFCI, the ICICI also guarantees loans raised by companies from other sources besides underwriting their issue of shares and debentures. Foreign currency loans can also be secured by companies from ICICI. In the context of the emerging competitive scenario in the finance sector, ICICI has merged with ICICI Bank Ltd., with effect from 3 May, 2002. Consequent upon the merger, the ICICI group's financing and banking operations have been integrated into a single full service banking company.

3. **Industrial Development Bank of India (IDBI):** It was set up in 1964 as a subsidiary of Reserve Bank of India for providing financial assistance to all types of industrial enterprises without any restriction on the type of finance and the amount of funds. It could also refinance loans granted by other financial institutions and offer guarantees for the loans raised from the capital market or scheduled banks. It also discounts and rediscounts the commercial bills of exchange and undertakes underwriting of the public issues. IDBI, like

ICICI, has also transformed into a commercial bank and has been retitled as IDBI Ltd. with effect from 1 October, 2004 with IDBI Bank merged into it.

4. **Industrial Investment Bank of India (IIBI):** The erstwhile Industrial Reconstruction Bank of India (IRBI), an institution which was set up for rehabilitation of small units has been reconstituted in 1997 as Industrial Investment Bank of India. It is a full fledged all purpose development bank with adequate operational flexibility and autonomy. After the reconstruction its focus has changed from rehabilitation finance to development banking.

5. **Small Industries Development Bank of India (SIDBI):** It was set up in 1990 as a principal financial institution for the promotion, financing and development of small-scale industrial enterprises. It is an apex institution of all the banks providing credit facility to small-scale industries in our country. It offers refinancing of bills, rediscounting of bills, and several other support services to Small Scale Industries (SSI). It undertakes a wide range of promotional and development activities for improving the inherent strength of SSI units and creating avenues for the economic development of the rural poor.

6. **State Financial Corporations (SFCs):** In order to provide financial assistance to all types of industrial enterprises (proprietary and partnership firms as well as companies) most of the states of our country have set up SFCs. The primary objective of these corporations is to accelerate the pace of Industrial development in their respective states. SFCs provide finance in the form of long-term loans or through subscription of debentures, offer guarantee to loans raised from other sources and take up underwriting of public issues of shares and debentures made by companies. However, they cannot directly subscribe to the shares issued by the companies. The SFC (Amendment) Act, 2000 has provided greater flexibility to SFCs to cope with the changing economic and financial environment of the country.

7. **State Industrial Development Corporations (SIDCs):** These corporations were set up in 1960s and early 1970s by most state governments for promotions and development of medium and large-scale industries in their respective states. In addition to providing financial assistance to industrial units, they also undertake a variety of promotional activities. They also implement the various incentive schemes of the central and state governments.

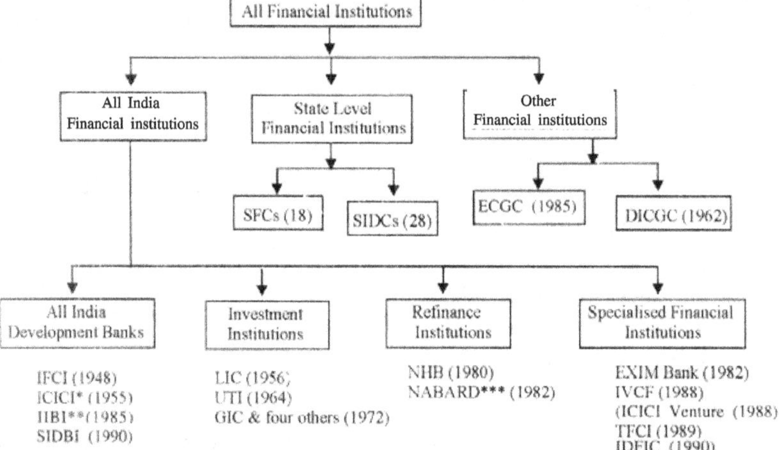

Note: * Industrial Credit and Investment Corporation of India (ICICI) was merged with ICICI Bank in 2002 and ceased to be a development finance institution.

** The Industrial Reconstruction Bank of India (IRBI) was set-up in 1985 but was renamed as Indistrial Investment Bank of India in 1997.

***NABARD took over the refinance functions performed earlier by Agricultural Refinance Development Corporation.

8. **Other Financial Institutions:** Apart from the above special financial institutions, there are a few other organizations, which act as important source of long-term finance. These are:

(a) **Life Insurance Corporation of India (LIC):** It was set up in 1956 on nationalisation of life insurance business in India. Primarily it carries on the business of life insurance and deploys the funds in accordance with national priorities and objectives. It invests mainly in government securities and shares, debentures and bonds of companies. It also extends financial assistance to banks and other institutions for social development and infrastructure facilities. It also underwrites new issues of shares and grant loans to the corporate sectors. Its performance with regard to assistance to corporate sector has been significant both in terms of sanctions and disbursements.

(b) **General Insurance Corporation of India (GIC):** It was established in 1973 on nationalization of general insurance business in India. Like LIC, its investment priority is socially oriented sectors of the economy, and invests its funds in government securities and share and debentures of companies. It also provides term loans and underwriting facility to new and existing industrial undertakings.

(c) **Unit Trust of India (UTI):** It was set up in 1964 as an investment trust with capital of Rs. 5 crore subscribed by Reserve Rank of India, LIC, State Bank of India and other financial institutions. It has been playing an important role in mobilizing the savings of the community through sale of units under various schemes (most well known being US-64 and master shares) and channalising them into corporate investments. It has also been extending financial assistance to the companies by way of term loans, bills rediscounting, equipment leasing and hire purchase financing.

(d) **Export and Import Bank of India (EXIM Bank):** The Export and Import Bank of India was set up on January, 1982 to take over the operations of international finance wing of the IDBI and act as an apex institutions in the field of financing foreign trade. The main functions of the Bank are: (i) financing of export and import of goods and services; (ii) granting deferred payment credit for medium and long term duration; (iii) providing loans to Indian parties to enable them to contribute to share capital of joint ventures in foreign countries and; (iv) extending refinance facilities to commercial banks in respect of export credit. Recently it has introduced production equipment finance programme under which it provides rupee term finance to export oriented units for acquisition of equipment. Apart from these, the Exim Bank also undertakes merchant banking and development banking functions as considered necessary to finance promotional activities and providing counseling services to persons engaged in export-import business.

(e) **Venture Capital Institutions:** Venture Capital is a form of equity finance designed specially for funding high risk and high reward projects of young entrepreneurs. It helps them to turn their research and development projects into commercial ventures by providing them the initial capital and managerial assistance. The initial capital is provided in the form of equity participation through direct purchase of the share and debentures of the enterprise set up for the purpose. The institutions providing venture capital also actively participate in the management of the entrepreneurs' business. By actively involving and supporting the enterprises, they able to protect and enhance the value of their investment.

The development of venture capital institutions is of recent origin in India. The concept was formally introduced in 1986-87 when the Government announced the creation of a venture fund to be operated by IDBI. It was followed by ICICI, IFCI and two public sector banks (State Bank of India and Canara Bank) who set up separate companies for the purpose. Some state government controlled development financial institutions viz., Gujarat Industrial Investment Corporation and Andhra Pradesh State Corporation also promoted their venture capital companies. In 1992-93, SIDBI also set up a venture capital fund for providing financial assistance for innovative ventures in small-scale sector.

NATIONAL BANK FOR AGRICULTURE AND RURAL DEVELOPMENT (NABARD)

It is the apex banking institution providing finance for agriculture and rural development. NABARD was established on July 12, 1982 with the *paid-up* capital of ₹ 100 crore (present level of ₹ 2000 crore) having 50 : 50 contribution of Indian Government and RBI. NABARD (Amendment) Bill 2000 was accepted by the President in January 2001. Under this act the authorised capital has been raised from ₹ 500 crore to ₹ 2000 crore.

Union Cabinet has approved the proposal of raising paid-up capital of NABARD. As per Union Cabinet decision the paid-up capital of NABARD has been increased from present level of ₹ 2,000 crore to 5,000 crore in two phases. In the first phase ₹ 1,000 crore was raised in 2011-12, while the remaining ₹ 2,000 crore was raised in second phase during 2012-13.

NABARD was established with the aim for providing credit for promotion of agriculture, small scale industries, cottage and village industries, handicrafts and other allied economic activities in rural areas with a view to promote integrated rural development and securing prosperity in rural areas.

As an apex institution in rural credit structure, NABARD provides refinance facilities to various such refinance facilities to various such financial institutions which provide loans to promote productive activities in rural areas. To meet its loan requirements, NABARD obtains funds from Government of India, Word Bank and other agencies. It also mobilises resources by issuing bonds and debentures guaranted by Union Government. Besides, it also utilises the funds of National Rural Credit Fund.

NABARD also provides loans to Commercial Banks and Regional Rural Banks for refinance purpose so that these banks may continue their various activities including granting finances for small irrigation, IRDP, dairy development, mechanisation of farms, etc.

Types of Finance

Types of Finance	Period of Repayment	Purpose
Short-term	Less than a year	Purchase of raw materials, payment of wages, rent, insurance etc.
Medium-term	One year to five years	Expenditure on modernisation, renovation, heavy advertising etc.
Long-term	More than five years	Purchase of land and building, plant and machineries, etc.

✩✩✩✩✩✩

Non-Banking Financial Companies (NBFCs)

INTRODUCTION

Non-banking financial companies (NBFCs) are fast emerging as an important segment of Indian financial system. It is an heterogeneous group of institutions (other than commercial and co-operative banks) performing financial intermediation in a variety of ways, like accepting deposits, making loans and advances, leasing, hire purchase, etc. They raise funds from the public, directly or indirectly, and lend them to ultimate spenders. They advance loans to the various wholesale and retail traders, small-scale industries and self-employed persons. Thus, they have broadened and diversified the range of products and services offered by a financial sector. Gradually, they are being recognised as complementary to the banking sector due to their customer-oriented services; simplified procedures; attractive rates of return on deposits; flexibility and timeliness in meeting the credit needs of specified sectors; etc.

A non-banking financial company (NBFC) is a company registered under the Companies Act, 1956 and is engaged in the business of loans and advances, acquisition of shares/stock/bonds/debentures/ securities issued by government or local authority or other securities of like marketable nature, leasing, hire-purchase, insurance business, chit business, but does not include any institution whose principal business is that of agriculture activity, industrial activity, sale/purchase/construction of immovable property.

A non-banking institution which is a company and which has its principal business of receiving deposits under any scheme or arrangement or any other manner, or lending in any manner is also a non-banking financial company (residuary non-banking company).

The working and operations of NBFCs are regulated by the Reserve Bank of India (RBI)within the framework of the Reserve Bank of India Act, 1934 (Chapter III B) and the directions issued by it under the Act. **As per the RBI Act, a 'non-banking financial company' is defined as:-** (i) a financial institution which is a company; (ii) a non banking institution which is a company and which has as its principal business the receiving of deposits, under any scheme or arrangement or in any other manner, or lending in any manner; (iii) such other non-banking institution or class of such institutions, as the bank may, with the previous approval of the Central Government and by notification in the Official Gazette, specify.

REGISTRATION OF NBFCs

In terms of Section 45-IA of the RBI Act, 1934, it is mandatory that every NBFC should be registered with RBI to commence or carry on any business of non-banking financial institution as defined in clause (a) of Section 45 I of the RBI Act, 1934.

However, to obviate dual regulation, certain category of NBFCs which are regulated by other regulators are exempted from the requirement of registration with RBI viz. venture capital fund/merchant banking companies/stock broking companies registered with SEBI, insurance company holding a valid certificate of registration issued by IRDA, Nidhi companies as notified under Section 620A of the Companies Act, 1956, chit companies as defined in clause (b) of Section 2 of the Chit Funds Act, 1982 or housing finance companies regulated by National Housing Bank.

DIFFERENCES BETWEEN BANKS & NBFCs

NBFCs are doing functions akin to that of banks, however there are a few differences:

(i) a NBFC cannot accept demand deposits (demand deposits are funds deposited at a depository institution that are payable on demand – immediately or within a very short period – like your current or savings accounts.)

(ii) it is not a part of the payment and settlement system and as such cannot issue cheques to its customers; and

(iii) deposit insurance facility of DICGC is not available for NBFC depositors unlike in case of banks.

Types of NBFCs

The types of NBFCs registered with the RBI are:

1. **Equipment leasing company:** is any financial institution whose principal business is that of leasing equipments or financing of such an activity.

2. **Hire-purchase company:** is any financial intermediary whose principal business relates to hire purchase transactions or financing of such transactions.

3. **Loan company:** means any financial institution whose principal business is that of providing finance, whether by making loans or advances or otherwise for any activity other than its own (excluding any equipment leasing or hire-purchase finance activity).

4. **Investment company:** is any financial intermediary whose principal business is that of buying and selling of securities.

Distinction between Cash Credit and Bank Overdraft
(*i*) Cash credit is an arrangement of credit granted by a bank to a firm. The firm may or may not have an account with the bank. Overdraft is granted to an accountholder purely on the basis of his credit-worthiness. Credit worthiness is decided by the financial soundness of past dealings of the customer with the bank.
(*ii*) In case of cash credit, the amount of credit is placed in a separate account of the borrower. Overdraft limit is generally granted to an existing account of the customer.
(*iii*) The amount of credit in case of cash credit depends upon the value of securities offered. But overdraft limit is decided on the average balance in the customers account.
(*iv*) Overdraft is granted without the security of any assets. But for cash credit, security of tangible assets is an essential requirement.

With effect from December 6, 2006 the above NBFCs registered with RBI have been reclassified as:

(i) Asset Finance Company (AFC)
(ii) Investment Company (IC)
(iii) Loan Company (LC)

AFC would be defined as any company which is a financial institution carrying on as its principal business the financing of physical assets supporting productive / economic activity, such as automobiles, tractors, lathe machines, generator sets, earth moving and material handling equipments, moving on own power and general purpose industrial machines.

Principal business for this purpose is defined as aggregate of financing real/physical assets supporting economic activity and income arising therefrom is not less than 60% of its total assets and total income respectively.

The above type of companies may be further classified into those accepting deposits or those not accepting deposits.Besides the above class of NBFCs the Residuary Non-Banking Companies are also registered as NBFC with the Bank.

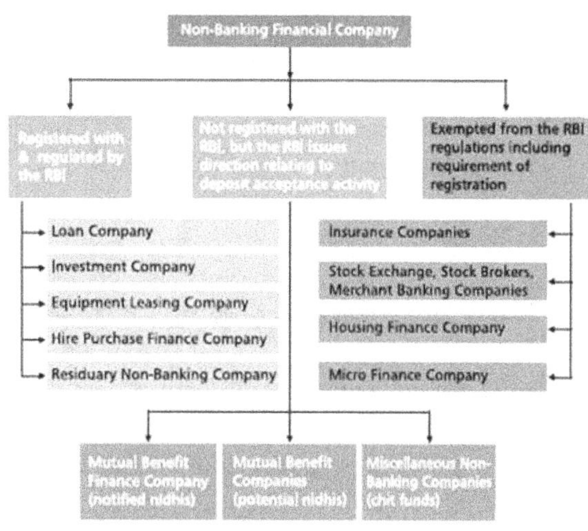

NBFCs by their Principle Business

Non-Banking Financial Companies (NBFCs)	Principle Business
Equipment Leasing Company (EL)	Equipment leasing or financing of such activity
Hire Purchase Finance Company (HP)	Hire purchase transaction or purchasing or such transactions
Investment Company (IC)	Acquisition of securities and trading in such securities to earn a profit
Loan Company (LC)	Making loans or advances for any activity other than its own; EL/HP/ Housing Finance
Residuary Non-Banking Companies (RNBCs)	Receives deposits under any scheme or arrangement, by whatever name called, in one lump-sum or in instalments by way of contributions or subsriptions or by sale of units or certificates or other instruments, or in any manner
Mutual Benefit Financial Companies (MBFC) i.e. Nidhi Company	Any company which is notified by the Central Government as a Nidhi Company under section 620A of the Companies Act, 1956. It is a NBFC doing the business of lending and borrowing with its members or shareholders.
Miscellaneous Non-Banking Company (MNBC) i.e. Chit Fund Company	Managing, conducting or supervising as a promoter, foreman or agent of any transaction or arrangement by which the company enters into an agreement with a specified number of subscribers that every one of them shall subscribe a certain amount in instalments over a definite period and that every one of such subscribers shall in turn, as determined by lot or by auction or by tender or in such manner as may be provided for in the arrangement, be entitled to the prize amount

Acceptance of Public Deposits

Only those NBFCs holding a valid Certificate of Registration can accept/hold public deposits. The NBFCs accepting public deposits should comply with the Non-Banking Financial Companies Acceptance of Public Deposits (Reserve Bank) Directions, 1998, as issued by the bank. Some of the important regulations relating to acceptance of deposits by the NBFCs are:-

- ❏ They are allowed to accept/renew public deposits for a minimum period of 12 months and maximum period of 60 months.
- ❏ They cannot accept deposits repayable on demand.
- ❏ They cannot offer interest rates higher than the ceiling rate prescribed by RBI from time to time.
- ❏ They cannot offer gifts/incentives or any other additional benefit to the depositors.
- ❏ They should have minimum investment grade credit rating.
- ❏ Their deposits are not insured.
- ❏ The repayment of deposits by NBFCs is not guaranteed by RBI.

MUDRA BANK

The **Micro Units Development and Refinance Agency** (known as the **MUDRA Bank**) has been launched on April 8, 2015 which would primarily be responsible for regulating micro and small enterprise financing business, and supporting them. The roles envisaged for MUDRA include laying down policy guidelines for micro enterprise financing business and registration of MFI entities as well as their accreditation and rating.

Prime Minister Narendra Modi launched the ₹ 20,000 crore (₹ 200 billion) MUDRA Bank that aims to provide refinancing to small and medium enterprises, particularly those belonging to members of scheduled castes and scheduled tribes. According to Narendra Modi, the bank would help over six crore families. The bank would also get an additional ₹ 3,000 crore (₹ 30 billion) in the budget to create a credit guarantee corpus for guaranteeing loans being provided to the micro enterprises.

MUDRA Bank will offer loans under three schemes-**Shishu**-upto ₹ 50,000, **Kishor** upto ₹ 5 lac and **Tarun** upto ₹ 10 lac-based on stage of micro business. MUDRA Bank will also register MFIs and be responsible for accreditation and rating of MFI. It will also lay down policies for proper last mile practices to be followed by MFI to prevent indebtedness and provide proper client protection.

Important features of MUDRA Bank can be summed up as follows:

- MUDRA Bank stands for Micro Units Development Refinance Agency (MUDRA). Also, Mudra, in Hindi, means currency.
- MUDRA Bank is being set up through a statutory enactment and will be responsible for developing and refinancing through a Pradhan Mantri MUDRA Yojana.
- Since small entrepreneurs are businesses are often cut off from banking system because of limited branch presence, MUDRA Bank will partner with local co-ordinators and provide finance to 'Last Mile Financiers' or small/ micro businesses.
- MUDRA has been targeted towards mainstreaming young, educated or skilled workers and entrepreneurs including women entrepreneurs.
- The bank will cater to 5.77 crore small business units that are spread all across India who currently find it difficult to access credit from the regular banking system.
- MUDRA Bank will ensure clients are properly protected and will lay down principles and methods of loan recovery in case of a default. The Bank will also rigidly follow 'responsible financing practices' so deter borrowers from indebtedness.
- The Bank will be set up with a corpus of ₹ 20,000 crore and a credit guarantee fund of ₹ 2,000 crore.
- The Bank will nurture small businesses through different stages of growth and development of businesses termed as Shishu, Kishor and Tarun.
- **Shishu:** This is the first step when the business is just starting up. The loan cover in this stage will be upto ₹ 50,000.
- **Kishor:** In this stage, the entrepreneur will be eligible for a loan ranging from ₹ 50,000 to ₹ 5 lakh.
- **Tarun:** This last and final category will provide loans for upto ₹ 10 lakh.

MERCHANT BANKING

Initially, commercial banks set up merchant banking divisions, which later became separate merchant banking subsidiaries. A few merchant banks have been set up by private financial service companies in association with foreign banking and money market institutions, and some have been set up by firms and individuals engaged in brokerage and financial advisory business.

Merchant banks in India manage and underwrite new issues; they undertake syndication of credit; they advise corporate clients on fund raising and other financial aspects, Unlike merchant banks abroad, Indian merchant banks do not undertake banking business, viz., deposit banking, lending and foreign exchange services.

The merchant banks were subject to two types of authorities:

(a) The Securities and Exchange Board of India (SEBI) sought to authorise and regulate all merchant banks on issue activity and portfolio management of their business; and

(b) RBI supervised those merchant banks which were subsidiaries or affiliates of commercial banks. If the merchant banks were to raise deposits, they would have to be subject to the guidelines issues by RBI.

The Narasimham Committee (1991) saw considerable potential for the operation of merchant banks in the framework of deregulated industrial economy. The merchant banks were emerging as financially strong and independent. The Committee would like the Government to encourage the formation of joint ventures with well-reputed international merchant and investment banks. The Committee would also like the merchant banks to have access, in course of time, to the market for deposits and borrowed resources, subject to the observance of prudential norms specially tailored to the conduct of prudential norms specially tailored to the conduct of their business.

Merchant banking has been statutorily brought under the regulatory framework of SEBI and has to be authorised by the latter. Merchant bankers have to adopt the stipulated capital adequacy norms, abide by a code of conduct which specifies a high degree of responsibility towards investors in respect or pricing and premium fixation of issues and disclosures in the prospectus or offer letters for fresh issues of capital. Merchant bankers have now a great degree of accountability in the offer document and issue process.

Bills Related to Banking and Insurance Sector	
● The Reserve Bank of India (Amendment) Bill 2005	For providing more operational flexibility to the Central Bank to fix SLR and CRR for different banks so as to make available more funds for productive growth.
● The Banking Regulation (Amendment) Bill 2004	For removing 10% Cap on voting rights and also encouraging foreign banks to set up subsidiaries and attract foreign investments.
● Credit Information Companies (Regulation) Bill 2004	For helping banks to deal with NPAs by providing information regarding credit worthiness of various categories of customers.
● The Securities Laws (Amendment) Bill 2004	The dematerialises stock exchanges and enhance panel provisions to protect investors interests.
● Insurance Regulatory Authority Bill 2004	For increasing the FDI Cap from 26% to 49% in private insurance companies.

★★★★★★

Mutual Funds

Mutual fund refers to a fund established in the form of a trust by a sponsor to raise money through one or more schemes for investing in securities. It is a special type of investment institution, which acts as an investment intermediary that collects or pools the savings of a large number of investors and invests them in a fairly large and well diversified portfolio of sound investments. This minimizes their risk and ensures good returns to the investors. Thus, they act as an investment agency for small investors and a good source for long-term finance for the business.

FEATURES OF MUTUAL FUNDS

The essential features of mutual funds are as follows:

1. It is a trust into which a number of investors invest their money in the form of units to form a large pool of funds.
2. The amount is invested in securities by the managers of the fund.
3. The amount is invested in different securities of reputed companies to ensure definite and regular income. Thus, it helps in minimizing the risk.
4. The mutual fund schemes often have the advantages of high return, easy liquidity, safety and tax benefits to the investors.
5. The net income received on the investments of the fund is distributed over the units held.
6. The managers of the fund are obliged to redeem the units on demand or on the expiry of a specified period.

CONCEPT OF MUTUAL FUNDS

↓

Many investors with common financial objectives pool their money

↓

Investors, on a proportionate basis, get mutual fund units for the sum contributed to the pool

↓

The money collected from investors is invested into shares, debentures and other securities by the fund manager

↓

The fund manager realizes gains or losses, and collects dividend or interest income

↓

Any capital gains or losses from such investments are passed on to the investors in proportion of the number of units held them

ADVANTAGES OF MUTUAL FUNDS

S.No.	Advantage	Particulars
1.	Portfolio Diversification	Mutual Funds invest in a well-diversified portfolio of securities which enables investor to hold a diversified investment portfolio (whether the amount of investment is big or small).
2.	Professional Management	Fund manager undergoes through various research works and has better investment management skills which ensure higher returns to the investor than what he can manage on his own.
3.	Less Risk	Investors acquire a diversified portfolio of securities even with a small investment in a Mutual Fund. The risk in a diversified portfolio is lesser than investing in merely 2 or 3 securities.
4.	Low Transaction Costs	Due to the economies of scale (benefits of larger volumes), mutual funds pay lesser transaction costs. These benefits are passed on to the investors.
5.	Liquidity	An investor may not be able to sell some of the shares held by him very easily and quickly, whereas units of a mutual fund are far more liquid.
6.	Choice of Schemes	Mutual funds provide investors with various schemes with different investment objectives. Investors have the option of investing in a scheme having a correlation between its investment objectives and their own financial goals. These schemes further have different plans/options.
7.	Transparency	Funds provide investors with updated information pertaining to the markets and the schemes. All material facts are disclosed to investors as required by the regulator.
8.	Flexibility	Investors also benefit from the convenience and flexibility offered by Mutual Funds. Investors can switch their holdings from a debt scheme to an equity scheme and vice-versa. Option of systematic (at regular intervals) investment and withdrawal is also offered to the investors in most open-end schemes.
9.	Safety	Mutual Fund industry is part of a well-regulated investment environment where the interests of the investors are protected by the regulator. All funds are registered with SEBI and complete transparency is forced.

DISADVANTAGES OF MUTUAL FUNDS

S.No.	Disadvantage	Particulars
1.	Costs Control Not in the Hands of an Investor	Investor has to pay investment management fees and fund distribution costs as a percentage of the value of his investments (as long as he holds the units), irrespective of the performance of the fund.
2.	No Customized Portfolios	The portfolio of securities in which a fund invests is a decision taken by the fund manager. Investors have no right to interfere in the decision making process of a fund manager, which some investors find as a constraint in achieving their financial objectives.
3.	Difficulty in Selecting a Suitable Fund Scheme	Many investors find it difficult to select one option from the plethora of funds/schemes/plans available. For this, they may have to take advice from financial planners in order to invest in the right fund to achieve their objectives.

TYPES OF MUTUAL FUNDS

Keeping in view the investment objectives of the investors the mutual funds usually have a large variety of schemes such as equity fund, debt fund, balanced fund, growth fund, income fund, liquid fund, tax saver fund, index fund and so on. These schemes are broadly classified into two categories as follows:

(a) **Open Ended Funds:** These funds have no fixed corpus and period. Such fund continuously offer units for sale and is ready to buy back the units surrendered.

In other words, investors are free to buy from, or sell to, the trust any number of units at any point of time at prices which are linked to the net asset value (NAV) of the units.

(b) **Close Ended Funds:** In case of these funds, subscriptions from the investors are collected during a specified time period and have a fixed corpus. Not only that, the investors cannot redeem their units till the specified maturity date. However, to provide liquidity, these are listed on the stock exchange and the investors can purchase and sell through the brokers at the market price without any difficulty.

It may be noted that Unit Trust of India was the first mutual fund started in India as early as 1964. Later, LIC, GIC and some nationalised banks also launched their mutual funds with high degree of success. However, during post liberalisation era, many private sector mutual funds have entered the fray. To mention a few, these are: Birla Sun Life, HDFC, HSBC, ICICI Prudential, DSP Merrill Lynch, DBS Chola Mutual Fund.

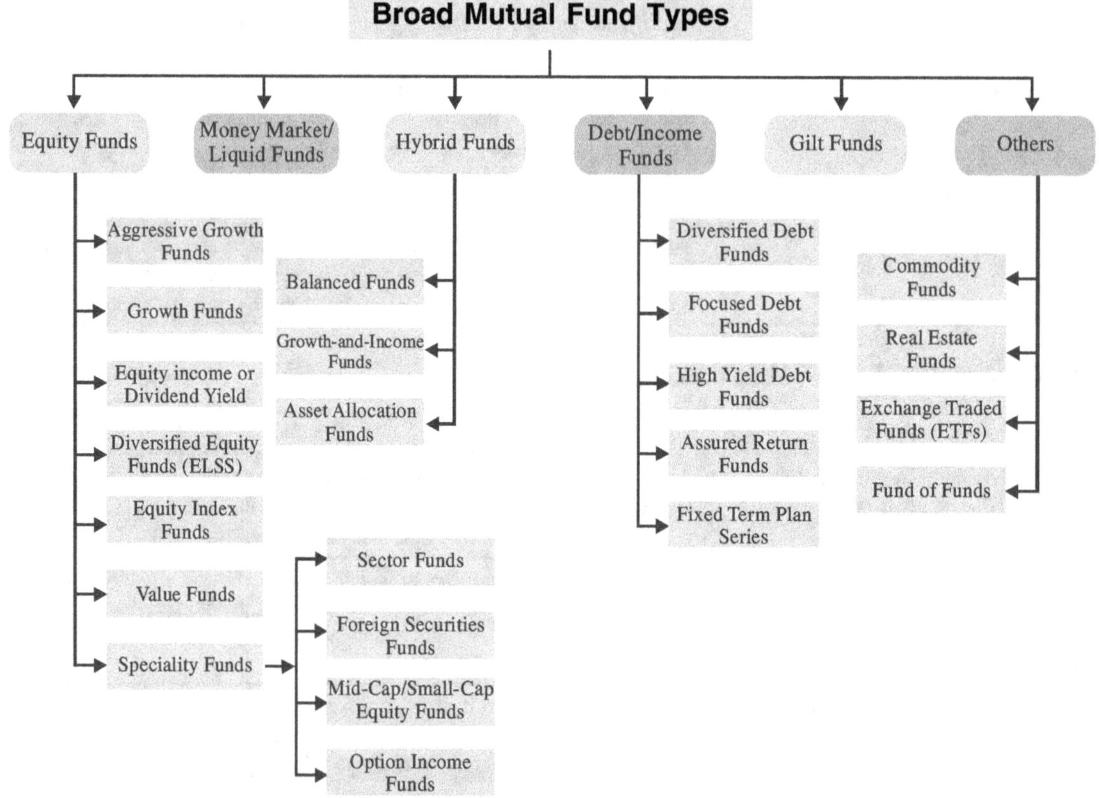

1. **Equity Funds:** Equity funds are considered to be the more risky funds as compared to other fund types, but they also provide higher returns than other funds. It is advisable that an investor looking to invest in an equity fund should invest for long term i.e. for 3 years or more. There are different types of equity funds each falling into different risk bracket.

2. **Debt/Income Funds:** Funds that invest in medium to long-term debt instruments issued by private companies, banks, financial institutions, governments and other entities belonging to various sectors (like infrastructure companies etc.) are known as Debt/Income Funds. Debt funds are low risk profile funds that seek to generate fixed current income (and not capital appreciation) to investors. In order to ensure regular income to investors, debt (or income) funds distribute large fraction of their surplus to investors. Although debt securities are generally less risky than equities, they are subject to credit risk (risk of default) by the issuer at the time of interest or principal payment. To minimize the risk of default, debt funds usually invest in securities from issuers who are rated by credit rating agencies and are considered to be of "Investment Grade". Debt funds that target high returns are more risky.

3. **Gilt Funds:** Also known as Government Securities in India, Gilt Funds invest in government papers (named dated securities) having medium to long term maturity period. Issued by the Government of India, these investments have little credit risk (risk of default) and provide safety of principal to the investors. However, like all debt funds, gilt funds too are exposed to interest rate risk. Interest rates and prices of debt securities are inversely related and any change in the interest rates results in a change in the NAV of debt/gilt funds in an opposite direction.

4. **Money Market/Liquid Funds:** Money market/liquid funds invest in short-term (maturing within one year) interest bearing debt instruments. These securities are highly liquid and provide safety of investment, thus making money market / liquid funds the safest investment option when compared with other mutual fund types. However, even money market / liquid funds are exposed to the interest rate risk. The typical investment options for liquid funds include Treasury Bills (issued by governments), Commercial papers (issued by companies) and Certificates of Deposit (issued by banks).

5. **Hybrid Funds:** As the name suggests, hybrid funds are those funds whose portfolio includes a blend of equities, debts and money market securities. Hybrid funds have an equal proportion of debt and equity in their portfolio.

6. **Commodity Funds:** Those funds that focus on investing in different commodities (like metals, food grains, crude oil etc.) or commodity companies or commodity futures contracts are termed as Commodity Funds. A commodity fund that invests in a single commodity or a group of commodities is a specialized commodity fund and a commodity fund that invests in all available commodities is a diversified commodity fund and bears less risk than a specialized commodity fund. "Precious Metals Fund" and Gold Funds (that invest in gold, gold futures or shares of gold mines) are common examples of commodity funds.

7. **Real Estate Funds:** Funds that invest directly in real estate or lend to real estate developers or invest in shares/securitized assets of housing finance companies, are known as Specialized Real Estate Funds. The objective of these funds may be to generate regular income for investors or capital appreciation.

8. **Exchange Traded Funds (ETF):** Exchange Traded Funds provide investors with combined benefits of a closed-end and an open-end mutual fund. Exchange Traded Funds follow stock market indices and are traded on stock exchanges like a single stock at index linked

prices. The biggest advantage offered by these funds is that they offer diversification, flexibility of holding a single share (tradable at index linked prices) at the same time. Recently introduced in India, these funds are quite popular abroad.

9. **Fund of Funds:** Mutual funds that do not invest in financial or physical assets, but do invest in other mutual fund schemes offered by different AMCs, are known as Fund of Funds. Fund of Funds maintain a portfolio comprising of units of other mutual fund schemes, just like conventional mutual funds maintain a portfolio comprising of equity/debt/money market instruments or non financial assets. Fund of Funds provide investors with an added advantage of diversifying into different mutual fund schemes with even a small amount of investment, which further helps in diversification of risks. However, the expenses of Fund of Funds are quite high on account of compounding expenses of investments into different mutual fund schemes.

Bank Rate
Bank Rate is the rate of discount at which the central bank of the country (RBI) discounts first class bills. It is the rate of interest at which the central bank lends money to the lower banking institutions. Bank rate is the direct quantities method of credit control in the economy.

REPO Rate
Repo Rate, or repurchase rate, is the rate at which RBI lends to banks for short periods. This is done by RBI buying government bonds from banks with an agreement to sell them back at a fixed rate. If the RBI wants to make it more expensive for banks to borrow money, it increases the repo rate. Similarly, if it wants to make it cheaper for banks to borrow money, it reduces the repo rate. Please not that Bank Rate and Repo Rate seem to be similar terms because in both of them RBI lends to the banks. However, Repo Rate is a short-term measure and it refers to short-term loans and used for controlling the amount of money in the market, Bank Rate is a long-term measure and is governed by the long-term monetary policies of the RBI. In broader term, bank rate is the rate of interest which a central bank charges on the loans and advances that it extends to commercial banks and other financial intermediaries. RBI uses this tool to control the money supply.

Reverse Repo Rate
Reverse repo rate is the rate of interest at which the RBI borrows funds from other banks in the short term. This is done by RBI selling governments bonds/securities to banks with the commitment to buy them back at a future date. The banks use the reverse repo facility to deposit their short-term excess funds with the RBI and earn interest on it. RBI can reduce liquidity in the banking system by increasing the rate at which it borrows from banks. Hiking the repo and reverse repo rate ends up reducing the liquidity and pushes up interest rates.

Cash Reserve Ratio (CRR)
The Cash Reserve Ratio is the amount of funds that the banks are bound to keep with Reserve Bank of India, with reference to the net demand and time liabilities (NDTL) to ensure the liquidity and solvency of the Banks. Please note that earlier RBI was empowered to fix CRR between 3-20% by notification.

Statutory Liquidity Ratio (SLR)
Every bank in India has to maintain at the close of business every day, a minimum proportion of their net demand and time liabilities as liquid assets in the form of cash, gold and un-encumbered approved securities. The ratio of liquid assets to demand and time liabilities is known as Statutory Liquidity Ratio (SLR). In simple words, it is the percentage of total deposits banks have to invest in government bonds and other approved securities. An SLR bond also qualifies for the portfolio maintained by banks to meet the liquidity requirement.

☆☆☆☆☆

Stock Exchange

Stock exchange is the term commonly used for a secondary market, which provide a place where different types of existing securities such as shares, debentures and bonds, government securities can be bought and sold on a regular basis. A stock exchange is generally organised as an association, a society or a company with a limited number of members. It is open only to these members who act as brokers for the buyers and sellers. **The Securities Contract (Regulation) Act has defined stock exchange as an** "association, organisation or body of individuals, whether incorporated or not, established for the purpose of assisting, regulating and controlling business of buying, selling and dealing in securities".

The main characteristics of a stock exchange are:

1. It is an organised market.
2. It provides a place where existing and approved securities can be bought and sold easily.
3. In a stock exchange, transactions take place between its members or their authorised agents.
4. All transactions are regulated by rules and by laws of the concerned stock exchange.
5. It makes complete information available to public in regard to prices and volume of transactions taking place every day.

It may be noted that all securities are not permitted to be traded on a recognised stock exchange. It is allowed only in those securities (called listed securities) that have been duly approved for the purpose by the stock exchange authorities. The method of trading now-a-days, however, is quite simple on account of the availability of on-line trading facility with the help of computers. It is also quite fast as it takes just a few minutes to strike a deal through the brokers who may be available close by. Similarly, on account of the system of scrip-less trading and rolling settlement, the delivery of securities and the payment of amount involved also take very little time, say, 2 days.

FUNCTIONS OF A STOCK EXCHANGE

The functions of stock exchange can be enumerated as follows:

1. **Provides ready and continuous market:** By providing a place where listed securities can be bought and sold regularly and conveniently, a stock exchange ensures a ready and continuous market for various shares, debentures, bonds and government securities. This lends a high degree of liquidity to holdings in these securities as the investor can encash their holdings as and when they want.

2. **Provides information about prices and sales:** A stock exchange maintains complete record of all transactions taking place in different securities every day and supplies regular information on their prices and sales volumes to press and other media. In fact, now-a-days,

you can get information about minute to minute movement in prices of selected shares on TV channels like CNBC, Zee News, NDTV and Headlines Today. This enables the investors in taking quick decisions on purchase and sale of securities in which they are interested. Not only that, such information helps them in ascertaining the trend in prices and the worth of their holdings. This enables them to seek bank loans, if required.

3. **Provides safety to dealings and investment:** Transactions on the stock exchange are conducted only amongst its members with adequate transparency and in strict conformity to its rules and regulations which include the procedure and timings of delivery and payment to be followed. This provides a high degree of safety to dealings at the stock exchange. There is little risk of loss on account of non-payment or nondelivery. Securities and Exchange Board of India (SEBI) also regulates the business in stock exchanges in India and the working of the stock brokers.

Not only that, a stock exchange allows trading only in securities that have been listed with it; and for listing any security, it satisfies itself about the genuineness and soundness of the company and provides for disclosure of certain information on regular basis. Though this may not guarantee the soundness and profitability of the company, it does provide some assurance on their genuineness and enables them to keep track of their progress.

4. **Helps in mobilisation of savings and capital formation:** Efficient functioning of stock market creates a conducive climate for an active and growing primary market. Good performance and outlook for shares in the stock exchanges imparts buoyancy to the new issue market, which helps in mobilising savings for investment in industrial and commercial establishments. Not only that, the stock exchanges provide liquidity and profitability to dealings and investments in shares and debentures. It also educates people on where and how to invest their savings to get a fair return. This encourages the habit of saving, investment and risk-taking among the common people. Thus it helps mobilising surplus savings for investment in corporate and government securities and contributes to capital formation.

5. **Barometer of economic and business conditions:** Stock exchanges reflect the changing conditions of economic health of a country, as the shares prices are highly sensitive to changing economic, social and political conditions. It is observed that during the periods of economic prosperity, the share prices tend to rise. Conversely, prices tend to fall when there is economic stagnation and the business activities slow down as a result of depressions. Thus, the intensity of trading at stock exchanges and the corresponding rise on fall in the prices of securities reflects the investors' assessment of the economic and business conditions in a country, and acts as the barometer which indicates the general conditions of the atmosphere of business.

6. **Better Allocation of funds:** As a result of stock market transactions, funds flow from the less profitable to more profitable enterprises and they avail of the greater potential for growth. Financial resources of the economy are thus better allocated.

ADVANTAGES OF STOCK EXCHANGES

Having discussed the functions of stock exchanges, let us look at the advantages which can be outlined from the point of view of (a) Companies, (b) Investors, and (c) the Society as a whole.

(a) To the Companies

(i) The companies whose securities have been listed on a stock exchange enjoy a better goodwill and credit-standing than other companies because they are supposed to be financially sound.

(ii) The market for their securities is enlarged as the investors all over the world become aware of such securities and have an opportunity to invest

(iii) As a result of enhanced goodwill and higher demand, the value of their securities increases and their bargaining power in collective ventures, mergers, etc. is enhanced.

(iv) The companies have the convenience to decide upon the size, price and timing of the issue.

(b) To the Investors

(i) The investors enjoy the ready availability of facility and convenience of buying and selling the securities at will and at an opportune time.

(ii) Because of the assured safety in dealings at the stock exchange the investors are free from any anxiety about the delivery and payment problems.

(iii) Availability of regular information on prices of securities traded at the stock exchanges helps them in deciding on the timing of their purchase and sale.

(iv) It becomes easier for them to raise loans from banks against their holdings in securities traded at the stock exchange because banks prefer them as collateral on account of their liquidity and convenient valuation.

(c) To the Society

(i) The availability of lucrative avenues of investment and the liquidity thereof induces people to save and invest in long-term securities. This leads to increased capital formation in the country.

(ii) The facility for convenient purchase and sale of securities at the stock exchange provides support to new issue market. This helps in promotion and expansion of industrial activity, which in turn contributes, to increase in the rate of industrial growth.

(iii) The Stock exchanges facilitate realisation of financial resources to more profitable and growing industrial units where investors

can easily increase their investment substantially.

(iv) The volume of activity at the stock exchanges and the movement of share prices reflect the changing economic health.

(v) Since government securities are also traded at the stock exchanges, the government borrowing is highly facilitated. The bonds issued by governments, electricity boards, municipal corporations and public sector undertakings (PSUs) are found to be on offer quite frequently and are generally successful.

LIMITATIONS OF STOCK EXCHANGES

Like any other institutions, the stock exchanges too have their limitations. One of the common evils associated with stock exchange operations is the excessive speculation. We know that speculation implies buying or selling securities to take advantage of price differential at different times. The speculators generally do not take or give delivery and pay or receive full payment. They settle their transactions just by paying the difference in prices. Normally, speculation is considered a healthy practice and is necessary for successful operation of stock exchange activity. But, when it becomes excessive, it leads to wide fluctuations in prices and various malpractices by the vested interests. In the process, genuine investors suffer and are driven out of the market.

Another shortcoming of stock exchange operations is that security prices may fluctuate due to unpredictable political, social and economic factors as well as on account of rumours spread by interested parties. This makes it difficult to assess the movement of prices in future and build appropriate strategies for investment in securities.

STOCK EXCHANGES IN INDIA

The first organised stock exchange in India was started in Mumbai known as Bombay Stock Exchange (BSE). It was followed by Ahmedabad Stock Exchange in 1894 and Calcutta Stock

Exchange in 1908. The number of stock exchanges in India went upto 7 by 1939 and it increased to 21 by 1945 on account of heavy speculation activity during Second World War. A number of unorganised stock exchanges also functioned in the country without any formal set-up and were known as kerb market. The Security Contracts (Regulation) Act was passed in 1956 for recognition and regulation of Stock Exchanges in India. At present we have 19 recognised stock exchanges in the country. Of these, the most prominent stock exchange that came up is National Stock Exchange (NSE). It is also based in Mumbai and was promoted by the leading financial institutions in India. It was incorporated in 1992 and commenced operations in 1994. This stock exchange has a corporate structure, fully automated screen-based trading and nation-wide coverage.

Another stock exchange that needs special mention is Over The Counter Exchange of India (OTCEI). It was also promoted by the financial institutions like UTI, ICICI, IDBI, IFCI, LIC etc. in September 1992 specially to cater to small and medium sized companies with equity capital of more than Rs.30 lakh and less than Rs.25 crore. It helps entrepreneurs in raising finances for their new projects in a cost effective manner. It provides for nationwide online ringless trading with 20 plus representative offices in all major cities of the country. On this stock exchange, securities of those companies can be traded which are exclusively listed on OTCEI only. In addition, certain shares and debentures listed with other stock exchanges in India and the units of UTI and other mutual funds are also allowed to be traded on OTCEI as permitted securities. It has been noticed that, of late, the turnover at this stock exchange has considerably reduced and steps have been afoot to revitalise it. In fact, as of now, BSE and NSE are the two Stock Exchanges, which enjoy nation-wide coverage and handle most of the business in securities in the country.

REGULATIONS OF STOCK EXCHANGES

As indicated earlier, the stock exchanges suffer from certain limitations and require strict control over their activities in order to ensure safety in dealings thereon. Hence, as early as 1956, the Securities Contracts (Regulation) Act was passed which provided for recognition of stock exchanges by the central Government. It has also the provision of framing of proper bylaws by every stock exchange for regulation and control of their functioning subject to the approval by the Government. All stock exchanges are required submit information relating to its affairs as required by the Government from time to time. The Government was given wide powers relating to listing of securities, make or amend bylaws, withdraw recognition to, or supersede the governing bodies of stock exchange in extraordinary/abnormal situations. Under the Act, the Government promulgated the Securities Regulations (Rules) 1957, which provided inter alia for the procedures to be followed for recognition of the stock exchanges, submission of periodical returns and annual returns by recognised stock exchanges, inquiry into the affairs of recognised stock exchanges and their members, and requirements for listing of securities.

SHARES

Share is the smallest unit into which the total capital of the company is divided. For example, when a company decides to raise Rs. 50 crores of capital from the public by issuing shares, then it can divide its capital into units of a definite value, say Rs. 10/- or Rs. 100/- each. these individual units are called as its share. After deciding the value of each share and number of shares to be issued, the company then invites the public to buy the shares. The investing public then buy the shares as per their capabilities. The investors who have purchased the shares or invested money in the shares are called the shareholders. They get dividend as return of their investment.

Investors are of different habits and temperaments. Some want to take lesser risk and are interested in a regular income. While others are ready to take greater risk in anticipation of huge profits in future. In order to tap the savings of different types of people, a company can issue two types of shares, viz. (a) Equity Shares, and (b) Preference shares.

EQUITY SHARES

Equity shares are shares, which do not enjoy any preferential right in the matter of claim of dividend or repayment of capital. The equity shareholders get dividend only after making the payment of dividends on preference shares. There is no fixed rate of dividend for equity shareholders. The rate of dividend depends upon the surplus profits. In case there are good profits, the company pays dividend to the equity shareholders at a higher rate. Again in case of winding up of a company, the equity share capital is refunded only after refunding the claims of others. In fact they are regarded as the owners of the company who exercise their authority through the voting rights they enjoy. The money raised by issuing such shares is known as equity share capital. It is also called as ownership capital or owners' fund.

Merits of Equity Shares

From Shareholders point of view	From Management point of view
• The equity shareholders are the owners of the company. • It is suitable for those who want to take risk for higher return. • The value of equity shares goes up in the stock market with the increase in profits of the concern. • Equity shares can be easily sold in the stock market. • The liability is limited to the nominal value of shares. • Equity shareholders have a say in the management of a company as they are conferred voting rights.	• A company can raise capital by issuing equity shares without creating any charge on its fixed assets. • The capital raised by issuing equity shares is not required to be paid back during the lifetime of the company. It will be paid back only when the company is winding up. • There is no binding on the company to pay dividend on equity shares. The company may declare dividend only if there are enough profits. • If a company raises more capital by issuing equity shares, it leads to greater confidence among the creditors.

Limitations of Equity Shares

From Shareholders point of view	From Management point of view
• Equity shareholders get dividend only when the company earns sufficient profits. The decision to declare dividend lies with the Board of Directors of the company. • There is high speculation in equity shares. This is particularly so in the time of boom when profitability of the companies is high. • Equity shareholders bear a very high degree of risk. In case of losses they do not get dividend, and in case of winding up of a company, they are the last to get the refund of their money invested. Equity shares actually swim and sink with the fate of the company.	• It requires more formalities and procedural delay to raise funds by issuing equity shares. Also the cost of raising capital through equity share is more as compared to debt. • As the equity shareholders carry voting rights, groups are formed to garner the votes and grab the control of the company. This may lead to conflict of interests, which is harmful for the smooth functioning of a company.

PREFERENCE SHARES

Preference Shares are those shares, which carry preferential rights in respect of dividend and return of capital. Before any dividend is paid to the equity shares, the dividend at a fixed rate must be paid on the preference shares. However, this dividend is payable only if there are profits. Again at the time of winding up, the holder of the preference shares will get the return of their capital before anything is paid to the equity shareholders. The holders of the preference shares do not have any voting right. So, they cannot take part in the management of the company. It is not compulsory on the part of the company to issue preference shares.

Types of Preference Share

A company has the option to issue different types of preference share. Let us see what are the different types of preference share a company can issue.

(i) Convertible and Non-convertible Preference Share: The preference shares which can be converted into equity shares after a specified period of time are known as convertible preference share. Otherwise, it is known as non-convertible preference share.

(ii) Cumulative and Non-cumulative Preference Share: In cumulative preference shares, the unpaid dividends are accumulated and carried forward for payment in future years. On the other hand, in non-cumulative preference share, the dividend is not accumulated if it is not paid out of the current year's profit.

(iii) Participating and Non-participating Preference Share: Participating preference shares have a right to share the profit after making payment to the equity shares. The non-participating preference shares do not enjoy such a right.

(iv) Redeemable and Irredeemable Preference Share: Preference shares having a fixed date of maturity is called as redeemable preference share. Here, the company undertakes to return the amount to the preference shareholders immediately after the expiry of a fixed period. Where the amount of the preference shares is refunded only at the time of liquidation, are known an irredeemable preference shares.

Difference between equity shares and preference shares

S.No.	Basis of difference	Equity shares	Preference Shares
1.	Choice	It is compulsory to issue these shares.	It is not compulsory to issue these shares.
2.	Payment of dividend	Dividend is paid on these shares only after paying dividend on preference shares.	Dividend is paid on these shares in preference to the equity shares.
3.	Return of capital	In case of winding up of the company the equity share capital is refunded only after the refund of preference share capital.	In case of winding up of the company the capital is refunded in preference over the equity shares.
4.	Voting Right	The equity shareholders enjoy voting rights.	The preference shareholders do not have voting rights.
5.	Accumulation of Dividend	The dividends on equity shares are not accumulated and therefore cannot be carried forward.	The unpaid dividends are accumulated and are carried forward to the future years in case of cumulative preference shares.

DEBENTURES

The companies can raise long term funds by issuing debentures that carry assured rate of return for investors in the form of a fixed rate of interest. It is known as debt capital or borrowed capital of the company. The debenture is a written acknowledgement of money borrowed. It specifies the terms and conditions, such as rate of interest, time of repayment, security offered, etc. These are offered to the public to subscribe in the same manner as is done in the case of shares.

The debentureholders are the creditors of the company and are entitled to get interest irrespective of profit earned by the company. They do not have any voting right. So they do not interfere in the day-to-day management of the business. Ordinarily, debentures are fully secured. In case the company fails to pay interest on debentures or repay the principal amount, the debentureholders can recover it from sale of its assets.

Merits of Debentures

(a) Debentures are secured loans. On winding up of the company, they are repayable before making any payment to the equity and preference shareholders.

(b) The debentureholders get assured return irrespective of profit.

(c) Issue of debentures enables the company to provide high return to equity shareholders when the earnings of the company are good. This is called Trading on Equity.

(d) Debentureholders have no right either to vote or take part in the management of the company. So by issuing debentures the company raises the additional capital without diluting the control over its management.

(e) Interest paid on debentures is treated as an expense and is charged to the profits of the company. The company thus, saves income tax.

Limitations of Debentures

(a) If the earnings of the company are uncertain and unpredictable, issue of debentures may pose serious problems due to fixed obligation to pay interest and repay the principal. So, when the company expects good and stable income, then only it should issue debentures.

(b) The company, which issues debentures, creates a charge on its assets in favour of debentureholders. So a company not having enough fixed assets cannot borrow money by issuing debentures.

(c) The assets of the company once mortgaged cannot be used for further borrowing. So, issue of debentures reduces the borrowing capacity of the company.

Trading on Equity

Trading on Equity refers to the use of high debt for ensuring higher returns for the equity shareholders. This is workable when the profitability is high and the rate of return on investment of funds is higher than the rate of interest to be paid on the borrowed money. Let us take an example. Suppose Rs. 5 crores is required to be invested on a project that may give 20% return per annum. If the management decides to raise Rs. 2.50 crores by issuing equity shares of Rs. 10 each and Rs. 2.5 crores by issuing 10% debentures, then the shareholders will get a return of 30% on their funds. Let us the see the calculation.

Total earnings   Rs.1,00,00,000
Interest on debenture @10%   Rs. 25,00,000

Earning after paying interest   Rs. 75,00,000
Return on Equity Share Capital

$$= \frac{75,00,000}{2,50,00,000} \times 100 = 30\%$$

Now if the company decides to raise 80% by debt and only 20% by shares (Rs. 4 crores by 10% debentures and Rs. 1 crore by shares), the return on equity share capital will be calculated as follows:

Total earnings   Rs. 1,00,00,000
Interest on debenture @10%   Rs. 40,00,000

Earning after paying interest   Rs. 60,00,000

Return on Equity Share Capital

$$= \times 100 = 60\%$$

We can see that with the use of higher proportion of debt the rate of return on equity capital has simply doubled. At the same time, it is also associated with high risk that, if the profitability declines to less than 10%, we shall still have to pay 10% on debentures. This will reduce the return on equity share capital to less than even 10%.

Types of Debentures

Debentures may be classified as:

(i) **Redeemable and Irredeemable Debentures:** The debentures which are repayable on a specified date, are called redeemable debentures. On the other hand, there is no fixed time by which the company is bound to pay back the money in case of irredeemable debentures. These debentureholders cannot demand to get back their money as long as the company does not make any default in payment of interest. So these debentures are also called perpetual debentures.

(ii) **Convertible and Non-convertible Debentures:** The holders of convertible debentures are given the option to convert their debentures into equity shares. But incase of non-convertible debentures the company does not give any such option.

(iii) **Secured and Unsecured Debentures:** Secured debentures are issued with a charge on the assets of the company as security. This charge may be fixed i.e., on specified asset, or it may be floating. Secured debentures are also known as mortgaged debentures. On the other hand, unsecured debentures are issued with merely a promise of payment without having any charge on any assets as security. So these debentures are also known as naked or simple debentures. Now-a-days debentures are invariably issued as secured debentured.

(iv) **Registered and Bearer Debentures:** For registered debentures the issuing company maintains a record of the debentureholders. Any sale or transfer of such debentures must be registered with the company. On the other hand, bearer debentures are just like negotiable instruments and transferable by mere delivery. The company keeps no record of such debenture-holders. Interest coupons are attached to them and anybody can produce the coupon to get the interest.

After having some idea about shares and debentures let us find out the difference between them.

Difference between Shares and Debenture

S.No.	Basis	Shares	Debentures
1.	Status	Shareholders are the owners of the company. They provide ownership capital which is not refundable unless the company is liquidated.	Debentureholders are the creditors of the company. They provide loans generally for a fixed period, which are to be paid back.
2.	Nature of return on investment	Shareholders get dividends. Its amount is not fixed as it depends on the profit of the company.	Interest is paid on debentures at a fixed rate. Interest is payable even if the company is running at a loss.
3.	Rights	Shareholders are the real owners of the company. They have the right to vote and determine the policies of the company.	Debentureholders do not have the right to attend meetings of the company. So they have no say in the management of the company.
4.	Security	No security is required to issue shares.	Generally debentures are secured. So, sufficient fixed assets are required when debentures are to be issued.
5.	Order of repayment	Share capital is paid back only after paying the debentureholders and creditors.	Debentureholders have the priority of repayment over shareholders.
6.	Risk	Risk is high due to uncertainty of returns.	Little risk due to certainty of return.

SECURITIES AND EXCHANGE BOARD OF INDIA (SEBI)

SEBI (Securities and Exchange Board of India) was initially constituted on 12 April, 1988 as a non-statutory body through a resolution of the Government for dealing with all matters relating to development and regulation of securities market and investor protection and to advise the Government on all these matters. SEBI was given statutory status and powers through an ordinance promulgated on January 30, 1992.

The statutory powers and functions of SEBI were strengthened through the promulgation of the Securities Laws (Amendment) ordinance on January 25, 1995 which was subsequently replaced by an Act of Parliament. In terms of this Act, SEBI has been vested with regulatory powers over corporates in the issuance of capital, the transfer of securities and other related matters. Besides, SEBI has been empowered to impose monetary penalties on capital market intermediaries and other participants for a range of violations.

SEBI is managed by six members—one chairman (nominated by Central Government), two members (officers of central ministries), one member (from RBI) and remaining two members are nominated by Central Government. The office of SEBI is situated at Mumbai with its regional offices at Kolkata, Delhi and Chennai. In 1988 the initial capital of SEBI was Rs. 7.5 crore which was provided by its promoters (IDBI, ICICI, IFCI). This amount was invested and with its interest amount day-to-day expenses of SEBI are met.

All statutory powers for regulating indian capital market are vested with SEBI itself.

Functions of SEBI

1. To safeguard the interests of investors and to regulate capital market with suitable measures.
2. To regulate the business of stock exchanges and other securities market.
3. To regulate the working of Stock Brokers. Sub-brokers, Share Transfer Agents, Trustees, Merchant Bankers, Underwriters, Portfolio Managers etc. and also to make their registration.
4. To register and regulate collective investment plans of mutual funds.
5. To encourage self-regulatory organisations.
6. To eliminate malpractices of security markets.
7. To train the persons associated with security markets and also to encourage investors' education.
8. To check insider trading of securities.
9. To supervise the working of various organisations trading in security market and also to ensure systematic dealings.
10. To promote research and investigations for ensuring the attainment of above objectives.

Recognised Exchanges (Stock & Commodity)

1. Ace Derivatives and Commodity Exchange Limited, Mumbai
2. Ahmedabad Stock Exchange Ltd.
3. Bombay Stock Exchange Ltd.
4. Bombay Commodity Exchange Ltd., Vashi
5. Calcutta Stock Exchange Ltd.
6. Chamber of Commerce, Hapur
7. Cotton Association of India, Mumbai
8. Delhi Stock Exchange Ltd.
9. India Pepper & Spice Trade Association, Kochi
10. Indian Commodity Exchange Limited, New Delhi
11. Magadh Stock Exchange Ltd.
12. Metropolitan Stock Exchange of India Ltd.
13. Multi Commodity Exchange of India Ltd., Mumbai
14. National Commodity & Derivatives Exchange Ltd., Mumbai
15. National Multi Commodity Exchange of India Limited., Ahmedabad
16. National Stock Exchange of India Ltd.
17. Rajkot Commodity Exchange Ltd., Rajkot
18. Spices and Oilseeds Exchange Ltd., Sangli
19. Universal Commodity Exchange Ltd., Navi Mumbai

CONCEPT OF DEPOSITORY SYSTEM

Depository system is that system in which ownership of security is changed by an electronic account entry and physical transaction of secutiries does not take place. The main functions of depository are as follows:

1. To accept deposits for ensuring safe custody of securities.

2. To make computerised account entry for ensuring evidence of ownership transfer.

3. To keep record of mortgaged securities.

Different countries possess generally two types of depository:

    (a) Securities immobilisation system of depositories.

    (b) Securities dematerialisation system of depository.

Depository System in India

Depository system, based on non-physical transfer of share certificates, was inторduced in the country on the recommendations of a technical committee. On September 21, 1995 the President of India gave his acceptance to Depository Ordinance 1995. This ordinance was passed in Lok Sabha but it could not obtain the acceptance of Rajya Sabha. Again on January 7, 1996, Ordinance was released for second time which cleared all obstacles of establishing depository in India. The objective of the depository services is to improve and modernise the market and to enhance the level of investor protection through eliminating bad deliveries, forgery of shares and expediting the transfer of shares. This is being done through electronic book entry form and scripless trading in stock exchanges thereby reducing settlement risk. The salient features of the system are as follows:

1. Legal provisions have been made for entry of account details relating to security ownership.

2. Investor can either continue with the existing share certificate system or opt for depository mode. The investors opting for depository system will have to get their registration with any participant in depository. These participants will be registered with SEBI. Generally commercial banks, financial institutions, custodians of securities and share brokers will work as participants in depository.

3. Every depository will be registered with SEBI and will work only after securing certificate to this effect from SEBI.

4. All payments, transactions and transfer under depository system will be free from stamp duty. Similarly, no stamp duty is payable at the time of joining or leaving depository system.

5. Companies issuing new shares will provide options to investors for obtaining securities or adopting depository system.

6. Under depository system, change of ownership will become as electronic book entry transfer.

CREDIT RATING AGENCIES

Credit Rating Agencies evaluate the debentures, fixed-deposits and other Short term credit documents of various companies after studying their financial status, industrial risks and market conditions. These agencies work on the request of companies.

At present four Credit Ration Agencies are working in the country—Credit Rating Information Services of India Limited (CRISIL), Investment Information and Credit Rating Agency of India Ltd. (ICRA), Credit Analysis and Research Ltd. (CARE) and Duff Falps Credit Rating India Private Ltd. (DCR India). CRISIL is the first Credit Rating Agency of the country which started its functioning since January 1988.

All the above mentoined credit rating agencies quote the credit rating only for a particular period of time. It may change according to the circumstances. This credit rating is meant only for debentures and not for equity issues. The different types of credit rating allotted by different credit rating agencies in India are shown in the following table:

S.No.	Investment Grades	Credit Rating		
		CRISIL	ICRA	CARE
	Long Term Debentures			
1.	Highest Safety	AAA	LAAA	CARE AAA
2.	High Safety	AA	LAA	CARE AA
3.	Adequate Safety	A	LA	CARE A
4.	Inadequate Safety	BB	LBB	CARE BB
5.	High Risk	B	LB	CARE B
	Mid Term Debentures			
1.	Highest Safety	FAAA	MAAA	CARE AAA
2.	High Safety	FAA	MAA	CARE AA
3.	Adequate Safety	FA	MA	CARE A
4.	Inadequate Safety	FB	MB	CARE BB
5.	High Risk	FC	MC	CARE C
	Short Term Debentures			
1.	Highest Safety	P_1	A_1	PR_1
2.	High Safety	P_2	A_2	PR_2
3.	Adequate Safety	P_3	A_3	PR_3
4.	Inadequate Safety	P_4	A_4	PR_4
5.	High Risk	—	—	—

MOODY'S RATING

Aaa— Shows that the bonds possess least investment risk.

Aa— Shows high grade bonds

A— Shows high mid-grade bonds with favourable investment factors.

Baa— Shows mid-grade bonds neither low grade nor high grade safety.

Ba— Shows bonds covered with speculative factors.

Main Share Price Index in Famous Share Market of the World

BSE (Mumbai)	SENSEX
NSE (Mumbai)	S & P CNX Nifty
NewYork	DOW JONES
Tokyo	NIKKEI
Frankfurt (Germany)	MID DAX
Hong Kong	HANG SENG
Singapore	SIMEX STRAITS TIMES

Note: The Bombay Stock Exchange (BSE) and Taqwaa Advisory and Shariah Investment Solutions have launched the BSE TASIS SHARIAH 50 Index since Dec. 27, 2010.

★★★★★★

E-banking refers to electronic banking. It is like e-business in banking industry. E-banking is also called as "Virtual Banking" or "Online Banking". E-banking is a result of the growing expectations of bank's customers.

E-banking involves information technology based banking. Under this I.T system, the banking services are delivered by way of a Computer-Controlled System. This system does involve direct interface with the customers. The customers do not have to visit the bank's premises.

POPULAR SERVICES COVERED UNDER E-BANKING

The popular services covered under E-banking include:

1. Automated Teller Machines,
2. Credit Cards,
3. Debit Cards,
4. Smart Cards,
5. Electronic Funds Transfer (EFT) System,
6. Cheques Truncation Payment System,
7. Mobile Banking,
8. Internet Banking,
9. Telephone Banking, etc.

ADVANTAGES OF E-BANKING

The main advantages of E-banking are:

1. The operating cost per unit services is lower for the banks.
2. It offers convenience to customers as they are not required to go to the bank's premises.
3. There is very low incidence of errors.
4. The customer can obtain funds at any time from ATM machines.
5. The credit cards and debit cards enables the Customers to obtain discounts from retail outlets.

The customer can easily transfer the funds from one place to another place electronically.

AUTOMATED TELLER MACHINE (ATM)

Banks have now installed their own Automated Teller Machine (ATM) throughout the country at convenient locations. By using this, customers can deposit or withdraw money from their own account any time.

DEBIT CARD

Banks are now providing Debit Cards to their customers having saving or current account in the banks. The customers can use this card for purchasing goods and services at different places in lieu of cash. The amount paid through debit card is automatically debited (deducted) from the customers' account.

CREDIT CARD

Credit cards are issued by the bank to persons who may or may not have an account in the bank. Just like debit cards, credit cards are used to make payments for purchase, so that the individual does not have to carry cash. Banks allow certain credit period to the credit cardholder to make payment of the credit amount. Interest is charged if a cardholder is not able to pay back the credit extended to him within a stipulated period. This interest rate is generally quite high.

PHONE BANKING

In case of phone banking, a customer of the bank having an account can get information of his account, make banking transactions like, fixed deposits, money transfers, demand draft, collection and payment of bills, etc. by using telephone. As more and more people are now using mobile phones, phone banking is possible through mobile phones. In mobile phone a customer can receive and send messages (SMS) from and to the bank in addition to all the functions possible through phone banking.

SMART CARD

A smart card usually contains an embedded 8-bit microprocessor (a kind of computer chip). The microprocessor is under a contact pad on one side of the card. Think of the microprocessor as replacing the usual magnetic stripe present on a credit card or debit card.

The microprocessor on the smart card is there for security. The host computer and card reader actually "talk" to the microprocessor. The microprocessor enforces access to the data on the card.

The chips in these cards are capable of many kinds of transactions. For example, a person could make purchases from their credit account, debit account or from a stored account value that's reload able. The enhanced memory and processing capacity of the smart card is many times that of traditional magnetic-stripe cards and can accommodate several different applications on a single card.

E-CHEQUE

- An E-cheque is the electronic version or representation of paper cheque.
- The Information and Legal Framework on the E-cheque is the same as that of the paper cheque's.
- It can now be used in place of paper cheques to do any and all remote transactions.
- An E-cheque work the same way a cheque does, the cheque writer "writes" the E-cheque using one of many types of electronic devices and "gives" the E-cheque to the payee electronically. The payee "deposits" the Electronic Cheque receives credit, and the payee's bank "clears" the E-cheque to the paying bank. The paying bank validates the E-cheque and then "charges" the check writer's account for the check.

PLASTIC MONEY

At the end of 20th century another form of money emerged which is called plastic money. The emergence of this money started from the introduction of credit cards. At the beginning economist classified credit card also as credit money but introduction of Debit Card and ATM cards compelled economist to admit that another form of currency has evolved that is "Plastic Money" Examples-Credit Cards, Debit Cards, ATM cards and Smart Cards.

A PIN (Personal Identification Number) code is used to perform transactions with plastic money.

INTERNET BANKING

Transaction at the convenience of customers, saving times and cost through computers is popularly known as Online Banking. It is also known as Net Banking or Internet Banking. It is done through a computer with internet facilities. Customers can monitor and control their funds through Internet Banking. They can check account

balance view their account, get summary statement, make bill payments and utility payments, request for cheque book, drafts, Bankers chequs, stop cheque payment, trans for funds, request for third party transfers, invest and renew deposits, issue standing instructions, register mobile number for SMS alerts and many more attractive features user-Id and password are given by the banks to the customer for operation of account after they successfully register with the bank.

ELECTRONIC COMMERCE

The growth of Internet into a global market place attracts more business firms to use this media for commerce. Business firms may use the Internet initially for communication. Websites are set up to provide information about its products and services. Business firms offer corporate information, product information, marketing related services etc,.

The Internet has integrated the fragment markets words over though in a modest way. But this interaction is growing rapidly. The most important advantage of the internet for business firms is that it allows reaching customers at very low costs.

Electronic commerce is the process of searching, choosing, buying and selling of product or service on the electronic network; it uses the computer and communication networks for promoting products, selling, delivery, collection and delivery service.

Electronic Commerce includes:

(a) Buying and selling on the internet

(b) Making payments electronically

(c) Business transaction in which there is no physical exchange or physical contact.

(d) It is transacting a business over am electronic network without physical contact.

FEATURES OF E-COMMERCE

E-Commerce has the following general features:

(a) It is a business strategy to cut down costs, while improving quality and increasing the speed of delivery of goods/services.

(b) It has ability to sell and purchase products/ services/information on computer networks.

(c) It is a solution for office automation and quick business transactions.

(d) It is a tool to improve intra business functioning like business re-engineering.

(e) It is tools to improve inter business communication through easy and accurate interaction and information interchange.

IMPORTANCE OF E-COMMERCE

E-Commerce becomes inevitable because of the following:

(a) **Low setup cost:** Any body can easily set up a website. In fact there are many organizations and training institutes who help customers in developing and launching websites. To market a product large retail showrooms are not required, just a web site showing the characteristics of the product including cost details are sufficient.

(b) **Global Free Market:** Nobody can dominate the global market as presence on the internet is easy not only for global giants, but even small organisations can participate actively at low costs and compete with stiff competition.

(c) **Global Access:** Since more than 200 countries are hooked onto the Internet, anybody who can afford a TV and a telephone can fully access the Internet and gain the information required.

(d) **Availability of Technology:** Since the same technology like web servers, browsers, engines, internet, etc., is used throughout the world therefore business can be easily conducted.

(e) **Multiple Opportunities:** By using E-Commerce multiple activities like selling, renting, purchasing etc. can be performed. In fact a whole variety of transactions can be provided all under one roof.

☆☆☆☆☆☆

International Financial Organisations [IBRD (World Bank), IDA, IFC, IMF, ADB]

INTERNATIONAL BANK FOR RECONSTRUCTION AND DEVELOPMENT (IBRD)

IBRD and its associate institutions as a group are known as the World Bank. IBRD was established in December 1945 with the IMF on the basis of the recommendation of the Bretton Wood Conference. That is the reason why IMF and IBRD are called 'Bretton Wood Twins'.

India is a member of four constituents of the World Bank Group *i.e.* IBRD, IDA, IFC and MIGA (*i.e.* Multilateral Investment Guarantee Agency) but not of its fifth institute ICSID (*i.e.* International Centre for the settlement of Investment Disputes).

The headquarter of World Bank is at Washington D.C.

IDA (established on September 24, 1960) and IFC (established in July 1956) are the two main associate institutions of IBRD. These institutions work under the supervision of Word Bank. MIGA is also an associate institution in the World Bank group.

Objectives of World Bank

1. To provide long-run capital to member countries for economic reconstruction and development World Bank provides capital mainly for following purposes.

   (i) To rehabilitate war ruined economies (this objective is fully achieved).

   (ii) To finance productive efforts according to peacetime requirements.

   (iii) To develop resources and production facilities in underdeveloped countries.

2. To induce long-run capital investment for assuring BOP equilibrium and balanced development of international trade. (This objective was adopted to increase the productivity of member countries and to improve economic conditions and standard of living among them).

3. To promote capital investment in member countries by following ways:

   (i) To provide guarantee on private loans or capital investment.

   (ii) If private capital is not available even after providing guarantee, then IBRD provides loans for productive activities on considerate conditions.

4. To provide guarantee for loans granted to small and large units and other projects of member countries.

5. To ensure the implementation of development projects so as to bring about a smooth transference from a war-time to peace economy.

IMF vs. WORLD BANK

IMF and the World Bank are Bretton Woods Twins. Both the institutions were established to promote international economic co-operation but a basic difference is found in the nature of economic assistance given by these two institutions. World Bank provides long-term loans for promoting balanced economic development, while IMF provides short-term loans to member countries for eliminating BOP disequilibrium.

Functions of the World Bank

1. Bank can grant loans to a member country upto 20% of its share in the paid up capital.

2. Bank also provides loan to private investors belonging to member countries on its own guarantee, but for this loan private investors have to seek prior permission from those countries where this amount will be collected. For such loans the consent of that country is also required whose currency is given is loans. For granting such guarantee, the Bank charges 1% to 2% as service charge.

3. The quantum of loans, interest rate and terms and conditions are determined by the Bank itself.

4. Generally, Bank grants loan for a patricular project duly submitted to the Bank by the member country.

5. The debtor nation has to repay either in reserve currencies or in the currency in which the loan was sanctioned.

Besides, granting loans for reconstruction and development, World Bank also provides various technical services to the member countries. For this purpose, the Bank has established. 'The Economic Development Institute' and a Staff College in Washington.

INTERNATIONAL DEVELOPMENT ASSOCIATION (IDA)

IDA is an associate institution of World Bank known as **soft loan window** of World Bank. IDA was established on September 24, 1960. IDA provides loan to its member countries and no interest is charged on these long-term loans. These soft loans are provided to the poor countries of the World.

INTERNATIONAL FINANCE CORPORATION (IFC)

World Bank established IFC in July 1956. This corporation provides loan to private industries of developing nations without any government guarantee and also promotes the additional capital investment in these countries. Thus, the main work of IFC is to ensure the financial support to private sector in developing countries.

Objectives

1. To provide loans to private sector.
2. To co-ordinate capital and management.
3. To induce capitalist countries to invest in developing countries.

INTERNATIONAL MONETARY FUND (IMF)

IMF is an international monetary organisation. It was established on December 27, 1945 in Washington on the recommendations of Bretton Woods Conference.

Objectives of IMF

1. To promote international monetary co-operation.
2. To ensure balanced internationl trade.
3. To ensure exchange rate stability.
4. To eliminate or to minimize exchange restrictions by promoting the system of multilateral payments.
5. To grant economic assistance to member countries for eliminating the adverse imbalance in balance of payments.
6. To minimize imbalances in quantum and duration of international trade.

The main source of IMF resources is the quotas allotted to member countries. Till 1971, all the amounts of quotas and the assistance provided were denominated in US dollar, but since December 1971 all the quotas and transactions of IMF are expressed in SDR (Special Drawing Right) which is also known as Paper Gold. In 1971, on SDR was assumed equivalent to 1 dollar but due to subsequent decline in dollar value SDR 1 became equivalent to $ 1.585 by the end of April 1995. Since January 1, 1981 the value of SDR is being determined by the basket of currencies of 5 largest exporting member countries : US Dollar, Deut-sche Mark, Yen, Franc and Pound Sterling.

The IMF's financial year is from 1 May to 30 April. IMF lends to various member countries in the form of various facilities (Extended Fund Facility, Standby Facility, Contingent Credit Lines, Compensatory Facility etc.) designed to serve specific purpose, but essentially aimed at balance of payments stablisation or meeting the emergent foreign exchange needs.

ASIAN DEVELOPMENT BANK (ADB)

ADB was established in Dec. 1966 on the recommendations of ECAFE (Economic Commission for Asia and Far East). The aim of this Bank is to accelerate economic and social development in Asia and Pacific regions. The Bank started its functioning on January 1, 1967. The head office of the Bank is located at Manila, Philippines.

International Organisations: A View

Organisation	Establishment Year	Headquarter	Imporant Features
1. **IMF and IBRD**	1945	Washington D.C.	IBRD, IFC, IDA, MIGA are associate institutions of World Bank. Initially IBRD was constituted in 1945. IFC and IDA were established in 1956 and 1960 respectively
2. **ADB**	1966	Manila	The aim of this Bank is to accelerate economic and social development in Asia and Pacific region.

Some New Guidelines of RBI

- RBI has decided to bring down the validity of cheque, draft, pay orders and banker's cheques to 3 months instead of current period of 6 months. This rule has become effective since April 1, 2012. As per the notification of RBI, with effect from April 1, 2012 bank now will not make payment of cheques bearing that date or any subsequent date, if they are presented beyond the period of three months from the date of such instrument.

  RBI noticed that these instruments were literally being used as cash and being rotated in the fact that this decision was made in the public interest and in the interest of banking policy, RBI has asked banks to inform holders of such instruments of the validity by printing suitable instructions on the instruments issued on or after April 1, 2012.

  The RBI has also directed banks to ensure that account payee cheques and drafts are credited only to accounts of the person named in the instrument.

- RBI has provided relief to a number of scheduled commerical banks by allowing them to include technical write offs while increasing the provision coverage ratio (PCR) to 70 per cent.

  In its second quarter review of the monetary policy, RBI had asked banks to increase the coverage ratio. In the guidelines issued now, RBI has allowed banks to include floating provisions that were not included in Tier-II Capital, in addition to provisions for NPAs while calculating the PCR.

★★★★★★

Important Acts and Committees Related to Banks

CHAPTER 12

❑ **Banking Regulation Act, 1949**

It is an Act that consolidates the law relating to banking and provide for the nature of transaction carried on by banks in India. It contains the provisions of power of RBI to control advances by banking companies, accounts and audit of banks, restrictions as to minimum paid up capital and reserves, restrictions as to payment of dividends, validation of license granted by RBI to multi state co-operative societies. It also contains provisions of suspension of business and winding up of banking business.

❑ **Banking Companies (acquisition and transfer of undertakings) Act, 1970**

This Act provide provisions for the acquisition and transfer of the undertakings of certain banking companies, having regard to their size, resources, coverage and organization, in order to control the heights of the economy and to meet progressively, and serve better, the needs of development of the economy in conformity with national policy and objectives and for matter connected therewith or incidental thereto.

❑ **Banking Companies (acquisition and transfer of undertakings) Act, 1980**

This Act provides provisions for the acquisition and transfer of the undertakings of certain banking companies, having regard to their size, resources, coverage and organisation, in order further to control the heights of the economy, to meet progressively, and serve better, the needs of the development of the economy and to promote the welfare of the people, in the conformity with the policy of the State towards securing the principles laid down in clauses (b) and (c) of article 39 of the Constitution and for matters connected therewith or incidental thereto.

❑ **State Bank of India Act, 1955**

It is an Act that constituted State Bank for India and transferred to it the undertaking of the Imperial Bank of India and to provide for other matters connected therewith or incidental thereto. Its purpose is to extend the banking facilities on a large scale, more particularly in the rural and semi-urban areas, and for diverse other public purposes.

❑ **State Bank of India (subsidiary banks) Act, 1959**

It is an Act that provides for the formation of certain Government or Government-associated bank as subsidiaries of the State Bank of India and for the constitution, management and control of the subsidiary banks so formed, and for matters connected therewith, or incidental thereto.

❏ **Regional Rural Banks Act, 1976**

It is an Act that provide for the incorporation, regulation and winding up of Regional Rural Banks with a view to developing the rural economy by providing, for the purpose of development of agriculture, trade, commerce, industry and other productive activities in the rural areas, credit and other facilities, particularly to the small and marginal farmers, agricultural labourers, artisans and small entrepreneurs, and for matters connected therewith and incidental thereto.

❏ **Companies Act, 1956**

As per section 2 of Banking Regulation Act, 1949 the provisions of Banking Regulation Act, 1949 shall be in addition to, and not, save as hereinafter expressly provided, in derogation of the Companies Act, 1956 (1 of 1956), and any other law for the time being in force. The Banking Regulation Act is to be read as supplemental to the Companies Act. Hence the provisions relating to appointment, qualification, disqualification under companies act for company auditor applies to bank auditors also.

❏ **Information Technology Act, 2000**

This act provide legal recognition for transactions carried out by means of electronic date interchange and other means of electronic communication, commonly referred to as "electronic commerce", which involve the use of alternative to paper-based methods of communication and storage of information to facilitate electronic filing of documents with the Government agencies and further to amend the Indian Penal Code, the India Evidence Act, 1872, the Banker's Books Evidence Act, 1891 and the Reserve Bank of India Act, 1934 and for matters connected therewith or incidental thereto.

❏ **Prevention of Money Laundering Act, 2002**

As per the provisions of the Act, every banking company, financial institution (which includes chit fund company, a co-operative bank, a housing finance institution and a non-banking financial company) and intermediary (which includes a stock-broker, sub-broker, share transfer agent, banker to an issue, trustee to a trust deed, registrar to an issue, merchant banker, underwriter, portfolio manager, investment adviser and any other intermediary associated with securities market and registered under section 12 of the Securities and Exchange Board of India Act, 1992) shall have to maintain a record of all the transactions; the nature and value of which has been prescribed in the Rules under the PMLA. Such transactions include:

(i) All cash transactions of the value of more than Rs. 10 lakhs or its equivalent in foreign currency.

(ii) All series of cash transactions integrally connected to each other which have been valued below Rs. 10 lakhs or its equivalent in foreign currency where such series of transactions take place within one calendar month.

(iii) All suspicious transactions whether or not made in cash and including, inter-alia, credits or debits into from any non monetary account such as Demat account, security account maintained by the registered intermediary.

❏ **Credit Information (companies regulation act), 2005**

This Act provides provisions for regulation of credit information companies and to facilitate efficient distribution of credit and for matters connected therewith or incidental thereto.

❏ **Securitisation and Reconstruction of Financial Assets and Enforcement of Security Interest act, 2002**

It is an Act to regulate securitisation and reconstruction of financial assets and enforcement of security interest and for matters connected therewith or incidental thereto.

❏ **Banking Cash Transaction Tax (chapter vii of finance act, 2005)**

The Finance Act, 2005 introduced a new levy, namely, the Banking Cash Transaction Tax (BCTT) on certain banking transactions. The provisions relating to levy of this tax are contained in Chapter VII (sections 93 to 112) of the Act. This Act came into force from 1st June 2005. The tax base for the purposes of BCTT is the value of taxable banking transaction. A taxable banking transaction has been defined in clause (8) of section 94 of the Finance Act, 2005. Broadly, there are two categories of transactions:

(i) Cash withdrawal - A cash withdrawal would fall within the scope of a taxable banking transaction if it satisfies the following conditions:

(a) The cash withdrawal (by whatever mode) is from an account other than a savings bank account.

(b) The account is maintained with any scheduled bank.

(c) The amount of cash withdrawn on a single day from the same account should exceed Rs.25,000 in the case of an individual or a HUF or Rs.1,00,000 in the case of any other person.

(ii) Receipt of cash on encashment of term deposits.

Similarly, a receipt of cash on encashment of term deposits would fall within the scope of a taxable banking transaction if it satisfies the following conditions:

(a) The cash is received on encashment of a term deposit or deposits.

(b) The term deposit or deposits are in any scheduled bank.

(c) The amount of cash received in a single day exceeds Rs. 25,000 in the case of a deposit or deposits in the name of an individual or a HUF or Rs.1,00,000 in case of any other person.

No BCCT shall be payable if amount of term deposit or deposits is credited to any account with the bank.

BCCT is charged at the rate of 0.1 percent of every taxable banking transaction.

❑ **Service Tax (chapter v of finance act, 1994)**

Chapter V of the Finance Act, 1994, introduced Service Tax in India in 1994. The Central Board of Excise & Customs (CBEC), Department of Revenue, Ministry of Finance, deals with the task of formulation of policy concerning levy and collection of Service Tax. Some of the services related to banking covered in the service tax net are credit card services, merchant baking services, financial leasing services, security and foreign exchange services, advisory services, financial service, ATM operation, maintenance or management related services

❑ **Income Tax Act, 1961**

The income of a Bank is chargeable to income tax under section 28, Profits and Gains of Business and Profession. Apart from normal deductions under section Chapter IV D. Certain Specific Sections deal with the income chargeable to tax of a banking company. Section 43D provides that interest income of bad and doubtful debts, i.e. NPAs shall be chargeable to tax in the year in which they are credited to the profit and loss account or the year in which they are received. Hence the banks are allowed to follow a Hybrid System of Accounting, which is banned in case of other assessees by virtue of section 145 of the Income tax act. The provision made on NPAs is also allowed as a deduction as against the normal rule under section 36(1)(viia) to the extent of 7.5% of Income (computed before any deduction under this clause and Chapter VI-A) under the act or 5% (10% in case of rural branch) of the NPAs as per books of account of the bank on the last day of previous year.

❑ **Securities Transaction Tax (chapter vii of finance (no 2) act, 2004)**

This is applicable from 1st October 2004 .The STT is applicable at different rates on the value of the "taxable securities transaction," which means a transaction of purchase and sale of securities entered into in a recognised stock exchange in India and is payable by the buyer and the seller of the securities.

The value of taxable securities transaction,

(i) in the case of taxable securities transactions relating to " option in securities", shall be the aggregate of the strike price and the option premium of such "options in securities";

(ii) in the case of taxable securities transaction relating to "futures", shall be the price at which such "futures" is traded; and

(iii) in the case of any other taxable securities transaction, shall be the price at which such securities are purchased.

IMPORTANT COMMITTEES

Narasimham Committee on Financial Reforms

The Government of India constituted a 9-member committee under the chairmanship of Mr. M. Narasimham, Retired RBI Governor, on Aug. 14, 1991 for making recommendations on existing financial system and to give suggestions for improving the existing structure. The committee submitted its report to the Finance Minister in November 1991 which was placed on the table of Parliament on December 17, 1991.

The salient recommendations are:

1. 4-tier banking system should be introduced in the country.

   I tier 3 or 4 International Banks

   II tier 8 or 10 National Banks

   III tier Regional Banks

   IV tier Rural Banks

2. Branch licensing system for opening new bank branches should be abolished.

3. A liberal view should be adopted for allowing foreign banks in the country. Both foreign and domestic banks should be treated at par.

4. SLR for banks should be curtailed to the level of 25% within next 5 years. CRR should also be curtailed in various phases.

5. Banks should be given more autonomy and the directed credit should be abolished.

6. Primary targets for credit should be redefined and such credit should not be more than 10% of total credit.

7. Computerisation in banks should be promoted.

8. Banks should be authorised to appoint banking official at their own discretion.

9. The dual control of RBI and Finance Ministry on banks should be abolished and RBI should function only as a regulatory authority of banking system in the economy.

10. RBI's representative should not be included in the management boards of banks. Only Government representative should be there.

11. Granting resources to development finance institutions on concessional rates of interest should be abolished in phases within next 3 years. These institutions should be allowed to mobilise resources from open market on competitive rates.

12. Quick and effective liberal attitude should be adopted in the policy related to capital market. System of getting prior permission by the companies for their new share issue should also be abolished.

Goiporia Committee on Consumer Service Improvements in Banks

RBI constituted a committee under the chairmanship of Sri M.N. Goiporia, the then President of SBI, in September 1990 on making recommendations for consumer service improvements in banks. The committee submitted its report on December 5, 1991. The main recommendations of the committee were as given below:

1. Extension of banking hours for all works excluding cash payment.

2. Re-adjustment of bank opening time for staff so as to ensure start of work at bank counters well in time.

3. Spot deposit of outstation cheques of Rs. 5000/- (instead of existing 2500/-) in bank accounts.

4. Increase in bank interest rates on saving accounts.

5. Providing tax benefit on bank deposit amounts.

6. To ensure optimum use of powers available with bank staff.

Jankiraman Committee

RBI set up a high level enquiry committee on April 30, 1992 under the Chairmanship of Mr. R.

Jankiraman. The committee submitted the fifth and final report on May 7, 1993. The committee identified several types of irregularities in securities transactions which were used to siphon off funds out of the banking system:

1. Purchases of securities and other instruments were made by banks and their subsidiaries where the counter party was ostensibly another bank but when in reality the proceeds were directly or indirectly credited to the accounts of brokers.

2. Ready forward (Sale and purchase) transactions were entered into either on their own or on client's accounts by banks with brokers who used these funds for speculative activity.

3. Brokers in the stock exchanges were directly financed by banks by discounting bills not supported by genuine transactions.

4. Banks and other institutions showed large payments as call money to other banks. However, in the books of the receiving banks, there was no record of call money acceptances. Instead, the amounts were credited to the accounts of individual brokers. On the due date, these alleged call loans were repaid by payment out of the broker's accounts in the name of other banks.

5. Banks and other institutions rediscounted bills of exchange held by other banks and institutions but the proceeds and repayments were routed through broker's accounts.

6. Sums received as inter-corporate deposits and under portfolio management sechemes (PMS) by merchant banking subsidiaries of public sector and other banks were passed on to brokers through ready forward deals.

Chandrashekhar Committee's on Transfer of Shares

SEBI constituted a committee under chairmanship of Mr. Chandrashekhar for improving the process of share ekhar transfers. The committee submitted its report in April, 1997. The committee put recommendations to regulate dealings of secondary market. Different recommendations have been made for different groups like Deptt. of Company Affairs, SEBI, Opener of New Issues, Registrar and Transfer Agents, Stock Exchanges and Share Brokers.

Malhotra Committee for Improving Insurance Sector

The Government of India constituted a committee for recommending improvements in insurance sector under the Chairmanship of Dr. R.N. Malhotra, Ex-Governor of RBI, in April 1993. On January 7, 1994 the committee submitted its recommendations to the Finance Minister. Some of the important recommendations are as follows:

1. **Liberalisation of Insurance Industry:** The committee has recommended for liberalising insurance industry:

   (i) The private sector should also be permitted in Insurance sector, but the same company should not be permitted to perform both life insurance and general insurance business.

   (ii) The minimum paid-up capital for the new company should be Rs. 100 crore including a minimum subscription of 26% and maximum of 40% from promoters.

   (iii) No other equity holder, excluding the promoters of private insurance companies, should be granted equity share exceeding 1% of total equity.

   (iv) Co-operative societies at state level should be permitted to perform business with the minimum paid-up capital of Rs. 100 crore.

   (v) Foreign insurance companies should be permitted to operate in India on selective basis and they should be granted permission only if they perform business by establishing a joint enterprise with Indian promoters.

2. **Restructuring of Insurances Industry:** The committee also put recommendations for restructuring insurance industry:

   (i) All the four associate companies of GIC should be granted permission to perform their business independently and GIC should work only as reinsurance company.

(ii) The existing share capital of GIC should be increased from Rs. 107.5 crore to Rs. 200 crore, which should include 50% share of the Government and the rest shares should be opened for the general public (though a certain percentage of share should be reserved for the employees of the Corporation).

(iii) The exising paid-up capital for all associate companies of GIC (which is at present Rs. 40 crore for every company and fully financed by GIC) should be increased upto Rs. 100 crore. The capital of all these companies should include the Government share of 50% and the remaining share should be opened for the general public.

(iv) The committee also recommended to increase the paid-up capital of LIC from existing level of Rs. 5 crore to Rs. 200 crore (again 50% for the Government and rest for the public).

3. **Regulation of Insurance Business:** The committee has put following recommendations for regulating insurance business:

(i) All old and new insurance companies should be regulated under similar rules.

(ii) Controller of insurance should be given all the responsibilities under Insurance Act.

(iii) Insurance Regulatory Authority (IRA) should be established in insurance sector on the lines of SEBI and IRA should be granted complete functional autonomy.

(iv) IRA should have a permanent source for financing its activities and for this IRA should be permitted to charge a levy of 0.5% on annual incomes of insurance companies.

4. **Rural Insurance:**

(i) New insurance companies entering into insurance industry should perform a minimum pre-determined insurance in rural sector and they should attain this limit compulsorily.

(ii) Postal Life Insurance should be used to promote life insurance business in rural areas.

5. **Insurance Surveyors:**

(i) Licence system for insurance surveyors should be abolished and insurance companies should be granted permission to recruit the surveyors of their own.

(ii) At present, any claim of Rs. 20,000 or above comes under the enquiry of the surveyor. The Committee has recommended to extend this minimum limit to Rs. 1 lakh.

(iii) Insurance companies should be permitted to settle the claims upto Rs. 1 lakh on primary survey basis.

Major Recommendations of Rajan Committee on Finanacial Sector Reforms

❑ Allow auction of securities with shorter period of listing.

❑ Allow exchange traded interest rate, exchange rate derivatives.

❑ RBI should use repo, reverse repo to manage inflation in the short term.

❑ Should limit role in currency markets to managing volatility.

❑ Allow more foreign investors in bond markets; let Indian insurance companies, PFs to invest overseas.

❑ Sell small under performing public sector banks, rope in private strategic investors in larger ones.

❑ Set up holding companies, sell stake to other PSUs.

❑ Exchange traded currency deriva-tives in all currencies with rupee settlement may trade on NSE and BSE.

❑ Exchange traded interest rate derivatives using both cash settlement and physical settlement with trading on NSE and BSE.

❑ Improvements in the market design including 'true auctions' for primary market sale of securities, reduction in period between auction and start of trading.

❑ Domestic hedge funds with large minimum investment should be recognised and registered.

❑ Three-tier world of financial markets, comprising public and professional exchanges and OTC market. Phase out STT.

- SEBI needs to establish a speedier and new product approval process and introduce new methods of price discovery, clearing and settlement.

Important Latest Committees

1. **R.V. Gupta Committee:** Agriculture Credit
2. **Narsimham Committee (Second):** Banking Reforms
   (Constituted in December 1997, Submitted Report on April 21, 1998.
3. **Khan Working Group:** Development Finance Institutions
4. **Chandrate Committee:** Delisting in Share Market
   (Constituted by SEBI in Feb. 1997)
5. **UK Sharma Committee:** NABARD's role in RRB
   (Constituted in January 1998, Submitted Report on April 27, 1998)
6. **C.B. Bhave Committee:** Company Information
   (Constituted by SEBI, Submitted Report on October 27, 1998)
7. **S.L. Kapoor Committee:** Credit & Flow Problems of SSIs
   (Constituted by RBI in December 1997)
8. **S.N. Verma Committee (1999):** restructuring the Commercial Banks.
9. **J.J. Irani Committee:** Company Law Reforms.
10. **Parekh Committee:** Infractructure Financing.

Reforms in Insurance Sector

Insurance Sector constitutes on important segment of financial market in India and plays a predominant role in the formation of capital in the country. The reforms in the insurance sector started with the enactment of Insurance Regulatory and Development Authority Act, 1999. The Act paved the way for the entry of private insurance companies into the insurance market and also constitution of insurance Regulatory and Development Authority (IRDA).

Insurance Regulatory and Development Authority: The Insurance Regulatory and Development Authority (IRDA) was constituted on 19 April, 2000 to protect the interest of ther holders of insurance policies and to regulate, promote and ensure orderly growth of the insurance industry. The authority consists of a Chairperson, three whole-time Members and four part-time Members.

For regulating the insurance sector, the Authority has been issuing regulations covering almost the entire segment of insurance industry, namely, regulation on insurance agents, solvency margin, re-insurance, registration of insurers, obligation of insurers to rural and social sector, accounting procedure, etc.

Insurance (Amendment) Act, 2002: The Government, functioning of the opened up insurance sector, has enacted Insurance (Amendment) Act, 2002. The Act relates to introduction of brokers as intermediaries, allowing more flexibility in the eligibility qualifications for corporate agents, allowing more flexible mode of payment of premium through credit cards, smart cards, over internet, etc., change in the allocation of surplus between shareholders and policy holders, direct entry of co-operatives in the insurance sector and some other consequential amendments which are of a technical nature for the smooth functions of the opened up sector.

General Insurance Business (Nationalisation) Amendment Act, 2002: With the enactment of IRDA Act, 1999 it was necessary to nominate Indian Re-insurer under Insurance Act, 1938. The Government decided that General Insurance Corporation (GIC) which was a holding company of four public sector insurance companies, should be declared as Indian Re-insurer. Since under the Act, a Reinsurer cannot underwrite general insurance business, it has been decided to retransfer the holding of GIC to the Government. To achieve these objectives, the Government has enacted General Insurance Business (Nationalisation) Amendment Act, 2002.

★★★★★★

Multiple Choice Questions

1. "BCSBI" stands for:
   A. Banking Codes and Standards Boards of India
   B. Board Code for Standards in Branches
   C. Board Code for Standards in Banking
   D. None of the above

2. A draft issued by the bank has been lost by the payee. He sends a letter to the issuing bank to stop payment. Bank will:
   A. note caution and will advise the payee to contact purchaser of the draft
   B. not act on the request
   C. stop payment
   D. None of the above

3. Across the face of a cheque bears the words 'Peoples Bank'. What is its significance:
   A. it is an extraneous matter appearing on the cheque. Hence should be returned
   B. the cheque is specially crossed in favour of Peoples Bank
   C. it is not a crossing as it does not contain two parallel lines
   D. None of the above

4. As per KYC Policy, the list of terrorist organizations is supplied to the Banks by the:
   A. Government of India   B. CIBIL   C. IBA   D. RBI

5. As per RBI directives which of the following areas/functions cannot be outsourced by the Banks:
   A. opening and closing of accounts   B. cash collection from the parties
   C. recovery of bad loans   D. credit and debit cards

6. As per RBI guidelines, when a counterfeit note is detected at the branch, it should be:
   A. Branded with a stamp "COUNTERFEIT BANKNOTE"
   B. Recorded in a separate register under authentication
   C. acknowledged in the prescribed format of RBI and issued to the tenderer
   D. All of the above

7. Asset Reconstruction Company is associated with:
   A. DICGC   B. ECGC   C. NPA   D. SEBI

8. Association of National Exchanges Members of India (ANMI) is a body consisting of:
   A. Bankers and SEBI   B. SEBI and IBA
   C. Brokers Operating in the National Exchanges   D. Bankers, SEBI, IBA and RBI

9. At what stage of opening of bank account is the checking of Politically Exposed Persons (PEP) carried out:
  A. at the first point of customer interaction
  B. at the Account Services Level
  C. at the Central Account Services Level
  D. one month after the account is opened

10. Authorized Dealers for foreign exchange transactions are appointed by:
  A. Reserve Bank of India
  B. Government of India
  C. Individual Banks
  D. FEDAI

11. Balance of Trade of a country is equivalent to:
  A. difference between the Inward and Outward remittances made in foreign exchange
  B. surplus generated shown in a Trading Account
  C. difference between exports and imports
  D. none of the above

12. Banker's right of set off can be exercised on receipt of:
  A. Income Tax Attachment Order
  B. Garnishee Order
  C. Both A and B
  D. None of the above

13. Banking services offered to units set up in Special Economic Zones (SEZs) have been exempted from paying ...... tax:
  A. Capital Gains Tax
  B. Income Tax
  C. Service Tax
  D. None of these

14. Banks generally prefer to extend finances to registered firms only, because:
  A. banks will have priority over creditors in case of liquidation of the firm
  B. the firm can sue the debtors in case of default on their part
  C. banks can sue the firm in case of default
  D. the creditors can sue the firm

15. Banks should not grant new loans for purpose of minor irrigation in:
  A. White Block
  B. Grey Block
  C. Dark Block
  D. All of these

16. Borrower's ability to meet the immediate liabilities is indicated by:
  A. Current Ratio
  B. Acid Test Ratio
  C. Debt Equity Ratio
  D. None of these

17. Branches receive Potential Linked Plan through:
  A. Block Level Banker's Committee
  B. State Level Banker's Committee
  C. District Consultative Committee
  D. Lead Bank Department

18. By "Deemed Exports" it means:
  A. supplies of goods and services to units within the country which can earn foreign currency to the country
  B. exports made by units situated in EPZ areas to out of country
  C. exports made by EOU out of the country
  D. anticipated value of exports

19. By devaluation we mean:
  A. A fall in the domestic value of a currency
  B. A fall in the external value of a currency caused by the market forces
  C. A fall in the external value of a currency caused by Government action
  D. None of the above

20. Capitalization of Reserves is carried out by issue of ...... to the existing shareholders:
    A. Additional shares   B. Bonus shares   C. Incentives   D. None of these

21. Certificate in respect of an SSI unit is given by:
    A. RBI   B. Chamber of Commerce
    C. District Industries Centre   D. None of these

22. Closed Economy is one in which:
    A. only export takes place   B. money supply is fully controlled
    C. deficit financing takes place   D. neither export nor import takes place

23. Commercial Papers are secured by:
    A. floating charge on stocks   B. unsecured loans
    C. fixed assets   D. book-debts

24. Concept of "Service Area Approach" was recommended by:
    A. R.V. Gupta   B. A.D. Gorawala
    C. Dr. P.D. Ojha Committee   D. Dr. Kalia

25. Credit Exposure does not include:
    A. Bridge Loans
    B. Working Capital Demand Loan
    C. Shares of the company underwritten by the bank
    D. Advances against the Bank's fixed deposits granted to a company

26. Currency Note containing political slogan is not a legal tender as per:
    A. Legal Tender (Inscribed Notes) Act, 1964
    B. Negotiable Instruments Act, 1881
    C. Reserve Bank of India Act
    D. None of the above

27. Demand draft for ₹ 20,000 and above:
    A. can be paid in cash
    B. should not be paid in cash
    C. mode of payment will depend on the status of the customer
    D. None of the above

28. Deposits under NRE/FCNB accounts are linked to:
    A. Base Rate   B. SIBOR   C. LIBOR   D. None of these

29. Electronic Fund Transfer scheme of RBI has been renamed as:
    A. Clearing   B. Core Banking Solutions
    C. Real Time Gross Settlement   D. National Electronic Fund Transfer

30. Escrow account is useful/helpful to:
    A. importers   B. exporters   C. both A and B   D. None of these

31. External Commercial Borrowings (ECBs) form part of:
    A. Current Account   B. Capital Account
    C. Either A or B   D. Balance of Payments

32. FEMA provides that a person becomes a resident if he stays in India for ...... or more in the previous year.
    A. 180 days   B. 181 days   C. 182 days   D. 183 days

33. Generally, the lead bank in a district is the bank which is:
   A. having government business
   B. having the largest deposits in the district
   C. identified to coordinate implementation of the District Credit Plan
   D. None of the above

34. Government policy to raise income by additional taxes and allocation of expenditure is called:
   A. Expenditure policy   B. Monetary policy   C. Income policy   D. Fiscal policy

35. Head Office of the Asian Development Bank located in:
   A. Jakarta   B. Manila   C. Nairobi   D. Tokyo

36. If a bank is unable to refund the short term deposits as funds are locked in long term loans, it involves:
   A. Interest Rate Risk   B. Operational Risk   C. Liquidity Risk   D. Market Risk

37. If a cheque presented through the Clearing House is returned unpaid for any reason, the banker has to enclose the cheque to a Returning Memo while returning the instrument to the customer. This provision has been prescribed under:
   A. Negotiable Instruments Act, 1881   B. Reserve Bank of India Act, 1934
   C. Banking Regulation Act, 1949   D. RBI Clearing House Rules

38. If a currency note is demonetized, it takes away the ...... of that currency:
   A. legal tender character   B. exchange rate   C. value   D. None of these

39. If credit facility applied for is rejected, the reasons therefor should be briefly mentioned in the:
   A. Loan Applications Received and Disposal Register
   B. Opinion Reports
   C. Loan Rejection Register
   D. None of the above

40. In case of Term Loans, the period of limitation is calculated as three years from:
   A. Date of documents   B. Date of sanction
   C. Date of default   D. Due date of each installment

41. In computer parlance, "FTP" means:
   A. File Transfer Protocol   B. File Transit Protocol
   C. File Translate Protocol   D. File Typing Protocol

42. In respect of "Door Step Banking", RBI has issued directives under the provisions of:
   A. Reserve Bank of India Act, 1934   B. Negotiable Instruments Act, 1881
   C. Banking Regulation Act, 1949   D. Shops and Establishments Act

43. ISO 14000 deals with quality standard for:
   A. Environmental Management   B. Technology Management
   C. Knowledge Management   D. Information Management

44. Legal heirs of a deceased customer approaches the bank with a copy of the Will left by the deceased and request for payment of the deposit standing in the name of the deceased depositor. Bank should
   A. obtain a probated Will and pay the amount to the legal heir
   B. obtain the Will and pay the amount to the legal heir
   C. both A and B
   D. None of the above

45. Loans against Shares/Debentures can be sanctioned against the security of:
 A. Preference Share and Covertible debentures
 B. fully paid Equity Shares and debentures in demat form
 C. all shares and debentures in physical form
 D. only Preference Share and partly paid debentures

46. Mutual Funds are required to be registered with:
 A. AMFI   B. SEBI   C. IBA   D. RBI

47. National Income of India is estimated by:
 A. Central Estimates Survey Committee   B. National Sample Survey Committee
 C. Central Statistical Organization   D. Finance Ministry

48. Net National Product is equivalent to:
 A. Gross Domestic Product minus Depreciation
 B. Gross National Product minus Indirect Taxes
 C. Net National Income minus Depreciation
 D. Gross National Product minus Depreciation

49. Nomination facility is available to:
 A. Individuals / Sole Proprietorship accounts / Private Limited Companies
 B. Individuals / Sole Proprietorship Accounts / Partnership Accounts
 C. Individuals / Sole Proprietorship Accounts
 D. All of the above

50. Off Shore Banking Unit is:
 A. a unit which is situated in Foreign country
 B. a unit which is situated in Special Economic Zones and deals in foreign currency only
 C. a unit which is actively participating in lending foreign currency loans and in joint ventures
 D. None of the above

51. One of the following is not correct in regard to Capital Market:
 A. It is a market for long term financial assets   B. Maturity Period less than one year
 C. Dealings take place at Stock Exchange   D. Unlimited number of players
 E. Regulated by SEBI

52. Providing various services relating to Capital Market is called:
 A. Merchant Banking   B. Retail Banking
 C. Narrow Banking   D. Modern Banking

53. RBI absorbs liquidity in the system through:
 A. Repo   B. Reverse Repo   C. Both A and B   D. Either A or B

54. RBI pays interest to banks on their balances kept with it for purposes of Cash Reserve Ratio at:
 A. Less than 3 per cent   B. 3.5 per cent on eligible balances
 C. At bank rate   D. No interest is paid

55. Remittance under the Guarantee Bond Scheme can be accepted from:
 A. only Associated Banks
 B. only Nationalized Banks
 C. only foreign Banks
 D. all Scheduled Banks and Co-operative Banks

56. Blue chip securities refer to:
   A. shares of any company
   B. shares of companies, which are listed at any of the stock exchanges
   C. shares of good companies
   D. all of the above

57. Which of the following is not included in government securities:
   A. Promissory Notes   B. Debentures   C. Bearer Bonds   D. All of these

58. A bearer bond is:
   A. an instrument evidencing a debt in the name of the holder
   B. an instrument of loan issued by scheduled commercial bank
   C. an instrument stating that the bearer thereof is entitled to receive payment of a certain sum on the maturity date as per the terms of the particular loan for which the bond is issued
   D. all of the above

59. Pledge means:
   A. advance against goods
   B. hypothecation of goods
   C. bailment of goods as security for payment of a debt or performance of a promise
   D. open limits

60. Which of the following statements is not correct:
   A. The rising interest rate increases the discount rate on cash flows and decreases the market value of that Asset
   B. Falling interest rates decrease the market value of Assets or Liabilities
   C. When a Bank holds longer term assets than liabilities and if interest rate rises, the market value of Assets falls by more amount than liabilities
   D. The above C may lead to economic loss

61. What is Yield Curve Risk:
   A. It is a line of graph plotting the yield of all maturities of a particular instrument
   B. Yield curve changes its slope and shape from time to time
   C. Yield curve can be twisted to the desired direction through the intervention of RBI
   D. All of the above

62. Currency Swaps are:
   A. common currency transactions involving borrowing and lending
   B. currency loans from a foreign country
   C. back-to-back loan
   D. None of the above

63. Reserve Bank of India has not authorized banks to approve limits relating to:
   A. Cash Reserve Ratio   B. Statutory Liquidity Ratio
   C. Foreign Exchange Operations   D. None of the above

64. Settlement risk can be avoided only if:
   A. settlements are made on real time basis
   B. there is a global settlement agency
   C. foreign exchange transactions are traded in Derivatives
   D. All of the above

65. Reverse Repo means:
- A. rate at which RBI borrows money from commercial banks
- B. rate offered to Blue chip companies
- C. a rate equal to Bank rate
- D. None of the above

66. S.L. Kapoor Committee relates to:
- A. financing of Small Scale Industries
- B. Agriculture financing
- C. both A and B
- D. None of the above

67. SEBI controls:
- A. Capital Market
- B. Money Market
- C. Both A and B
- D. None of these

68. Securitization is:
- A. non-performing loans are acquired from banks and financial institutions at a discounted value and security receipts issued to them so that these loans are removed from their balance sheet enabling them to reduce the provision in respect of such loans and improve profitability
- B. converting the illiquid loans of banks and financial institutions by Securitization Companies into tradable securities, after they are acquired and sold to the investors
- C. a process of acquisition of non-performing loans from banks by a Securitization company and covert them into tradable securities and sold to the investors
- D. all of the above

69. Shares of companies notified by SEBI can be traded only when these are in ...... form:
- A. physical
- B. dematerialized
- C. either A or B
- D. None of these

70. TDR offered as security for an advance is transferred to the bank by way of:
- A. pledge
- B. charge
- C. assignment
- D. all of these

71. The amendment to Section 41 of Reserve Bank of India Act, 1934 was carried out of the purpose of:
- A. RBI's decision to do away payment of interest on CRR balances
- B. empowering NGOs involved in environmental protection
- C. asking banks/financial institutions not to use coercive methods for recovery of loans
- D. none of the above

72. The Bank which has entered into carbon credit trading advisory services is:
- A. ICICI Bank
- B. UCO bank
- C. IDBI Bank
- D. Yes Bank

73. The Base Rate system has replaced BPLR with effect from:
- A. 01.05.2010
- B. 01.06.2010
- C. 01.07.2010
- D. 01.08.2010

74. The buyer or the importer who procures a Letter of Credit from his banker is called:
- A. opener of the credit
- B. beneficiary of the credit
- C. negotiator of the credit
- D. None of the above

75. The coverage of Right to Information Act (RTI), 2005 is:
- A. whole of India
- B. whole of India, except North Eastern States
- C. whole of India, except the State of Jammu & Kashmir
- D. None of the above

76. The difference between a Term Loan and a Deferred Payment Guarantee relates to:
- A. end use of funds
- B. outlay of funds
- C. both A and B
- D. None of these

77. The expansion for BIFR, in the context of the Indian Industry is:
  A. Board for Industrial and Financial Reconstruction
  B. Bureau for Industrial and Financial Reconstruction
  C. Board for Investment and Financial Reconstruction
  D. Bureau for Investment and Financial Reconstruction

78. The Financial Year of RBI starts from:
  A. 1st April   B. 1st June   C. 1st July   D. 1st December

79. The Government has approved framework for "Mobile-linked No-Frills Accounts" by banks. Which of the following is/are correct regarding the Government's expectations in this regard.
  A. nearly 500 million should be able to access financial services through mobile phones
  B. each bank to start its implementation from 31st July and complete it by 31st December 2010
  C. this will be a core micro payment platform for payment transfer of benefits of Government Schemes, and financial inclusion of target groups
  D. All of the above

80. The largest financial conglomerate of India is:
  A. HDFC Bank   B. ICICI Bank   C. IFCI   D. SBI

81. The major shareholders in Asset Reconstruction Company of India Limited (ARCIL) other than SBI are:
  A. IDBI & Canara Bank   B. ICICI & HDFC   C. IDBI & HDFC   D. IDBI & ICICI

82. The minimum and maximum court fee that is required to be paid for filing a suit in a Debt Recovery Tribunal is:
  A. ₹ 5,000; ₹ 1,00,000   B. ₹ 10,000; ₹ 1,00,000
  C. ₹ 12,000; ₹ 1,50,000   D. ₹ 12,000; no ceiling

83. The practice of reducing NPAs through cross-lending to square off loans from bank is known as:
  A. "Ever-Greening" of advances   B. "Take Over" of advances
  C. Compromise Settlement   D. None of the above

84. The risks involved in paying a post-dated cheque are:
  A. the drawer may issue other cheques which bear a date prior to the date of such a cheque and if the balance is insufficient, the bank may be held liable
  B. an Attachment Order may be received attaching the balance in the account
  C. the drawer may become insolvent or die
  D. the drawer may stop payment
  E. All of the above

85. The single largest component of external debt is:
  A. Commercial borrowings   B. Multilateral debt
  C. Short term debt   D. NRI deposits

86. The term "Holder" under an Option Contract refers to:
  A. Buyer of the Option   B. Seller of the Option
  C. Middleman/broker   D. Dealer

87. The type of charge created on LIC Policy is:
  A. pledge   B. hypothecation   C. assignment   D. all of these

88. To revitalize RRBs, the Central Government has taken some significant steps. One of these is not such a step:

A. made SARFAESI Act applicable to RRBs
B. permitted RRBs to accept NRI deposits
C. permitted RRBs for Branch Expansion
D. RRBs can undertake Insurance Business

89. Under CDR Mechanism, Category-I CDR System is applicable to accounts classified as under in the books of at least 90 per cent of the creditors (by value):

A. Standard

B. Standard and Sub-Standard

C. Sub-Standard or Doubtful

D. Standard or Sub-Standard or Doubtful

90. Under Section [S.2(h)] of the RTI Act, 2005 ''Other Public Authority'' means:
A. by notification issued or by order of the appropriate government
B. all bodies owned, controlled or subsequently financed by the government
C. all non governmental organizations substantially financed by the government
D. all of the above

91. Under the Corporate Debt Restructuring (CDR) mechanism, loan assets of banks have been categorized. Which one of the following statements is not correct:
A. Assets belonging to Standard and Sub-Standard category come under Category I
B. Assets belonging to Doubtful category come under Category 2
C. Assets belonging to Doubtful and Loss categories come under Category 2
D. Out of total Loan Assets, 90 per cent is Standard and Sub-standard and Doubtful is 10 per cent - this lot comes under Category I

92. Under which of the following methods of depreciation, amount of depreciation varies every year:
A. Written Down Value Method
B. Straight Line Method
C. Amount of depreciation does not vary on year to year basis
D. None of the above

93. Usually, the validity period of an Income Tax Refund Order is:

A. 1 months   B. 2 months   C. 3 months   D. 6 months

94. What do you mean by ''Outcome Budget'':
A. It denotes reaction of the media after Budget Papers are approved in the Parliament
B. It aims to measure performance of the Government in various departments
C. It is a report submitted by the Government of India indicating strides made in different projects by ministries and departments as a first step towards converting outlays into income
D. None of the above

95. What is ''Stagflation'':

A. inflation with growth

B. deflation with growth

C. inflation after deflations

D. inflation with depression

96. What is POP-SP in relation to New Pension System introduced on the 1st May 2009:
A. Point of Presence Service Provider for registering the citizens under the Scheme and remitting their subscriptions
B. Popular Service Provider for registering the citizens under the Scheme and remitting their subscriptions
C. Both A and B
D. None of the above

97. What is true about "White Card":
A. It is related to companies producing milk products
B. It does not carry on its face, the brand of the issuer
C. It is meant to covert blank money into the economy
D. None of the above

98. When a country decides to conduct trade on favorable terms with another country for mutual benefits, this is called:
A. FTA System　　　　　　B. MFN Status　　　　　　C. Bilateral Trade　　　D. Counter Trade

99. When a security is not treated in the Stock Exchange for a period of ...... days prior to the date of valuation, it is treated as "Non-Traded" security:
A. 30 days　　　　　　　　B. 45 days　　　　　　　　C. 60 days　　　　　　　D. 90 days

100. When banks invest their deposit accruals in Government securities, it is called:
A. Asset Securitization　　B. Hedging　　　　　　　　C. Narrow Banking　　D. Forfaiting

101. When we discuss Negotiated Dealing System, it denotes:
A. Settlement of Security dealing
B. Trading in Stock Markets
C. Trading in Government Securities
D. None of the above

102. Where banker pays a cheque in which amount or other particulars were chemically altered and such alteration is not visible to the naked eye, is any statutory protection available to the paying banker:
A. yes, provided the payment was a payment in due course and satisfies the condition as per Section 10 of the Negotiable Instruments Act, 1881
B. yes, provided the alteration is not visible and the banker has paid it in good faith
C. yes, provided the payment was made without any negligence on his part
D. all of the above

103. Which category of accounts are opened under Financial Inclusion:
A. Senior Citizens Deposit　　　　　　　　　　　B. Super Saver Accounts
C. No-Frill Accounts　　　　　　　　　　　　　D. SBI Vishesh

104. Which is the first bank in India to launch its interactive banking service through Dish TV:
A. SBI　　　　　　　　　　B. ICICI Bank　　　　　　C. HDFC Bank　　　D. Axis Bank

105. Which is the first bank in India to produce Green Power for captive use through wind mills:
A. HDFC　　　　　　　　　B. ICICI　　　　　　　　　C. SBI　　　　　　　　D. Axis Bank

106. While opening a current account, an introductory reference is absolutely necessary:
A. the introducer can be held responsible if the account becomes irregular
B. this is required under directions from the Reserve Bank of India
C. if it is not taken, the bank may be held responsible for being negligent and may, therefore, lose statutory protection available under Section 131 of the Negotiable Instruments Act, 1881
D. none of the above

107. A cheque, payment of which was stopped by the customer, was paid through oversight:
A. the bank is not responsible as such a responsibility was disclaimed at the time the stop order was registered
B. the bank is responsible and cannot debit the amount of the cheque to customer's account

    C. the bank is not responsible as the customer cannot stop the payment of a cheque which was properly issued

    D. the payment of a cheque, once issued cannot be stopped

108. Who was the first Indian Governor of the Reserve Bank of India:

    A. C. D. Deshmukh   B. Sachindra Ray   C. S. Mukherjee   D. I. G. Patel

109. There is a joint account in the names of A and B, to be operated by both of them jointly. There is a debit balance of ₹ 23,100 when the bank receives a notice of A's death:

    A. the amount can be recovered from B only

    B. the amount can be recovered from the estate of the deceased A only

    C. the amount can be recovered from B and/or the estate of the deceased A

    D. None of the above

110. Mohan, who will be 18 next December, approaches the bank for a loan of ₹ 1,00,000 to be repaid out of the property that will vest in him on his attaining majority:

    A. the loan may be granted provided the value of the property in question is sufficient

    B. the bank's head office will be approached for necessary guidance

    C. the loan may be granted provided, in addition to the security of the property in question, a third party's guarantee is arranged

    D. a minor's agreement being void *ab-initio* the proposal in question will not be entertained

111. There is a joint account in the name of Khem Singh and his wife Kartar Kaur with a mandate: "to be operated by either or survivor". Both are in dispute and each of them has instructed the bank not to honour the signature of the other in future:

    A. the balance of the account will be paid to Khem Singh against a proper receipt

    B. further operations on the account will be stopped, but the cheques already drawn by either of them and yet not presented will be honoured

    C. further operations on the account will be stopped till a fresh mandate signed by both of them is received

    D. the account will be closed and the balance remitted to them

112. The term "kite flying" in banking refers to:

    A. drawing a cheque without providing sufficient funds to meet it

    B. drawing and acceptance of a bill of exchange without consideration with a view to accommodate the other party

    C. the practice of paying usance bills before they become due

    D. drawing a post-dated cheque

113. The re-endorsement of unpaid bills of exchange in favour of the remitting bank or the constituent to whom they are returned must be followed by the words:

    A. in case of need please refer to   B. without recourse to us

    C. payable at the State Bank of India   D. None of the above

114. The amount of advance which may be granted against the security of a life insurance policy depends on:

    A. the amount of the insurance policy   B. the surrender value of the policy

    C. the paid-up value of the policy   D. the total amount of premiums paid

115. The primary relationship between the banker and the customer is that of:

    A. trustee and beneficiary   B. debtor and creditor

    C. principal and agent   D. lesser and lessee

116. The purpose of providing depreciation on the bank's property is:
   A. to reduce the profit of the bank
   B. to make usual allowances for annual wear and tear
   C. to enable the bank to recover this amount from the Reserve Bank of India
   D. to strengthen the financial position of the bank

117. A debt becomes time-barred after:
   A. one year   B. two and a half years   C. three years   D. five years

118. Bank rate is:
   A. a rate of interest charged by the commercial banks from the borrowers for advances against Government Securities
   B. the lowest rate of interest charged by the commercial banks from the borrowers
   C. the rate at which the Reserve Bank of India would rediscount bills of exchange or other eligible commercial papers, or advance against eligible securities to the scheduled banks
   D. the rate at which commercial banks discount bill of exchange for their customers

119. A cheque which was returned with the remarks: "Effects drawn against not yet cleared. Please present again", has been represented and there are no funds in the account to pay it:
   A. the cheque should be paid as the banker is under obligation to it
   B. the cheque should be paid and the customer asked to put the account in order
   C. the cheque should be returned with the answer: "Refer to drawer"
   D. none of the above

120. In case of a Hindu Undivided Family, when Karta dies leaving overdraft account:
   A. old account is closed and a new account opened
   B. fresh HUF letter is obtained
   C. all the co-parceners will operate on the account
   D. none of the above

121. In the Balance Sheet of a bank, contingent liabilities are shown:
   A. on the liabilities side of the Balance Sheet
   B. by way of a deduction from the assets
   C. by way of a footnote
   D. in the Schedule on the Assets side of the Balance Sheet

122. Village Adoption Scheme means:
   A. adopting a village for opening the branch of the bank
   B. adopting a village for intensive deposit mobilisation campaign
   C. selection of a village devastated by floods or natural calamities for providing financial help
   D. none of the above

123. When a cheque with forged drawer's signature is paid by the bank, the paying banker:
   A. is protected if the cheque is paid in good faith and without negligence
   B. is protected if the forgery could not have been detected with the exercise of reasonable care and prudence
   C. is not entitled to debit the drawer's account with the amount of the cheque
   D. is liable to the drawer only if there has been no contributory negligence on the part of the draer

124. In the matter of handling bills of exchange for collection, the relationship between customer and the bank is:
   A. trustee and the beneficiary   B. principal and agent
   C. bailor and bailee   D. None of the above

125. A scheduled bank is one:
   A. which conforms to the requirements of schedule III of the Banking Regulation Act, 1949
   B. which has been declared as a scheduled bank by the Government of India
   C. which has deposits exceeding Rs. 10 crore
   D. which has its name added to the second schedule of the Reserve Bank of India Act, 1934

126. When a cheque duly signed by the drawer, with particulars written therein in a hand-writing different from that of the drawer, is presented for payment:
   A. the bank will refuse payment of the cheque as there is a distinct possibility of the cheque signed in blank having been stolen from the drawer and hence, the branch is put on enquiry
   B. the bank will make the payment provided the cheque is otherwise in order
   C. the bank will make payment only to the authorised representative of the drawer
   D. none of the above

127. Hypothecation is:
   A. a transaction of conditional sale
   B. a legal transaction whereby goods may be made available as security for a debt
   C. transfer of ownership by the borrower to the lender
   D. none of the above

128. Crossing denotes:
   A. that the cheque will not be paid across the counter but will be credited to the account of the holder
   B. that the cheque will be paid through clearing only
   C. that the cheque can not be transferred by the payee named therein
   D. it is a direction to the paying banker to pay the cheque not in cash, but only through a banker by credit to bank account of payee

129. Where the signature of the drawer of a cheque is not genuine, such a cheque is called:
   A. post dated cheque
   B. stale cheque
   C. forged cheque
   D. all of these

130. Account payee crossing is addressed to:
   A. collecting banker
   B. paying banker
   C. payee
   D. all of these

131. 'Not Negotiable' crossing refers to:
   A. the cheque can not be negotiated
   B. the collecting bank should satisfy itself as to the title of the holder before collecting the cheque
   C. the cheque can not be collected as the protection under Section 131 of the Negotiable Instruments Act, 1881 is not available in such cases
   D. the transferee shall not have and shall not be capable of giving a better title to the cheque than that of the transferer

132. Stop payment instructions remain in force for a period of:
   A. one year
   B. three months
   C. six months unless revoked by the customer
   D. until the account is closed by the customer

133. Payment of a cheque may be countermanded by the:
   A. payee
   B. drawer
   C. true owner
   D. drawee

134. In case the advising bank is unable to establish the authenticity of Letter of Credit it must:
A. immediately inform the buyer
B. immediately inform the seller
C. immediately inform the issuing bank
D. none of the above

135. Examination of the documents before making payments is the prime responsibility of:
A. sellers bank in the seller's country
B. buyers bank in the seller's country
C. negotiating bank
D. None of the above

136. The beneficiary of the LC draws a bill of exchange on:
A. Issuing Bank
B. Advising Bank
C. Negotiating Bank
D. None of these

137. Invoice is a:
A. Accounting document
B. Legal document
C. Commercial document
D. All of these

138. The currency of the issuance of the insurance policy:
A. must be as the currency of the seller's country
B. must be same as the currency of the issuing bank's country
C. must be the same as that of the currency of the LC
D. none of the above

139. Stand by Letter of Credit is a substitute of:
A. Letter of Credit
B. Guarantee
C. Advise note
D. None of these

140. Many banks have adopted/launched 'Core Banking Solutions' (CBS). Core Banking Solution is:
A. A marketing strategy adopted by the banks
B. A new type of ATM useful for rural population
C. A delivery channel for quick and fast delivery
D. A new product launched to help senior citizens only as they are not able to visit branches/ATMs frequently

141. Banking Sector will fall under which of the following:
A. Agricultural Sector
B. Service Sector
C. Manufacturing Sector
D. Industrial Sector

142. Which of the following Acts was framed specially to deal more effectively with the problem of Non-Performing Assets in Banking system:
A. SARFAESI Act
B. Banking Regulation Act
C. Foreign Exchange Management Act
D. Industrial Disputes Act

143. Many Banks these days are entering into business of offering loans against property. This business of the banks can be categorized under which of the following heads of banking:
A. Corporate Banking
B. Personal Banking
C. Merchant Banking
D. Portfolio Management Services

144. ''e-stamping'' denotes:
A. replacement of the traditional system of affixing postal stamps in postal services
B. doing away with the need of banks to brand stamps on negotiable instruments manually
C. sending message through e-mail, where no stamping is necessary
D. replacing stamp duty required for payment of registration of properties and documents

145. In which of the following situations can a bank issuing a Bank Guarantee may withhold payment of the Guarantee invoked by the beneficiary:

A. when it is not satisfied that there was default on the part of the party because of which the beneficiary suffered

B. bank can withhold payment of the guarantee upon being served an injunction by the Court restraining payment under the guarantee

C. there is no provision for withholding payment of a Bank Guarantee when invoked

D. none of the above

146. Please identify the statement which is not true, from out of the following in respect of Guarantee Cover under Credit Guarantee Trust for Medium & Small Enterprises:

A. retail traders are eligible for cover

B. Small Road and Water Transport Operators are eligible for the cover

C. Small Business entities, Professional & Self-Employed persons are eligible for cover

D. other service enterprises under the scope of Micro and Small Enterprises are eligible for the cover

147. Under the Credit Guarantee Trust for Medium & Small Enterprises, loans and advances to Educational Institutions are:

A. covered

B. not covered

C. CGTMSE is silent about covering the loans to Educational Institutions

D. none of the above

148. When a Bank Guarantee is invoked by the beneficiary either in writing or by telex or telegram, the Bank issuing the Guarantee:

A. will have to effect payment without delay or demur

B. will have ot pay within three working days

C. will pay after being satisfied that the beneficiary suffered loss

D. none of the above

149. Which of the following banks enjoys the reputation of being at the top in market capitalization among all the private banks:

A. ICICI Bank   B. HDFC Bank   C. Axis Bank   D. Yes Bank

150. Which of the following categories of persons is not eligible for being engaged as Business Facilitation in the Bank:

A. retired employees of banks

B. retired bank employees and Government employees

C. bank employees who retired voluntarily

D. ex-servicemen

151. "Apiary" is:

A. export of pearls   B. export of fish

C. place where bees are reared for honey   D. export of diamonds

152. "Claused Bill of Lading" is one which indicates:

A. no defects in packaging or condition of goods   B. defective condition of package and goods

C. no documents attached to it   D. None of the above

153. "Cost Overrun" means:

A. Remaining constant in Project Cost   B. escalation in Project Cost

C. decrease in Project Cost   D. None of the above

154. "Dark Block" is an area:
  A. where literacy rate is below 15 per cent
  B. where people below the poverty line are more than 90 per cent
  C. where underground source of water is not available
  D. where more than 85 per cent exploitation has taken place on the available underground water

155. "Gearing" in accounting parlance refers to:
  A. Break Even Sales   B. Current Ratio   C. Debt/Equity   D. DSCR

156. "Hedging" denotes:
  A. protecting against fluctuations/uncertainty risk in forex markets
  B. credit risk assessment in respect of advances
  C. speculative buying/selling of foreign currency
  D. None of the above

157. "Order Nisi" is:
  A. an order to freeze or stop all transactions of the customer in his account
  B. also a direction to the banker to explain why the funds in the customer's account so freezed should not be used for payment of the judgment debt
  C. both A and B
  D. None of the above

158. "Pomology" is associated with:
  A. mushroom cultivation   B. study of fruit crops
  C. fish farming   D. vegetable production

159. "Working Capital" means:
  A. Own Capital of the Proprietor   B. Borrowed Capital
  C. All Assets minus All Liabilities   D. Current Assets minus Current Liabilities

160. "Working Capital Gap" means:
  A. excess of current assets over current liabilities other than bank borrowings
  B. excess of current assets over current liabilities including WCTL
  C. excess of current assets over current liabilities
  D. none of the above

161. Which of the following types of ATMs eliminates the need for PIN entry and authenticated customer transactions by thumb impressions:
  A. White Label ATMs   B. Biometric ATMs
  C. On-site ATMs   D. Off-site ATMs

162. A cheque dated 31-4-2009 cannot be paid before:
  A. 30-04-2009   B. 01-05-2009
  C. either A or B   D. such cheque cannot be paid

163. Which of the following sources of income for a bank is most significant:
  A. service Charges   B. loans   C. deposits   D. fees

164. A Usance Bill when presented for acceptance has to be accepted/dishonoured within:
  A. 24 hours   B. 36 hours   C. 48 hours   D. 60 hours

165. As per Nayak Committee, the margin contribution of SSI units is ...... per cent the annual projected turnover.
  A. 5   B. 10   C. 20   D. 25

166. Authority to prescribe retention period of records of banks vests with:
A. IBA   B. RBI   C. GOI   D. SEBI

167. Authorized Dealers for foreign exchange transactions are appointed by:
A. Reserve Bank of India   B. Government of India
C. Individual Banks   D. FEDAI

168. Bill of Lading is a:
A. Negotiable Instrument   B. Non-negotiable Instrument
C. Quasi-Negotiable Instrument   D. None of the above

169. Brazil, Russia, India and China are called:
A. Nuclear Power countries   B. Industrialized countries
C. Developed countries   D. BRIC countries

170. By ''Repository'' we mean:
A. balance held in non Currency Chest branch   B. same as Currency Chest
C. a part of Currency Chest   D. None of the above

171. Code of Bank's Commitment deals with our commitments in the area of:
A. sanction of advances   B. steps taken against Frauds
C. standard Banking Practices in customer service   D. None of the above

172. Commercial Paper is a:
A. Demand Promissory Note   B. Usance Promissory Note
C. Government Promissory Note   D. Bond issued by a Company

173. Consent of RBI is necessary before transferring funds from one chest to another; because:
A. RBI is the owner of the Chest   B. RBI arranges transit insurance
C. police protection is arranged   D. details to be kept a secret

174. Currency Chest is the property of:
A. State Bank of India   B. Government of India
C. Reserve Bank of India   D. None of these

175. Due date for repayment of a crop loan is crop growing period, plus:
A. 4 months for marketing   B. 3 months for marketing
C. 2 months for marketing   D. 1 month for marketing

176. EEFC account can be opened in the form of:
A. Current Account, SB Account and TDR   B. Current Account and SB Account
C. Current Account only   D. None of the above

177. Factors influencing customer behaviour in banking are:
A. location and range of services   B. safety and return
C. custormer service   D. both B and C

178. For violation of FEMA, prosecution is done by:
A. RBI   B. DGFT
C. FEDAI   D. Enforcement Directorate

179. Format of cheque has been prescribed under:
A. Negotiable Instruments Act, 1881   B. Banking Transactions Act
C. Banking Regulation Act, 1949   D. None of the above

180. Garnishee Order can be issued by:
   A. a competent court   B. a debtor   C. a creditor   D. a bank

181. If a bill of exchange is not drawn for consideration, such a bill is called:
   A. Trade Bill   B. Accommodation Bill
   C. Clean Bill   D. Documentary Bill

182. If a Demand Promissory Note is obtained unstamped:
   A. penalty of 10 times the deficiency has to be paid and the proper stamp has to be affixed
   B. the Note has to be presented to the Collector/District Commissioner for adjudication
   C. unstamped/under-stamped DP Note can never be rectified
   D. the Note has to be properly stamped at the earliest

183. In respect of which of the following account, Interest rate is controlled by RBI:
   A. overdraft in Per-segment   B. Recurring Deposits Account
   C. Savings Bank Account   D. FCNRB. Account

184. Loan is not granted by bank against security of:
   A. Gold Ornaments   B. Certificate of Deposits
   C. Term Deposit Receipts   D. National Savings Certificate

185. Mutual Fund Scheme that operates continuously without any limit entry for subscriptions and redemptions is:
   A. Fixed Income   B. Specific Fund   C. Close Ended   D. Open Ended

186. One Rupee Coin forms part of:
   A. Currency Chest   B. Small Coin Depot
   C. Branch Cash Balance   D. All of the above

187. Paid cheques can be returned to a customer on request. It is provided for in the:
   A. Partnership Act, 1932   B. Indian Contract Act, 1872
   C. Banking Regulation Act, 1949   D. Negotiable Instruments Act, 1881

188. Pillars of BASEL-II are:
   A. Minimum capital ratio   B. Supervisory review
   C. Market discipline   D. All of these

189. PMRY is applicable to:
   A. rural area   B. agriculture
   C. rural and urban areas   D. all over India

190. Process of inviting subscriptions to a public issue through a tendering process is known as:
   A. Market Capitalization   B. Book-building   C. Under Writing   D. None of these

191. RBI manages liquidity with:
   A. Bank Rate   B. Cash Reserve Ratio
   C. Statutory Liquidity Ratio   D.   None of these

192. When the date of the cheque is later than the date on which it is presented for payment, the cheque is known as:
   A. stale cheque   B. invalid cheque
   C. ante-dated cheque   D. post dated cheque

193. Services associated with banking, insurance and securities are called:
   A. Financial Services   B. Banking Services   C. Credit Services   D. Debt Services

194. Subsidy under PMRY is reimbursed to banks by:
- A. Government of India
- B. State Government
- C. NABARD
- D. RBI

195. Term Deposit Receipt is:
- A. transferable by endorsement and delivery
- B. transferable by assignment
- C. cannot be transferred
- D. not negotiable

196. The concept of "Narrow Banking" was recommended by:
- A. Khan Committee
- B. Nayak Committee
- C. Sodhani Committee
- D. Tarapore & Narasimham Committee

197. The cut off limit for loans under Multiple Banking/Syndication/Consortium to be covered under Corporate Debt Restructuring Mechanism is:
- A. Rs. 10 crore and above
- B. Rs. 15 crore and above
- C. Rs. 20 crore and above
- D. Rs. 50 crore and above

198. The level of activity at which total revenue cost equals total sale value or when there is a "no profit" or "no loss" situation, it is known as:
- A. Break Even Point
- B. Operating Profit
- C. Gross Profit
- D. Net Profit

199. When does a Savings Bank account becomes dormant:
- A. if there is no transaction for a period of 12 months
- B. if there is no withdrawal for a period of 12 months
- C. if there is no withdrawal for a period of 6 months
- D. if there is no credit for a period of 12 months

200. The minimum amount of withdrawal/deposit in the Currency Chest permissible is:
- A. Rs. 1,000 in multiples of Rs. 500
- B. Rs. 10,000 in multiples of Rs. 1,000
- C. Rs. 1,00,000 in multiples of Rs. 10,000
- D. Rs. 1,00,000 in multiples of Rs. 50,000

201. The term "Trial Netting" is associated with:
- A. vermiculture
- B. sericulture
- C. bee-keeping
- D. pisciculture

202. The words "At Sight" and "After Sight" in a Bill of Exchange refers to:
- A. both mean on demand
- B. both mean after acceptance
- C. "at sight" means on demand and "after sight" means after acceptance
- D. None of the above

203. A lien is the right to:
- A. sell the goods or securities if the debt or loan is not repaid by the borrower
- B. retain goods or securities belonging to a debtor until he has discharged a debt to the retainer thereof
- C. dispose of the goods or securities in case of default on the part of the borrower
- D. None of the above

204. A bank reconciliation statement is prepared with the help of:
- A. bank pass book and bank column of cash book
- B. bank pass book and cash column of cash book
- C. bank pass book and petty cash book
- D. All of the above

205. Which one of the following statements is true:
   A. Normally if Cash Book shows a debit balance, Pass Book also shows a debit balance
   B. A credit entry in Pass Book means a credit entry in Cash Book
   C. For a dishonoured cheque, bank account is debited
   D. When a customer directly pays into bank, bank account is debited

206. The main purpose of preparing a Bank Reconciliation Statement is:
   A. to know the Cash Book Balance
   B. to know the Pass Book Balance
   C. to compare the transactions in the Cash Book and Pass Book
   D. to correct the Cash Book
   E. to reconcile Balance as per Cash Book with the Pass Book Balance

207. What are the main objectives of Consumer Protection Act, 1986:
   A. To provide better protection of the interest of consumers
   B. Settlement of consumer disputes
   C. To deal with other connected matters
   D. All of the above

208. Consumer Means:
   A. Any person who buys any goods
   B. Any person who hires or avails of any services
   C. Any person who makes payment in full or in instalments or under Hire Purchase system
   D. All of the above

209. The goods in the Consumer Protection Act, includes:
   A. every kind of movable property except money
   B. actionable claims, stocks and shares
   C. growing crops and things attached to or forming a part of the land
   D. all of the above

210. The services under the Consumer Protection includes:
   A. Banking, Financing and Insurance   B. Transport and Processing
   C. Supply of electrical and other energy   D. All of the above

211. Under the Basel-II Accord capital requirement for credit risk can be calculated:
   A. Standardised manner which is based on external credit rating assessment
   B. Internal rating system for credit risk
   C. Both A and B
   D. None of the above

212. The features of Standardised credit rating approach are:
   A. The risk can be measured in standardised manner based on external credit assessment
   B. The Risk weights are inversely related to the rating of counterparty
   C. Lower the rating, higher the risk
   D. All of the above

213. The objective of cash management is to:
   A. reduce bank overdraft   B. minimise cost of borrowings
   C. earn maximum interest income   D. maintain cash at optimum levels

214. Economic Order Quantity is a method of:
   A. managing raw materials
   B. managing finished goods
   C. managing debtors
   D. managing creditors

215. The term 'Working Capital Cycle' refers to:
   A. money invested in current assets
   B. rotation of money invested in working capital
   C. the periodic increase or decrease in the requirements of working capital funds
   D. conversion of cash of the business again into cash through the stages of inventory and receivables

216. A cheque can be paid in cash even after business hours when it is presented by:
   A. a person known to bank officials
   B. any person
   C. the drawer
   D. the payee

217. A Letter of Credit which is issued in lieu of a guarantee, is called:
   A. Back to Back Credit   B. Red Clause Credit   C. Standby Credit   D. None of these

218. A mortgage involves:
   A. transfer of ownership
   B. transfer of possession
   C. transfer of interest
   D. All of the above

219. A person is not interested in buying the right issue and prefers to give this right to one of his friends. This is called:
   A. renunciation   B. surrender   C. rejection   D. transfer

220. A private sector bank should have a minimum paid-up capital of:
   A. Rs. 100 crore   B. Rs. 200 crore   C. Rs. 300 crore   D. Rs. 500 crore

221. A reduction of Cash Reserve Ratio (CRR) will result in:
   A. increase in lendable resources of banks
   B. will not impact the level of bank credit
   C. increase in bank credit
   D. decrease in bank credit

222. A Self Help Group may become eligible for bank loan and subsidy:
   A. after First Grading
   B. after Second Grading
   C. soon after the registration
   D. 6 months after opening of Savings Bank account

223. A time barred debt can be revived by obtaining:
   A. a letter of undertaking to pay the time barred debt   B. time-barred debt cannot be revived
   C. a back-dated Revival Letter
   D. Revival Letter

224. Agricultural Term Loan is repaid out of:
   A. cash accrual
   B. sale proceeds of crop
   C. net incremental income
   D. annual savings of the farmer

225. An agricultural advance given for allied activity, viz., poultry, is classified as NPA if:
   A. interest and installments remain unpaid beyond 90 days
   B. interest and installments remain due for 2 crop seasons
   C. interest remains outstanding for 2 and a half years
   D. none of the above

226. An asset will be immediately categorized as Loss Asset, when the realizable value is:
   A. more than 15 per cent
   B. less than 10 per cent
   C. 10 per cent or more
   D. None of these

227. Appeal under Consumer Protection Act, 1986 is entertained, if submitted within:
  A. 90 days of the decision
  B. 30 days of the decision
  C. there is no provision for any appeal
  D. none of the above

228. Authority to prescribe retention period of records of banks vests with:
  A. IBA
  B. RBI
  C. GOI
  D. SEBI

229. Bank guarantee is a:
  A. Demand Liability
  B. Contingent Liability
  C. Term Liability
  D. None of these

230. Bank holidays under Section 25 of the Negotiable Instruments Act, 1881 are declared by:
  A. State Government for the respective State
  B. Banking Operations Department
  C. Central Government
  D. RBI

231. Banker's right of set off can be immediately exercised in case of:
  A. insolvency of the borrower
  B. lunacy of the borrower
  C. death of the borrower
  D. all of the above

232. Banks do not purchase/discount:
  A. Accommodation Bills
  B. Documentary Bills
  C. Usance Bills
  D. Clean Bills

233. Busy Season Credit Policy refers to the period:
  A. February and August
  B. June and December
  C. March to September
  D. October to March

234. Capital Adequacy Ratio measures Capital against:
  A. total deposits and total advances
  B. total deposits
  C. total assets
  D. total risk weighted assets

235. Ceiling for settlement through Lok Adalats is:
  A. Rs. 10 lakh
  B. Rs. 15 lakh
  C. Rs. 20 lakh
  D. Rs. 25 lakh

236. Consumer Protection Act, 1986 does not cover:
  A. failure to open accounts
  B. failure to issue drafts
  C. sanction of loans
  D. ATMs

237. Currency Chest Slip is serially numbered at the beginning of each year from:
  A. January to December
  B. March to April
  C. April to March
  D. July to June

238. Difference between buying and selling rates of a currency is known as:
  A. Forward Rate
  B. Bid-ask Rate
  C. Spot Rate
  D. None of these

239. EEFC account can be opened in the form of:
  A. Current Account, SB Account and TDR
  B. Current Account and SB Account
  C. Current Account only
  D. None of the above

240. Government securities are issued for a maximum period of:
  A. 10 years
  B. 15 years
  C. 25 years
  D. 30 years

241. If a bank wants to introduce a new deposit scheme, the same is now approved by:
  A. RBI
  B. IBA
  C. respective Bank's Board
  D. both A and B

242. Limitation period of a Demand Promissory Note is:
  A. 3 years from the date of execution
  B. 5 years from the date of execution
  C. 12 years from the date of execution
  D. 30 years from the date of execution

243. The Securities and Exchange Board of India (SEBI), which has been accorded statutory status, has its Headquarters in:
A. Mumbai   B. Kolkata   C. Delhi   D. Chennai

244. What is true with regard to MIGA:
1. It stands for Multilateral Investment Guarantee Agency
2. It encourages the flow of foreign investment into developing member countries
3. It is an affiliate of the World Bank, and was set-up in 1988
4. India joined MIGA in April as its 113th member
A. 1, 2, 3   B. 1, 2, 4   C. All of these   D. None of these

245. The main watchdog of international trade is:
A. IMF   B. World Bank   C. GATT   D. IFC

246. A common currency for the members of the Common Market in Europe is known as:
A. Dollar   B. Euro   C. Franc   D. Pound

247. The biggest international financial centre in the world is:
A. Frankfurt   B. Geneva   C. London   D. New York

248. The Securities and Exchange Board of India (SEBI), a statutory autonomous body, aims to:
A. promote a fair and healthy securities market
B. protect investor's rights
C. prevent malpractices in a mobilisation of resources through capital
D. all of the above

249. Which one of the following has largest network, accounts and annual deposits:
A. IDBI   B. ICICI
C. Post office saving bank   D. IOB

250. Under the new guidelines issued by the Government for regulation of merchant banking activities, all merchant bankers, both existing as well as those proposing to enter into this business, would have to obtain authorisation from:
A. BIFR   B. RBI   C. ICICI   D. SEBI

251. Which of the following Institutions extends maximum term loan to States:
A. NABARD   B. LIC   C. IDBI   D. IFCI

252. The creation of over the counter exchange of India (OTC) would help the introduction of a multi-tiered market for:
A. Exports   B. Securities
C. Small Scale Industries   D. Housing

253. The Stock Holding Corporation of India Ltd. (SHCIL) sponsored by the seven all India Financial Institutions (viz., IDBI, IFCI, ICICI, UTI, LIC, GIC and IRBI) was established in:
A. 1980   B. 1985   C. 1988   D. 1989

254. The Interest Rate Policy is a component of:
A. Fiscal Policy   B. Monetary Policy   C. Trade Policy   D. Direct Control

255. Truncation of cheques means:
A. The cheques in the paper form will be retained by the collecting banker and he will submit only a computerised statement to the Clearing House
B. Entire clearing operations would be done only through computers
C. Cheques will be scanned and the electronic image, instead of physical cheque, will be transmitted in the clearing cycle
D. Debiting the drawer's account through internet banking

256. 'Conversion' means:
   A. converting an order cheque into bearer or vice versa
   B. encashment of a cheque drawn on another branch of the same bank
   C. unlawful taking, using, disposing or destroying of goods which is inconsistent with the owner's right of possession
   D. none of the above

257. Which one of the followings is not correct:
   A. Debenture and Bonds can be issued with redemption in instruments over a period
   B. They can be issued with a premium or redemption
   C. There are no Bonds with put and call option
   D. Bonds secured by stocks or other collateral are called collaterised obligations

258. Which of the followings is relevant regarding issue of Bonds and Debentures:
   A. The holders have prior legal claim over the equity and preference stock holders
   B. The Trustee appointed by issuing company protects the rights of debenture holders
   C. The Trustee can initiate legal action against the company in case of any default
   D. All of the above

259. What is a convertible Bond:
   A. It is a mix of Debt and Equity
   B. Bond holder has an option to convert debt into equity on a fixed date
   C. The conversion price is pre-determined
   D. All of the above

260. What is External Commercial Borrowings:
   A. Indian companies can borrow on global market through Bank loan or issue of debt paper
   B. The debt can be repaid by reconversion of rupee funds into foreign currency
   C. A and B both
   D. None of the above

261. What is Gilts:
   A. Securities issued by government or Treasuries   B. They do not have any credit Risk
   C. A and B both   D. None of the above

262. SGL Account is:
   A. Subsidiary General Ledger
   B. It is maintained by Public Debt Office of RBI
   C. Banks maintain exclusively Government Securities Accounts
   D. All of the above

263. Credit Guarantee Fund Trust for Small Industries has been set up on the recommendations of:
   A. Narasimham Committee   B. Ghosh Committee
   C. Chore Committee   D. Kapoor Committee

264. For which of the following purpose can banks grant Working Capital Term Loan:
   A. Meeting margin for term loan
   B. Meeting margin for working capital loan
   C. Meeting contingent expenses
   D. Meeting credit needs for peak season in an industry

265. In respect of composite term loans granted to village industries, refinance is obtained from:
   A. NABARD   B. SIDBI   C. IDBI   D. RBI

266. J. S. Verma Committee Report relates to:
  A. Strengthening of weak banks
  B. Corporate Governance
  C. Bank Mechanization
  D. None of the above

267. Job rotation of employees is carried out periodically with a view to:
  A. Ensure that each employee gets an opportunity to be acquainted with various spheres of banking
  B. Ensure that knowledge required in a particular desk is not restricted to one employee
  C. Ensure against perpetration of frauds/forgeries
  D. It is a common banking practice

268. Know Your Customers (KYC) guidelines are as per the provisions of:
  A. Section 35 of Negotiable Instruments Act, 1881
  B. Section 35A of Banking Regulation Act, 1949
  C. Section 35A of RBI Act, 1934
  D. IBA guidelines

269. Loan System of Advances has been recommended by:
  A. Rashid Jilani Committee
  B. Narasimham Committee
  C. Goiporia Committee
  D. Tandon Committee

270. Maximum period for which a commercial paper can be issued is:
  A. 3 months
  B. 6 months
  C. 1 year
  D. 2 years

271. One of the following is not correct in regard to Capital Market:
  A. It is a market for long term financial assets
  B. Maturity Period less than one year
  C. Dealings take place at Stock Exchange
  D. Unlimited number of players
  E. Regulated by SEBI

272. Out of the "non-customer facing activities" given below, which of the following has been moved out of the branch to the maximum extent:
  A. Issue of demand drafts
  B. Processing of loans
  C. Clearing of cheques
  D. Opening of Savings Bank Accounts

273. RBI had introduced Advanced Approaches for Basel II Framework in India. Accordingly, the three Approaches are:
  A. Standardized Approach
  B. Basic Indicator Approach
  C. Standardized Duration Approach
  D. All of the above

274. The approaches suggested by Basel Committee for purpose of computing Credit Risk under Basel-II are:
  A. Advance Standard Approach, Internal Rating-Based Foundation Approach and Internal Risk-Based Advance Approach
  B. Standard Approach, Internal Rating-Based Foundation Approach, and Internal Rating-Based Advance Approach
  C. Basic Indicator Approach, Internal Rating-Based Foundation Approach, and Internal Risk-Based Advance Approach
  D. Standard Approach, Internal Rating-Based Foundation Approach and Internal Risk-Based Advance Approach

275. The duration of Ways & Means Advances (WMAs) is:
  A. 10 working days for Central Government 14 days for State Government
  B. 10 consecutive working days for Central Government and 14 days for State Government
  C. 14 working days for Central Government and 18 days for State Government
  D. 14 consecutive working days for Central Government and 18 days for State Government

276. The term ''Rolling Settlement'' is associated with:
   A. Settlement of overdues of large borrowers through process other than through a Compromise
   B. A Settlement system where the dates are frequently changing
   C. Trading in Stock Exchanges
   D. Money Market operations

277. Under the Corporate Debt Restructuring (CDR) mechanism, loan assets of banks have been categorized. Which one of the following statements is not correct:
   A. Assets belonging to Standard and Sub-Standard category come under Category 1
   B. Assets belonging to Doubtful category come under Category 2
   C. Assets belonging to Doubtful and Loss categories come under Category 2
   D. Out of total Loan Assets, 90 per cent is Standard and Sub-Standard and Doubtful is 10 per cent — this lot comes under Category 1

278. What are ''Z Group Shares'':
   A. These are shares of companies which comply with the Stock Exchange Listing Agreement fully
   B. These are shares of companies which do not comply with the Stock Exchange Listing Agreement fully
   C. A special category of shares reserved for high net worth individuals
   D. None of the above

279. What are the characteristics of Treasury Bills:
   A. These are borrowings by the Central/State Government
   B. These are in the form of Promissory Notes
   C. These are issued at a discount and for a fixed period of time
   D. All of the above

280. What does ''Round Tripping'' in Foreign Direct Investment (FDI) relate to:
   A. Using FDI funds inside the country
   B. Using FDI funds outside the country
   C. Domestic funds used outside the country
   D. None of the above

281. What does Collateral Security mean:
   A. Securities in the form of goods pledged for Cash Credits
   B. Securities given to banks for loans against approved securities
   C. Securities in the form of shares blue chip companies
   D. Security given to banks over and above the primary security

282. When does a person become insolvent:
   A. When he is left with no property of his own
   B. When he is declared an insolvent by the Court
   C. When he is terminated from a job he was holding
   D. When he declares himself to be an insolvent

283. When trading takes place among members of a Stock Exchange as a cartel to create false volumes and rigging the prices of shares, it is known as:
   A. Spot Trading   B. Future Trading   C. Circular Trading   D. Insider Trading

284. When two parties make an arrangement to exchange future cash flows, it is called:
   A. Options   B. Arbitrage   C. Swap   D. Futures

285. Which Act confers on banks their Right of set off:
   A. Banking Regulation Act, 1949
   B. Reserve Bank of India Act, 1934
   C. Negotiable Instruments Act, 1881
   D. Indian Contract Act, 1872

286. Which Committee had recommended the introduction of Electronic Funds Transfer (EFT) System:
A. C. Rangarajan Committee
B. Narasimham Committee
C. Y. V. Reddy Committee
D. K. S. Shere Committee

287. Which Committee was formed to review the system of lending under Consortium Arrangement:
A. Kapoor Committee
B. Khan Committee
C. J. V. Shetty Committee
D. Share Committee

288. Which of the following Acts prohibits stapling of bank/currency notes:
A. Section 35A of RBI Act, 1934
B. Section 35A of BRA Act, 1949
C. Section 35A of N I Act, 1881
D. None of the above

289. Which of the following cannot issue a Commercial Paper:
A. Companies
B. Primary Dealers
C. Commercial Banks
D. All India Financial Institutions

290. Which of the following categories of risks is taken care of by RTGS:
A. Systemic Risk and Credit Risk
B. Legal Risk and Credit Risk
C. Settlement Risk and Systemic Risk
D. Systemic Risk and Legal Risk

291. Which of the following is correct regarding Inter-Bank Liabilities (IBL):
A. IBL of a bank not to exceed 200 per cent of its net worth as on 31st March of the previous year
B. Where a bank is with a CRAR of at least 25 per cent more than minimum CRAR as on 31st March of the previous year, it can have a higher limit of up to 300 per cent of the net worth for IBL
C. IBL limit includes only fund-based IBL within India (including IBLs in foreign currency to banks operating within India)
D. All of the above

292. Which of the following is not an indicator of productivity for a bank branch:
A. Business Per Employee
B. Accounts (both deposits and advances) Per Employee
C. Net Profit Per Employee
D. Neat and clean ambience

293. Which of the following provisions empowers RBI to fix service charges on various payment or settlement services of Banks:
A. Section 12 of PMLA Act
B. Section 18 of Payment and Settlement Act, 2007
C. Section 35A, Banking Regulation Act, 1949
D. Section 22 of RBI Act, 1934

294. Which of the following statements is true regarding a Deferred Payment Guarantee (DPG):
A. It is a type of guarantee where no cash payment is involved
B. It is a type of guarantee which is given for purchase of immovable property
C. It is a type of guarantee where payment would have to be made in installments is guaranteed
D. None of the above

295. Who is a ''Proxy'' in relation to Companies:
A. A person who acts on behalf of another in a Company's meeting
B. A Proxy has no right to speak at a meeting
C. Both A and B
D. None of the above

296. 'Know Your Customer Guidelines' issued by RBI helps in:
A. customer identification while opening accounts   B. adopting anti-money laundering measures
C. identifying suspicious transactions   D. All of these

297. ''Allonge'' is:
A. a piece of paper for making endorsements
B. a piece of paper attached to a negotiable instrument for making available more space for further endorsements
C. both A and B
D. none of the above

298. ''Banking Ombudsman'' means a person:
A. appointed to settle dispute between employees and management
B. to whom customer can approach for redressal of his grievances
C. appointed to recover dues from defaulting borrowers
D. none of the above

299. ''Bid-Ask Price'' is:
A. quotation of the foreign currency
B. rate at which the traders bid for foreign currency
C. rate at which the traders ask for foreign currency
D. none of the above

300. ''Hundi'' is a:
A. Draft   B. Cheque   C. Bill of Exchange   D. Promissory Note

301. ''Islamic Banking'' is a term used for:
A. interest Free deposits, investment   B. covering Banking to Muslims
C. covering Islamic nations   D. none of the above

302. ''Service Area Approach'' was recommended by:
A. Dr. P. D. Ojha Committee   B. A. D. Gorawala
C. R. V. Gupta   D. Dr. Kalia

303. Banking Industry has been declared as public utility service for purpose of:
A. Negotiable Instruments Act, 1881   B. Reserve Bank of India Act, 1934
C. Banking Regulation Act, 1949   D. Industrial Disputes Act

304. Banks would prefer to mobilize deposits under Savings Bank accounts, because:
A. account holders will be motivated to save since savings account offer interest also
B. it is a low cost deposit for the bank and banks can profitably deploy such funds
C. banks want to inculcate the savings habit among the public
D. all of the above

305. Cash drawings under Kisan Credit Cards can be permitted at:
A. designated branches   B. at issuing branches
C. all branches   D. None of these

306. Currency Chest is the property of:
A. State Bank of India   B. Government of India
C. Reserve Bank of India   D. None of these

307. Customer Day in the bank is on and customers are allowed to meet the top officials of the bank on this day in every month:
A. 5th   B. 10th   C. 15th   D. 30th

308. Expand "ROCE":
    A. Return Over Capital Expenditure   B. Return Over Capital Employed
    C. Return On Capital Employed   D. None of the above

309. For a foreigner temporarily residing in India, type of account to be opened is:
    A. Resident Account   B. NRO   C. NRE   D. None of these

310. Generally banks borrow in Call Money Market for:
    A. maintaining Cash Reserve Ratio (CRR)   B. investment with Central Government
    C. credit for infrastructure   D. none of the above

311. Mutual Fund Scheme that operates continuously without any limit entry for subscriptions and redemptions is:
    A. Fixed Income   B. Specific Fund   C. Close Ended   D. Open Ended

312. PAN number is required for all transactions above:
    A. Rs. 25,000   B. Rs. 30,000   C. Rs. 1 lac   D. Rs. 10 lacs

313. Please indicate the change(s) which have been introduced to "Service Area Approach":
    A. no dues certificate from the Service Area branch for lending by non-service area branch need not be obtained hereafter
    B. a borrower's declaration or affidavit may be obtained to the effect that he has not borrowed from any other bank
    C. commercial banks are free to lend in any rural/semi-urban area under their normal schemes
    D. All of the above

314. Records, as per Banking Regulation Act, 1949 means:
    A. Vouchers   B. Account Opening Forms
    C. Ledgers / Registers   D. All of these

315. The components of Tier I capital of a banking company include:
    A. capital reserves representing surplus arising out of sale proceeds of assets
    B. paid-up capital, statutory reserves and other disclosed free reserves, if any
    C. both A and B
    D. none of the above

316. The government has stipulated that quoting Permanent Account Number is mandatory for:
    A. Current Accounts   B. Demat Accounts
    C. Term Deposits   D. Savings Bank

317. The Indicative Time Norm for issue of demand draft has been stipulated at:
    A. 5 minutes   B. 10 minutes   C. 15 minutes   D. 20 minutes

318. With a view to further widening the range of money market instruments and to give investors greater flexibility in the deployment of their short-term surplus funds, Reserve Bank of India permitted banks to issue:
    A. Certificate of Deposit   B. Commercial Paper
    C. 180 Days Treasury Bills   D. All of the above

319. Certificate of Deposit is:
    A. a certificate issued by IDBI about the financial soundness of a company to accept deposits from public
    B. a certificate issued by a bank to income-tax authorities stating that a particular amount was paid as interest to the depositor during the relevant financial year

C. a certificate issued by Reserve Bank of India, stating the amount of deposit held by a bank

D. a negotiable money market instrument and issued in dematerialised form or as a Usance Promissory Note, for funds deposited at a bank or other eligible financial institution for a specified time period

320. Certificates of Deposit may be issued by:

A. Select all-India Financial Institutions that have been permitted by RBI to raise short-term resource within the umbrella limit fixed by RBI

B. Local Area Banks (LABs)

C. Scheduled commercial banks excluding Regional Rural Banks

D. All of the above

321. Which was the first committee recommended for establishment of Special Recovery Tribunals for Books and Financial Institution:

A. Tiwari Committee   B. Ojha Committee

C. Narasimham Committee   D. Rangarajan Committee

322. In which year the Tiwari Committee recommanded for establishment of Special Tribunals for Banks dues recovery:

A. 1981   B. 1987   C. 1991   D. 1995

323. Which of the following committees also recommended the set up of Debt Recovery Tribunals:

A. Committee on Financial Sector Reforms   B. Committee on Customer Service

C. Committee on RRBs   D. None of the above

324. In which year the Recovery of Debts Due to Banks and Financial Institutions Act, was enacted:

A. 1991   B. 1993   C. 1994   D. 1995

325. The material difference between debentures and bonds is:

A. Debentures are governed by relevant provisions of company law

B. Debentures are transferrable on registration

C. Bonds are negotiable instrument governed by law of Contract

D. All of the above

326. The Bond can be:

A. Zero Coupon Bond   B. Deep Discount Bond

C. Floating Rate Bond   D. Any of these

327. Service Tax was introduced in India for the first time in the year:

A. 1990-91   B. 1991-92   C. 1994-95   D. 1996-97

328. As per the guidelines issued by the SEBI the Permanent Account Number (PAN) is a must for which of the following:

A. Demat Accounts   B. All Savings Bank Accounts

C. All Housing Loan Accounts   D. All Current Accounts

329. The first Indian RRB that is sponsored by the Union Bank that has achieved core banking solution is:

A. Kheladi Grameen Bank   B. Riddhi Siddhi Grameen Bank

C. Rewa Siddhi Grameen Bank   D. The Rewa-Dahej Bank

330. The biomonthly survey that the Federal Reserve undertakes to make its monetary policy is commonly called:

A. The Biege Book   B. The Yellow Book   C. The White Book   D. The Binge Book

331. "Account Payee" crossing is a:
  A. Restricted crossing   B. Special crossing
  C. General crossing   D. None of these

332. "Bridge Loan" denotes:
  A. interim finance by a bank pending disbursement of term loan by financial institutions
  B. loan granted to Public Works Department for construction of bridges over big rivers
  C. a product aimed at financing construction companies for construction of bridges
  D. loan granted for building of bridges which has been aided by World Bank

333. "Cost Overrun" means:
  A. Project Cost remains constant   B. Escalation in Project Cost
  C. Reduction in Project Cost   D. None of the above

334. Bad loans in banking terminology are generally known as:
  A. Prime Loans   B. Prime Asset
  C. BPOs   D. NPAs

335. "Refund Banker Scheme" has been launched by:
  A. IBA   B. RBI
  C. SEBI   D. Income Tax Department

336. Bank can issue a duplicate of a lost demand draft at the request of the:
  A. payee   B. holder   C. purchaser   D. either A or C

337. Banker may reduce lending risk by:
  A. ensuring that there will be no default on account of lack of liquidity and lack of willingness to pay on the part of the borrower
  B. ensuring that there will be no problem of liquidity with the borrower
  C. obtaining adequate security
  D. all of the above

338. Banks can raise up to ...... per cent of their total Tier I Capital in the form of perpetual debt.
  A. 50   B. 25   C. 15   D. 10

339. Commercial Paper is a:
  A. Money Market Instrument   B. Capital Market Instrument
  C. Negotiable Instrument   D. None of the above

340. Counter-Guarantee is obtained when:
  A. a Bank Guarantee is issued   B. a Fixed Deposit is issued
  C. a Bond is issued   D. None of the above

341. Currency notes issued by RBI are fully covered by:
  A. Approved assets   B. Gold   C. Foreign exchange   D. All of these

342. Expand BIFR:
  A. Board for Industrial and Financial Reconstruction
  B. Bureau for Industrial and Financial Reconstruction
  C. Board for Investment and Financial Reconstruction
  D. Bureau for Investment and Financial Reconstruction

343. Funds locked up in domestic Credit Sales can be traded and are called:
  A. Hire Purchasing   B. Forfaiting   C. Factoring   D. Leasing

344. Government of India has granted greater flexibility to RBI in setting Cash Reserve Ratio (CRR) after passing the ...... Amendment Bill:
  A. RBI
  B. Banking Regulation Act, 1949
  C. Finance
  D. None of the above

345. If neither the word "Bearer" nor "Order" is written on a cheque, payment will be made by treating it as:
  A. a Bearer cheque
  B. an Order cheque
  C. at bank's discretion
  D. cannot be paid at all

346. Import documents received under Letter of Credit established by the bank have been received from the negotiating bank. The cash credit account has been debited. The document which needs to be obtained from the customer before delivery of the important documents is:
  A. Trust Receipt
  B. Hypothecation letters
  C. No letter obtained; delivered as it is
  D. None of the above

347. In case of Life Insurance policies for whole-life, the insured amount is payable:
  A. after a specified period
  B. on the death of the policy-holder
  C. on demand by the policy- holder
  D. upon maturity of the policy or death of the policy-holder whichever happens earlier

348. Interest rates charged by banks are not subject to scrutiny by Courts on the ground of being excessive. It is provided for under Section ...... of Banking Regulation Act, 1949.
  A. 21
  B. 22
  C. 23
  D. 24

349. Lending under Call Money Funds are made with a maturity period of:
  A. one day
  B. one day to seven days
  C. one day to a fortnight
  D. one month

350. Which of the following terms is NOT used in the world of finance, banking and insurance:
  A. Devlauation
  B. Amnesty
  C. Hard currency
  D. Preference share

351. Mortgage has been defined under:
  A. Section 57 of Transfer of Property Act
  B. Section 58 of Transfer of Property Act
  C. Section 57 of Sale of Goods Act
  D. Section 58 of Sale of Goods Act

352. Net Interest Income means:
  A. Interest generated from bank's assets less interest paid on liabilities
  B. Interest earned on advances
  C. Miscellaneous Income
  D. None of these

353. RBI can inspect branches of banks as per the powers vested in it under:
  A. Section 35 of RBI Act
  B. Section 35 of BR Act
  C. SEBI
  D. None of these

354. Reverse Repo means:
  A. rate RBI charges on funds lent to banks
  B. rate offered to Blue chip companies
  C. a rate equal to Bank rate
  D. None of the above

355. Safe Custody Account in the name of minor can be opened only in respect of:
  A. Government Securities
  B. Company shares
  C. A Fixed Deposit Receipt
  D. All of the above

356. SEBI guidelines have prescribed that giving Permanent Account Number (PAN) is a must for:
A. All Current A/c
B. All Housing Loan A/c
C. All Savings Bank A/c
D. All Demat A/c

357. SHCIL deals in:
A. Scripts – Maintained in electronic form
B. Electronic Funds transfer
C. Risk Operations
D. Treasury Bills

358. The apex body for providing policy directions in the area of payment and settlement systems like RTGS, NEFT, ECS is:
A. Board for Regulation and Supervision of Payment and Settlement System (BPSS)
B. Banking Codes and Standards Board of India (BCSBI)
C. Securities and Exchange Board of India (SEBI)
D. Consumer Protection Act (COPRA), 1986

359. Against the currency issued by the Reserve Bank of India, it has to maintain certain assets as prescribed in the Reserve Bank of India Act, 1934. Which of the following is not an eligible asset in this regard:
A. Gold
B. Foreign Exchange Reserves
C. Government Securities
D. Shares and Debentures of Joint Stock Companies

360. Scheduled Commercial banks maintain an account with every office of the Reserve Bank of India primarily with a view to:
A. conforming to the requirements of the Reserve Bank of India Act, 1934
B. conducting business on Government Account
C. facilitating borrowings from the Reserve Bank of India
D. facilitating inter-bank clearing and transfer of funds from one centre to another

361. While taking book debts as a security against banker's advances, an appropriate form of charge is:
A. mortgage
B. pledge
C. hypothecation
D. assignment

362. In line with the international practices and as per the recommendations made by the Committee on the Financial System (Chairman Shri M. Narashimham), the Reserve Bank of India has introduced, in a phased manner, prudential norms for income recognition, asset classification and provisioning for the advances portfolio of the banks:
A. with a view to clean-up the balance sheets of banks
B. so as to move towards greater consistency and transparency in the published accounts
C. with a view to enhancing the profitability of banks
D. so that weak banks may be merged or amalgamated with strong banks

363. An asset, including a leased asset, becomes non-performing when:
A. it ceases to generate income for the bank
B. a Performance Guarantee issued by the bank on behalf of the borrower is invoked
C. it is rendered useless due to wear and tear or its becoming obsolete
D. the borrower dies

364. An account should be treated as 'out of order' if:
A. the outstanding balance remains continuously in excess of the sanctioned limit/drawing power
B. there are no credits continuously for 90 days as on the date of Balance Sheet even though the outstanding balance in the account is less than the sanctioned limit/drawing power

C. credits are not enough to cover the interest debited during the same period

D. all of the above

365. Any amount due to the bank under any credit facility is termed as 'overdue' if it is not:

A. paid on the due date fixed by the bank B. paid within 30 days from the due date

C. paid within 45 days from the due date D. paid with 24 hours from the due date

366. A Non-performing Asset (NPA) has been defined as a credit facility, in respect of which interest has remained unpaid for a period of:

A. four quarters B. three quarters C. three years D. three months

367. As per the directives issued by RBI, a cash credit or overdraft account will be treated as Non-performing Asset if:

A. the account remains 'out of order'

B. there are no credits in the account in the month in which interest is applied

C. the debit balance in the account has exceeded the sanctioned limit during the reporting month

D. any of the above

368. A loan granted for short duration crops would be treated as NPA, if the instalment of principal or interest thereon remains overdue for:

A. two crop seasons B. two quarters C. two half-years D. whichever is less

369. The capital adequacy norms in Banks were introduced in:

A. April 1991 B. March 1992 C. April 1992 D. July 1992

370. Capital adequacy ratio is the ratio of:

A. Capital as compared to Total Deposits

B. Capital as compared to Total Advances

C. Capital as compared to Total Assets

D. Capital as compared to Risk Adjusted Assets

371. Which of the following is correct regarding Capital Adequacy ratio:

A. The objective of Capital Adequacy is to strengthen the financial stability of banks

B. Capital is divided into two tiers, tier-I and tier-II

C. Assets are assigned risk weight from 0-100 based on intensity of risk

D. All of the above

372. The concept of Capital Adequacy in banks was introduced by:

A. Narasimham Committee B. Basle Committee

C. Reserve Bank of India D. Ministry of Finance

373. Which of the following is accounted for Tier-I Capital of a Bank:

A. Paid up Capital

B. Statutory Reserve

C. Disclosed Free Reserves and Capital Reserves arising out of Sale of Assets

D. All of the above

374. Which of the following is accounted for Tier-II Capital of a Bank:

A. Undisclosed Reserves

B. Revaluation Reserve and general provisions

C. Hybrid debt capital instrument and subordinated debt

D. All of the above

375. Which of the following ratios of Capital Adequacy ratio is prescribed for Indian Banks which have branches abroad:

A. 9 per cent B. 10 per cent C. 8 per cent D. 15 per cent

376. The 'CAMELS' Rating for Banks was recommended by:

A. Narasimham Committee B. Padmanabhan Committee
C. Nayak Committee D. Rangrajan Committee

377. What is the concept of 'CAMELS' Rating:

A. It deals with supervision of Banks by RBI
B. It is a method of performance evaluation of Banks
C. It is the process of internal audit
D. All of the above

378. Which of the following is not included in 'CAMELS':

A. Capital Adequacy and Asset Quality B. Management and Earning Performance
C. Employees Performance D. Liquidity and Systems

379. The RBI issued the following guidelines for effective Asset Liability Management System:

A. Banks should set up an internal Asset Liability Committee
B. The Committee should be headed by CMD or ED
C. The Management Committee of the Board should oversee implementation of the system
D. All of the above

380. The major responsibilities of Asset Liability Committee are:

A. Product pricing for deposits and advances
B. The level of maturity profile and mix of the incremental assets and liabilities
C. The Committee should also review the results and progress of implementation
D. All of the above

381. Which of the following is not a responsibility of Asset Liability Committee:

A. Fixing responsibility for CMD
B. To decide on source and mix of liabilities or sale of Asset
C. To decide on funding mix between fixed vs floating rate funds
D. The Committee would also decide about various sources of funding

382. Which of the Bank's department are not necessary to include in Asset Liability Committee:

A. Credit Resources Management B. Premises and Estate
C. Funds Management/Treasury D. Economic Research Division

383. SEBI is a:

A. Statutory body B. Advisory body
C. Constitutional body D. Non-statutory body

384. What is 'NIKKEI':

A. Share Price Index of Tokyo share market
B. Name of Japanese Central Bank
C. Japanese name of the country's Planning Commission
D. Foreign Exchange Market of Japan

385. NABARD was established on the recommendation of:

A. Public Accounts Committee B. Shivaraman Committee
C. Narasimham Committee D. Khandelwal Committee

386. What do we mean by Green Shoe Option:
   A. It is the shoe which is green in colour
   B. It is type of carbon credit rights that the nation have to purchase to get the right to emit carbon
   C. It gives the underwriter the right to sell investors more shares than originally planned
   D. The global warming of the earth

387. ''Micro Credits'' are loans:
   A. granted to distressed persons (other than farmers) to pre-pay their debt to non-institutional lenders against appropriate collateral or group security
   B. not exceeding ₹ 50,000 per borrower provided by banks
   C. both A and B
   D. none of the above

388. Rural Infrastructure Development Fund (RIDF) is financed by:
   A. Selected group of Public Sector Banks   B. Ministry of Rural Development
   C. Reserve Bank of India   D. NABARD

389. The term ''Credit Management'' covers:
   A. pre-sanction, appraisal, sanction, documentation, disbursement and post lending supervision and control
   B. management of all short term, medium and long term loans and on balance sheet transactions
   C. management of the credit portfolio (advances) of banks and financial institutions
   D. all of the above

390. ''Ways and Means'' advances are provided by Reserve Bank of India only to:
   A. Central Government   B. State Government
   C. Both A and B   D. None of the above

391. Debit Card serves the purpose of carrying:
   A. cash   B. cheque book   C. both A and B   D. none of these

392. Which of the following has become the first Regional Rural Bank issuing debit card in the country?
   A. Punjab Gramin Bank   B. Nanital/Almora Bank
   C. Kashi Gomti Sanyukta Gramin Bank   D. Baroda RRB

393. Which of the following Acts govern a Bank Guarantee?
   A. Negotiable Instruments Act, 1881   B. Indian Contract Act, 1872
   C. Sale of Goods Act, 1930   D. Indian Companies Act, 1956

394. Which of the following types of ATMs eliminates the need for PIN entry and authenticated customer transactions by thumb impressions:
   A. White Label ATMs   B. Biometric ATMs
   C. On-site ATMs   D. Off-site ATMs

395. Number of nationalised banks in India are:
   A. 14   B. 20   C. 25   D. 28

396. In which year six more commercial banks (in addition to the first lot of 14) were nationalised in India:
   A. 1976   B. 1979   C. 1980   D. 1982

397. Who was the Finance Minister when 14 Banks were nationalised on 19th July, 1969:
   A. Mrs. Indira Gandhi   B. Morarji Desai
   C. C. Subramaniam   D. Pranab Mukherjee

398. Which agency is exclusively concerned with the credit needs of all types of agricultural and rural development:
A. State Bank of India
B. Industrial Development Bank of India
C. Reserve Bank of India
D. NABARD

399. What is the name of technology given to the recently introduced computerised clearance of cheques:
A. Automatic clearance
B. MICR
C. Speedline System
D. Special clearning

400. Against Warehouse Receipts (W.H.Rs.) bank grants credit facility by way of:
A. cash credit account
B. demand loan account
C. both A and B
D. None of these

401. The term ''Multi-agency approach to rural lending'' means:
A. provision of funds for rural development by the NABARD through various lending agencies spread over the rural areas
B. provision of rural credit by commercial banks, regional rural banks and cooperative credit institutions
C. provision of finance for rural development by various central and state government agencies
D. the whole structure of rural finance-institutional as well as non-institutional

402. Who among the following is the chairman of the Group constituted by the RBI to examine major issues relating to restructuring of Regional Rural Banks:
A. M. C. Bhandari
B. N. K. Thingalaya
C. Y. S. P. Thorat
D. Sudhir Srivastava

403. NABARD is a:
A. Board
B. Bureau
C. Bank
D. Department

404. Loan against commodities:
A. are not allowed by banks except with the prior approval of RBI
B. are not popular in India
C. have been one of the earliest forms of bank advances
D. are allowed only to approved parties

405. Counter guarantee means a guarantee obtained:
A. by banks from customers on whose behalf the banks have to issue guarantees in favour of third parties, such as Government department, Public bodies, Corporations etc.
B. by banks from ECGC covering export risk
C. by banks from the beneficiary of the guarantee in whose favour the guarantee is to be issued
D. All of the above

406. PKIX means:
A. Public Key Infrastructure Extension
B. Public Key Infrastructure X. 509
C. Public Key Information Exercise
D. Public Key Infrastructure Exclusive

407. CPS is:
A. Certificate Practice Software
B. Certificate Practice System
C. Certificate Practice Statement
D. Certificate Public Structure

408. CRL is:
A. Certificate Retention List
B. Certificate Revocation List
C. Certificate Reduction List
D. None of the above

409. By ''Technical NPA'', it means:
  A. a loan account becoming NPA for non-renewal
  B. a loan account becoming NPA for not obtaining stock statements
  C. non-recording the due date after re-phasing/restructuring of a loan account
  D. All of the above

410. Cash Reserve Ratio (CRR) is maintained in the form of:
  A. Investment in Money Market   B. Government Securities
  C. Balance with RBI   D. All of the above

411. Computer system failure is classified in the risk category of:
  A. Credit Risk   B. Operational Risk   C. Technology Risk   D. Security Risk

412. CRA is applicable in:
  A. C&I, SSI and Agriculture Segments
  B. C&I, SSI, Agriculture, Trade & Services Sectors
  C. C&I, SSI and SBF Segments
  D. None of the above

413. Credit facility sanctioned for purchasing, processing and packing of goods meant for export is
known as:
  A. packing credit   B. bridge finance   C. forfaiting   D. none of these

414. Cyber Law is:
  A. that cipher is the starting point in arithmetic   B. law relating to electronic media
  C. testing of atomic weapons   D. law relating to space

415. Foreign citizen of Indian origin is:
  A. Person of Indian Origin (PIO)   B. Non Resident Indian (NRI)
  C. Ordinary Non Resident   D. Foreign National

416. How is Base Rate calculated:
  A. a host of factors, like cost of deposits, administrative costs, profitability of a bank in the previous
     financial year are taken into account
  B. certain parameters with stipulated weights are considered while calculating a lender's Base Rate
  C. cost of deposit has the highest weight in calculating Base Rate
  D. all of the above

417. The bank conducts Government business as an agent of:
  A. Union and State Governments   B. Reserve Bank of India
  C. State Bank of India   D. Both A and B

418. Out of the following who is not a customer of the bank:
  A. term-deposit account holder
  B. ''Cash Credit on hypothecation'' account holder
  C. outstation party from whom the bank has received a bill of exchange for collection
  D. local party from whom the bank has received a bill of exchange for collection

419. Which of the following statement is correct:
  A. a draft can be cancelled only by the drawee branch
  B. a draft can be cancelled only by the issuing branch
  C. a draft can be cancelled only if both the issuing branch and the drawee branch agree to do so
  D. a draft can be cancelled only after obtaining permission from the controlling authority

420. The statutory definition of the term "banking" is given in:
- A. The Negotiable Instruments Act, 1881
- B. The Reserve Bank of India Act, 1934
- C. The Companies Act, 1956
- D. The Banking Regulation Act, 1949

421. The term "Licensed banks" means:
- A. Banks licensed to deal in foreign exchange business under the Foreign Exchange Regulation Act, 1973
- B. Banks licensed to participate in the "Clearing house"
- C. Foreign banks which are licensed to establish branch officers in India
- D. Banks licensed by the Reserve Bank of India under Section 22 of the Banking Regulation Act, 1949 for carrying on or commencing banking business in India

422. When was the first commercial bank in India named 'Hindustan Bank' set up in Calcutta (now Kolkata):
- A. 1690
- B. 1770
- C. 1805
- D. 1890

423. Modern commecial banking in India begins with the setting up of the first Presidency Bank, The Bank of Bengal in ...... in Calcutta (now Kolkata):
- A. 1790
- B. 1806
- C. 1825
- D. 1910

424. Regional Rural Banks were established in the year:
- A. 1968
- B. 1970
- C. 1975
- D. 1977

425. A commercial bank is prohibited from issuing a bank draft payable to bearer by the provisions contained in:
- A. The Negotiable Instruments Act, 1881
- B. The Reserve Bank of India Act, 1934
- C. The Companies Act, 1956
- D. The Banking Regulation Act, 1949

426. Which of the following is a form of "Small Savings Bank" popular among the poor or children:
- A. Core Banking
- B. Credit Banking
- C. Debit Card
- D. Piggy Banking

427. Which of the following terms is not used in the world of economics/finance:
- A. Sinking Fund
- B. Third World
- C. Open Door Policy
- D. Devaluation

428. Which of the following organisations/agencies controls the monetary policy of our country:
- A. SEBI
- B. Planning Commission
- C. RBI
- D. Union Ministry of Finance

429. Which of the following is the name of the organization created specifically to develop small scale industrial sector in our country:
- A. NABARD
- B. SEBI
- C. SIDBI
- D. AMFI

430. Which of the following organisation/agencies is specifically set up to boost overall rural development in India:
- A. RBI
- B. SIDBI
- C. NABARD
- D. SEBI

431. Who is to certify that any bill is a Money Bill:
- A. Finance Minister
- B. Speaker of Lok Sabha
- C. Prime Minister
- D. None of the above

432. The RBI has asked the banks to step up legal action against wilful defaulters whose default money is over:
- A. one crore
- B. two crore
- C. three crore
- D. five crore

433. The credit-deposit (CD) ratio of ...... is highest in the banking sector.
- A. Foreign Banks
- B. Regional Rural Bank
- C. Public Sector Bank
- D. Private Sector Banks

434. Banks are not allowed to accept any fresh deposits or open any fresh account by way of renewal or otherwise under the two schemes — Non-Resident Non-Repatriable (NRNR) and Non-Resident Special Rupee (NRSR) with effect from:
A. January 1, 2002   B. April 1, 2002   C. January 1, 2003   D. April 1, 2003

435. The methods of credit control by the Reserve Bank of India may be broadly divided into two parts. These are:
A. open and close   B. quantitative and qualitative
C. monetary and fiscal   D. rural and urban

436. Committee on decontrolling the prices of petrol and diesel was headed by:
A. Kelkar Vijai   B. C. Rangrajan   C. Abhijit Sen   D. Kirit S. Parekh

437. What is the minimum number of directors in a public limited company:
A. 2   B. 3   C. 5   D. 7

438. Kisan Credit Cards (KCC) Scheme was formulated in the year:
A. 1996   B. 1997   C. 1998   D. 1999

439. Borrowings by scheduled commercial banks in the call/notice money market, on a daily basis should not exceed ...... of their owned funds or 2.0 per cent of aggregate deposits as at the end of March of the previous financial year, whichever is higher.
A. 25 per cent   B. 50 per cent   C. 75 per cent   D. 100 per cent

440. 'Pure Banking, Nothing Else' is a slogan raised by:
A. ICICI Bank   B. HDFC Bank   C. SBI   D. UTI Bank

441. 'Smart Money' is a term used for:
A. Internet Banking   B. Cash with Public   C. Cash with Bank   D. Credit Card

442. The government has allowed issue of Long-Term Bonds for Insurance Companies and others upto:
A. 10 years   B. 15 years   C. 25 years   D. 30 years

443. In the case of advance against fixed deposit receipts issued by banks:
A. the deposit receipts are assigned to the bank
B. the deposit receipts are hypothecated to the bank
C. the deposit receipts are mortgaged to the bank
D. a lien is created in favour of the bank on the deposit receipts

444. Negative lien is:
A. a right of the bank to take possession of all the assets hypothecated to the bank in the case of default by the borrower
B. a special type of lien on the shares of public limited companies
C. a declaration of the borrower to the effect that his assets are free from encumbrance and that he shall not encumber or dispose them of without bank's permission
D. none of the above

445. Discount on issue of shares is a:
A. revenue loss   B. capital loss
C. deferred revenue expenditure   D. revenue and capital loss both

446. Which of the following Committee recommanded a separate Act, for Securitisation and Reconstruction of Financial Assets and Enforcement of Security Interest Act:
A. Rangarajan Committee   B. T. R. Andhyarajuna Committee
C. Narashimham Committee   D. Nayak Committee

447. The essential features of securitisation are:
   A. Acquisition of Financial Assets by a Securitisation or Reconstruction Company
   B. The Assets may be NPA or standard
   C. On sale the Assets go out of the Books of the Originator
   D. All of the above

448. What are the Rights available to a secured creditor:
   A. To sell the Assets
   B. File application with DRT for recovery of full or remaining dues
   C. To proceed against the guarantor
   D. All of the above

449. The significance of index linked bonds is:
   A. It provides protection against inflation rate rise
   B. It is inbuilt in the process
   C. Both A and B
   D. None of the above

450. Why the corporates prefer to issue debt paper than to Bank credit:
   A. The cost of debt paper is much lower
   B. The procedure is easy
   C. Both A and B
   D. None of the above

451. A Bank may prefer to invest in corporate Bonds because:
   A. Bond is more liquid Asset
   B. Bond has an easy exit
   C. Bond can be sold at discount
   D. All of the above

452. Which of the following is not credit substitute:
   A. Commercial Paper
   B. Mortgage Loan
   C. Corporate Bond
   D. Certificate of Deposit

453. The difference between a Bond and Loan is:
   A. The loan has normally fixed rate of interest. Bond price is dependent on market interest rate movements
   B. Bonds are more liquid
   C. Yield to maturity value can be known easily in a bond
   D. All of the above

454. What is securitisation:
   A. A process which converts conventional credit into tradable Treasure Assets
   B. Credit receivable of the Bank can be converted into Bonds i.e., pass through certificates
   C. These certificates can be traded in the market
   D. All of the above

455. The advantages of securitisation for a Bank is:
   A. It provides liquidity to the issuing Bank
   B. The Bank capital does not get blocked
   C. Securitisation proceeds can be used for fresh lending
   D. All of the above

456. Which of the following is true:
   A. Surplus funds with the banks can be invested in pass through certificates
   B. This will be indirect expansion of credit portfolio
   C. Both A and B
   D. None of the above

457. The process of credit Derivative involves:
- A. The Protection Seller guarantees payment of principal and interest or both of the Asset owned by the Protection Buyer in case of credit default
- B. The Protection Buyer pays a premium to the Protection Seller
- C. Both A and B
- D. None of the above

458. Which one of the following statements is incorrect:
- A. Advances against gold ornaments are exempt from NPA norms
- B. Classification of NPA should be done borrower wise and not facility wise
- C. An NPA need not go through the various stages of classification
- D. The existance of security should be ignored if the value is less than 10 per cent of the outstanding in the borrowal account

459. Which one of the following statements is 'false':
- A. The provision on standard assets can be included as Tier-II Capital
- B. Statutory reserves kept by foreign banks in India are eligible for inclusion under Tier-I Capital
- C. Nationalised banks can raise 51 per cent of their capital funds from the public
- D. For foreign banks in India, foreign currency loans granted to Indian parties are not eligible for inclusion in capital funds

460. Specially Developed Economic Zones (SEZs) in India where some of the economic laws and restrictions of the land are relaxed with the purpose of giving incentives to investors are commonly known as:
- A. Preferential Zones
- B. Economic Corridors
- C. Industrial Parks
- D. Special Economic Zones

461. Advanced payment of tax is in the nature of:
- A. Asset
- B. Liability
- C. Prepaid Expenses
- D. Revenue Expenses

462. CSO has changed its base year for National Income estimation. The new base year is:
- A. 1990-91
- B. 2011-12
- C. 1994-95
- D. 1995-96

463. First share market in India was established in:
- A. Delhi
- B. Kolkata
- C. Mumbai
- D. Chennai

464. Matching the following:

List-I	List-II
1. Indian Contract Act	(a) 1872
2. Companies Act	(b) 1956
3. Banking Regulation Act	(c) 1949
4. Indian Partnership Act	(d) 1932
	(e) 1930

Codes :

	1	2	3	4
A.	(b)	(d)	(a)	(c)
B.	(a)	(c)	(b)	(d)
C.	(c)	(a)	(b)	(d)
D.	(a)	(d)	(c)	(b)

465. In India, bank is regulated by:
   A. Indian Contract Act, 1872
   C. Indian Companies Act, 1956
   B. Banking Regulation Act, 1949
   D. None of these

466. In SWOT analysis, 'S' stands for:
   A. Strengths   B. Strategies   C. Smart card   D. None of these

467. EOQ stands for:
   A. Evaluation-on-Quantity
   C. Economic Order Quantity
   B. Even-on-Quality
   D. Economic-on-Quality

468. 'MRO' means:
   A. Money Rate Over
   C. More Rate Over
   B. Maintenance Repair and Operating
   D. None of these

469. Example of the product line of a Bank is:
   A. Car loan   B. Personal loan   C. Home loan   D. Above all

470. Which of the following is the example of product diversification of Bank?
   A. Credit Card
   C. Debit Card
   B. International Credit Card
   D. Above all

471. VAT stands for:
   A. Value Added Tax
   C. Volume And Tax
   B. Value After Tax
   D. None of these

472. BPO stands for:
   A. Budget Product Online
   C. Business Process Outsourcing
   B. Balance of Payment
   D. None of these

473. Personal Banking includes:
   A. Deposits   B. Insurance   C. Investment   D. Above all

474. Micro Finance is related to:
   A. Poor class   B. Rich class   C. Industry   D. None of these

475. Which of the following is the example of the brand of SBI?
   A. SBI Mutual Fund
   C. Car Loan
   B. Saving and Current Deposits
   D. Home Loan

476. DSA stands for:
   A. Division Sales Act
   C. Direct Sales Association
   B. Direct Selling Agent
   D. None of these

477. The product of HDFC Bank includes:
   A. Credit Card   B. Personal Loan   C. Life Insurance   D. Above all

478. Internet marketing involves:
   A. Online marketing   B. e-marketing   C. Both A and B   D. None of these

479. MOS means:
   A. Marginal Operation System
   C. Margin on sale
   B. Margin of Safety
   D. None of these

480. Who is Prospect Customers?
   A. Potential Customer   B. Present Customer   C. Staff   D. None of these

481. Consumer loan taken by a customer on any consumer item, it is a contract of:
   A. Hire Purchase Agreement
   B. Contract of Sale
   C. Capital
   D. None of these

482. R & D means:
   A. Rate and Division
   B. Research and Development
   C. Research and Department
   D. None of these

483. Full form of PAN is:
   A. Product Account Number
   B. Permanent Account Number
   C. Payment Account Number
   D. Above all

484. PLR stands for:
   A. Product Low Rate
   B. Prime Lending Rate
   C. Permanent Lock Number
   D. None of these

485. Which of the following is the Private Bank?
   A. SBI   B. PNB   C. HDFC   D. Above all

486. Central bank of India is:
   A. SBI
   B. Reserve Bank of India
   C. UTI
   D. None of these

487. The Reserve Bank of India was established in:
   A. 1940   B. 1935   C. 1945   D. None of these

488. In Stock Market:
   A. Stock are kept
   B. Share are purchased and sold
   C. Capital is disposed
   D. Above all

489. In Bullion Market:
   A. Golds are purchased and sold
   B. Books are purchased and sold
   C. Animals are purchased and sold
   D. None of these

490. Non Banking assets include:
   A. Property seized by the bank
   B. Auction sale of the customer's property
   C. Band Building
   D. Both A and B

491. Which of the following is the largest commercial bank in India?
   A. SBI   B. PNB   C. ICICI Bank   D. Above all

492. Micro credit started from:
   A. USA   B. India   C. Bangladesh   D. Japan

493. .... can be done through digital Banking:
   A. Mobile Phone   B. Internet   C. Telephone   D. Above all

494. The International Bank for Reconstruction and Development (IBRD) is better known as:
   A. World Bank
   B. IMF
   C. ADB
   D. It is known by its name

495. The Bank of Calcutta, Bank of Bombay and Bank of Madras were merged in 1921 to form:
   A. Imperial Bank of India
   B. Reserve Bank of India
   C. Bank of India
   D. Union Bank of India

496. Which of the following is known as plastic money?
   A. Credit Cards   B. Bearer Cheque   C. Demand Drafts   D. Above all

497. Production and consumption takes place at about the same time. This is a characteristic of:
A. Manufacturing sector
B. Agriculture sector
C. Service sector
D. None of these

498. The tertiary sector of economy is called as:
A. Manufacturing Industry
B. Service Industry
C. Agro and Fishing Industry
D. None of these

499. FDR is:
A. Fix Date Rate
B. Fixed Deposit Receipt
C. Full Date Rate
D. None of these

500. NBA stands for:
A. Net Banking Assets
B. Net Book Act
C. National Banking Act
D. National Banking Association

501. Which among the following terms describe the 'universal banking'?
A. Branches of Bank in all major form of the world
B. A bank providing services in all geographical territories of its country
C. A bank providing combination of commercial banking and investment banking
D. None of these

502. Which among the following is called life blood of Business?
A. Marketing
B. Product
C. Finance
D. None of these

503. In the financial market, which among the following has provided the investors profitable and safe debt capital?
A. Globalisation
B. Credit Rating
C. Financial Sector Reform
D. None of these

504. Among which of the following is related to Bank Risks?
A. Deposits
B. Bank Funds
C. NPA
D. None of these

505. Opening of maximum number of ATMs is an example of:
A. Indirect Marketing
B. Direct Marketing
C. Social Marketing
D. None of these

506. Which among the following are called final accounts of a Bank?
A. Trading Account, Profit and Loss Account and Balance Sheet
B. Profit and Loss Account and Balance Sheet
C. Balance Sheet Only
D. None of these

507. Loan and Advances of a bank come under which of the following category?
A. Assets
B. Liabilities
C. Costs
D. None of these

508. What is the full form of ECB?
A. Extra Commercial Banking
B. Extra Commercial Borrowings
C. External Commercial Borrowings
D. None of these

509. Which among the following is correct regarding call option and put option in currency markets?
A. Call option is for sellers and put option is for buyers
B. Call option is for buyers and put option is for sellers
C. Both A and B
D. None of these

510. All the foreign exchange of the country ultimately goes to which of the following?
A. Ministry of Finance
B. Reserve Bank of India
C. Finance Secretarial
D. None of these

511. In the Banking Environment, which among the following is the internal factor?
A. Customer   B. Staff   C. Market   D. None of these

512. The following does not represent a market situation:
A. A bank run dispensary located in its staff quarters
B. A fund raising charity show for the members of an NGO
C. A meditation camp of a religious organization conducted for its members
D. A stall distributing Kada Prasad in a Gurudwara:

513. The following offering is not a service:
A. Fixed Deposit Receipt
B. Postage Stamp
C. Gift coupon of a chain share
D. Insurance policy

514. A bank has a special product for senior citizens which provides cheque book on saving account with customer name on cheque book, free of cost debit card with overdraft facility of Rs. 15,000, a special punch for holding pass book, cheque book and debit card facility for withdrawal and deposits at any branch of the bank, free of cost remittances to any branch of the bank, and free of cost remittance to any branch of another bank covered under RTGS facility.
Which of the following is the core product in this of offering?
A. Overdraft
B. Remittances
C. Saving Account
D. None of these

515. In 'Double-win' strategy:
A. Customer gets an additional benefit
B. Customer gets price debate
C. Both customers and the sales person come out with sense of satisfaction
D. Both A and B

516. A lead means:
A. Target Customer
B. Bank's Chairman
C. A religious Leader
D. A bank's Marketing Staff

517. ATMs are:
A. Branches of banks
B. Manned counters of banks
C. Unmanned, cash dispensers
D. Above all

518. Home loans are granted to:
A. Individuals   B. Institutions   C. Builders   D. Above all

519. Credit Cards are used for:
A. Cash withdrawals
B. Purchase of air tickets
C. Purchase of consumable items from retail outlets
D. Above all

520. A prospect means:
A. An employee of the bank
B. Any customer who walks into the bank
C. A customer who is likely to be interested in bank's product or service
D. A depositor of the bank

521. A call means:
   A. Calling on friends
   B. Calling on bank employees
   C. Calling on prospective customers
   D. To make telephone calls

522. Financial Inclusion means:
   A. Opening accounts of finance companies
   B. Financial analysis of balance sheet figures
   C. Opening accounts of HNIs
   D. Opening accounts of underprivileged persons

523. Customisation results in:
   A. Customer exodus
   B. Customer retention
   C. Customer complaints
   D. All of these

524. The target group for Education Loans is:
   A. All Parents
   B. All Professors
   C. All Research Scholars
   D. All College Students

525. The target group for car loans is:
   A. Auto manufacturing companies
   B. Car dealers
   C. Taxi drivers
   D. Car purchasers

526. 'Benchmark' means:
   A. Products lined upon a bench
   B. Salesmen sitting on a bench
   C. Set standards
   D. None of these

527. CRM means:
   A. Customer Relationship Management
   B. Customer Retention Manager
   C. Customer's Relatives Meet
   D. Channel Route Market

528. Bancassurance means:
   A. Assurance give by banks of Loanees
   B. Assurance to bank with one bank
   C. Assurance to repay loans
   D. Selling insurance products through banks

529. "HNI" means:
   A. Highly Non-interested Individuals
   B. Highly Needy Individuals
   C. High Networth Individuals
   D. None of these

530. What is the full form of LIC?
   A. Life Insurance Corporation
   B. Life Insurance Commission
   C. Life India Corporation
   D. All of these

531. SME means:
   A. Small And Medium Enterpries
   B. Small Marketing Enterpries
   C. Small Scale Marketing Entifics
   D. All of these

532. 'Out sourcing' means service rendered by:
   A. outside agencies
   B. other departments of the company
   C. employees, other than the sales persons
   D. All of these

533. ''Deemed Export'' denotes:
   A. supplies of goods and services to units within the country that can earn foreign currency to the country
   B. exports made by units situated in EPZ areas to out of country
   C. exports made by EOU out of the country
   D. anticipated value of exports

534. "Once a bearer is always a bearer" means that:
- A. where a cheque is originally expressed to be payable to the bearer, the banker is discharged by payment in due course to the bearer
- B. banker can pay the cheque to the bearer irrespective of any endorsement whether in full or in blank appearing thereon, notwithstanding that any such endorsement purports to restrict or exclude further negotiation
- C. both A and B
- D. None of the above

535. Banking Ombudsman entertains complaints involving:
- A. delay in collection of cheques
- B. deficiency in cash transactions
- C. non-issue of demand drafts
- D. all of the above

536. Banks in India can establish Offshore Banking Units in:
- A. EPZ
- B. SEZ
- C. STP
- D. EHTP

537. Banks stipulate interest rates on loans and advances based on:
- A. borrower's experience
- B. track record
- C. credit rating
- D. None of these

538. Expand "VIRUS" in computer parlance:
- A. Variable Integrated Risks Under Surveillance
- B. Vital Information Resource Under Siege
- C. Very Independent Resource Under Seizure
- D. None of the above

539. Expand "EPZ":
- A. Economical Plus Zone
- B. Entertainment Plus Zone
- C. Export Promotion Zone
- D. Electronic Promotion Zone

540. Expand "SHPI":
- A. State Bank Heritage Private Institute
- B. SBI Handicapped Promotion Institute
- C. Self Help Promotion Institutions
- D. None of the above

541. Expand IASB:
- A. International Accounting Standards Board
- B. Indian Accounting Standards Board
- C. Internal Accounting Standards Bureau
- D. Indian Accounts Standards Board

542. In Foreign Exchange transactions, "Value Date" refers to:
- A. the date of agreement between two parties for exchange of foreign currency
- B. the date of credit of proceeds to Correspondent's account
- C. the date of adjudication of cheque
- D. none of the above

543. INFINET stands for:
- A. Internal Financial Networking
- B. International Financial Networking
- C. Indian Financial Network
- D. Inland Financial Network

544. Which of the following is not the name of a Banking Organisation:
- A. HDFC
- B. IDBI
- C. YES
- D. SEBI

545. Cheap Money means:
- A. Low Rate of Interest
- B. Low Level of Savings
- C. Low Level of Income
- D. Excess of Black Money

546. Consequent upon the recommendations of the Working Group on Rural Banks, 5 Rural Regional Banks were initially set up in the year:

A. 1973   B. 1974   C. 1975   D. 1976

547. E.P.S. in share market stands for:

A. Earnings per share   B. Electronic Payment System
C. Employee Pension Scroll   D. Equated Payment System

548. The currency, Euro, has been introduced w.e.f.:

A. 01.01.1999   B. 01.01.2000   C. 01.08.2001   D. 01.03.2002

549. Who is authorised to issue coins in India:

A. RBI   B. Ministry of Finance
C. SBI   D. None of these

550. The full form of RBS is:

A. Risk Based Supervision   B. Rating by System
C. Role Based Supervision   D. Rating Bank Security

551. State Bank of India has ...... circles:

A. 9   B. 12   C. 14   D. 16

552. A saving Bank Deposit Account is one where:

A. Amounts are deposited and are withdrawan as per requirement of the customers
B. The deposits are made only once in a year
C. Periodical Fixed amount are deposited month wise and withdrawals are allowed after a fixed period
D. All of the above

553. Under hire-purchase system, the asset can be got insured by:

A. Buyer   B. Seller   C. Both A and B   D. None of these

554. Under the Hire-purchase System, the buyer becomes the owner of goods:

A. immediately after the delivery of goods
B. immediately after the down payment
C. immediately after the signing of the agreement
D. immediately after the payment of the last instalment

555. What is DBMS:

A. Database Management System   B. Database Marketing System
C. Data Bank Management Software   D. None of these

556. Which of the following is the body/agency set up by Government of India to increase the flow of foreign investment in the country:

A. FEMA   B. FCCB   C. NSDL   D. FIPB

557. National Income of India is estimated by:

A. Central Estimates Survey Committee   B. National Sample Survey Committee
C. Central Statistical Organization   D. Finance Ministry

558. Net Interest Income means:

A. Interest generated from bank's assets less interest paid on liabilities
B. Interest earned on advances
C. Miscellaneous Income
D. None of these

559. Pannir Selvam Committee Report relates to:
   A. Customer service   B. Exposure Norms   C. Frauds   D. NPAs

560. Perpetual Non-Cumulative Preference Shares are part of:
   A. Tier-I Capital   B. Tier-II Capital   C. Both A and B   D. None of these

561. RBI absorbs liquidity in the system through:
   A. Repo   B. Reverse Repo   C. Both A and B   D. None of these

562. Regional Rural Banks (RRBs) are managed by:
   A. NABARD   B. Reserve Bank of India
   C. Sponsoring Bank   D. Board of respective RRBs

563. Reverse Repo means:
   A. rate RBI charges on funds lent to banks   B. rate offered to Blue chip companies
   C. a rate equal to Bank rate   D. None of the above

564. The definition of ''Customer'' is available under:
   A. Negotiable Instruments Act, 1881   B. Consumer Protection Act, 1986
   C. Banking Regulation Act, 1949   D. KYC Guidelines

565. The electronically operated commodity exchange at national level is:
   A. National Commodity and Derivative Exchange
   B. National Multi-commodity Exchange of India
   C. Multi-commodity Exchange of India
   D. Commodity Exchange of India

566. The Settlement Agent for RTGS is:
   A. Reserve Bank of India   B. State Bank of India
   C. Indian Banks' Association   D. National Clearning Corporation

567. What is TIN and CIN in OLTAS:
   A. Tax Information Network and Customer Identification Number
   B. Tax Information Number and Customer Identification Number
   C. Tax Information Number and Challan Identification Number
   D. Tax Information Number and Challan Information Number

568. Which of the following is a feature of Spot Trade:
   A. Spot Trade is a process of settlement where payments and receipts of funds are settled in
      respective currencies
   B. under Spot Trade, settlement takes place within two working days from the date of trade
   C. under Spot Trade, a currency can be bought or sold with settlement on the same date
   D. under Spot Trade, settlement can happen on the next date

569. Which of the following is considered a material alternation:
   A. converting a cheque from ''Bearer'' to ''Order''
   B. converting a cheque from ''Order'' to ''Bearer''
   C. filling in the date on an undated cheque
   D. crossing an open cheque by the holder

570. Which of the following is correct regarding ''Rabi Season'';
   A. April to September   B. October to February
   C. June to December   D. None of these

571. Which of the following is true regarding "Retail Banking":
   A. credit facilities extended to retail traders
   B. providing basic services of a bank to the individuals
   C. collection of large number of Dividend/Interest Warrants
   D. providing services to the employees of large organizations

572. Which sector has the maximum quantum of disguised unemployment in India:
   A. Agriculture   B. Industry   C. Trade   D. Transport

573. Ten Rupee notes contain the signature of:
   A. Finance Secretary, GoI   B. Chairman, SBI
   C. Governor, RBI   D. Finance Minister, GoI

574. Under provisions of which one of the following Acts, the RBI issues directibes to the Banks in India:
   A. RBI Act   B. Banking Regulation Act
   C. Essential Commodities Act   D. Both A and B above

575. For which one of the following Loan Products 'Teaser Loans' are offered by Banks:
   A. Education Loans   B. Commercial Loans
   C. Loans against security of Gold   D. Home Loans

576. Currency notes of ₹ 2 denomination and above are liabilities of:
   A. Government of India   B. Reserve Bank of India
   C. State Bank of India   D. All of these

577. The main function of IMF is to:
   A. Finance investment loans to developing countries
   B. Act as a private sector lending arm of the World Bank
   C. Help to solve balance of payment problems of member countries
   D. None of the above

578. RBI has asked banks to make a plan to provide banking services to all villages having a population upto 2000. This directive issued by the RBI will fall in which of the following categories:
   A. Plan for Financial Inclusion
   B. Efforts to meet the targets of Priority Sector Lending
   C. Extension of Relief Packages to the Farmers
   D. Plan for opening more rural branches

579. The Export-Import Bank of India (Exim Bank) is a public sector financial institution created by an Act of Parliament viz:
   A. the Banking Regulation Act, 1949   B. the Companies Act, 1956
   C. the Export-Import Bank of India Act, 1981   D. the Exim Act, 1948

580. The Exim Bank has been set up for the purpose of:
   A. functioning as a specialised institution for providing comprehensive credits on international competitive terms for export of capital goods, engineering goods, manufactured produced, projects and services
   B. offering advisory services to exporters for non-traditional exports
   C. providing refinance facilities in regard to export financing by banks and other financial institutions
   D. all of the above

581. Euro Money is the official currency of:
   A. SAFTA   B. NATO   C. European Union   D. OPEC

582. The Headquarters of NABARD is situated in:
A. Delhi   B. Mumbai   C. Lucknow   D. Kolkata

583. Many a time we read in newspapers about the ''Doha Round'' of talks. It was related with the talks of which of the following organizations:
A. European Union
B. World Trade Organization (WTO)
C. International Atomic Energy Agencies (IAEA)
D. G-8 talks

584. What is the full form of ASBA:
A. Allotment supported by Blocked Amount
B. Application supported by Blocked Amount
C. Application supported by Bank Amount
D. Allotment supported by Bank Account

585. Financial Action Task Froce has an office in India at which place:
A. Mumbai   B. Chennai   C. Kolkata   D. New Delhi

586. National Savings Certificate matures at the end of:
A. Six years   B. Six and half years
C. Seven years   D. Eight years

587. ''Aadhaar'' is the new name of:
A. PMRY   B. NREGP   C. UID   D. None of these

588. ''Green Tax'' is being proposed by the Maharashtra State Government. Green Tax relates to:
A. tax to be levied to all car/vehicle users
B. tax to be levied to all categories of motor vehicles
C. tax to be levied to old motor vehicles
D. none of the above

589. ''Whistle Blowing Policy'' denotes:
A. starting banking operations at the blow of a whistle
B. an arrangement by a company (including banking and insurance companies) to put in place a procedure to help employees raise concern internally about possible irregularities, to the Chairman or a Committee of the Board or the external auditor in confidence
C. a situation, where bad advances of a banking company crosses certain fixed level
D. a situation, where a bank has to sound alert because of massive fraud taking place

590. A cheque drawn on a Treasury is treated as a:
A. Cheque   B. Negotiable instrument
C. Bill   D. Government cheque

591. A marginal farmer is one who owns:
A. up to 2.5 acres of dry land   B. up to 1.25 acres wet land
C. either A or B   D. None of the above

592. A short term crop loan becomes NPA if:
A. loan and interest remains unpaid for one year
B. loan and interest remains unpaid for two years
C. loan and interest remains unpaid for one crop season
D. loan and interest remains unpaid for two crop seasons

593. An organization has been established to protect the interests of investors in securities and to regulate the securities market. Please identify the organization from out of the following:
A. RBI   B. IRDA   C. SEBI   D. IBA

594. As per RBI directives, the complaints relating to cash not dispensed at ATMs although deposit account is debited, etc. should be disposed of within a period of:
A. 3 days   B. 7 days   C. 15 days   D. 30 days

595. As per RBI, which of the following categories of advances are included in "Sensitive Sector":
A. advances to Real Estate
B. advances against Stock Exchange securities
C. advances against commodities
D. all of the above

596. Association of National Exchanges Members of India (ANMI) is a body consisting of:
A. Bankers and SEBI
B. SEBI and IBA
C. Brokers operating in the national Exchanges
D. Bankers, SEBI, IBA and RBI

597. Bank branches need to report suspicious transactions to:
A. Controllers concerned   B. RBI
C. CVC   D. FIU-IND, New Delhi

598. Bank for International Settlement (BIS) is headquartered at:
A. Manila   B. Chicago
C. Basle, Switzerland   D. None of these

599. Banks are focusing on financing small borrowers through Self Help Groups. Which of the following is correct in this regard:
A. financing Self Help Groups are treated as financing to weaker sections within the Priority Sector
B. financing of Self Help Groups promotes the habit of thrift and concept of credit management
C. financing such activities is cost effective and will facilitate easy flow of credit to rural sector
D. all of the above

600. Banks stipulate interest rates on loans and advances based on:
A. borrower's experience   B. track record
C. credit rating   D. None of these

601. Base Rate (BR) is:
A. the minimum rate of interest that a bank is allowed to charge from its customers
B. unless mandated by the Government, RBI rule stipulates that no bank can offer loans at a rate lower than Base Rate to any of its customers
C. both A and B
D. None of the above

602. Inside Trading is related to:
A. Horse racing   B. Share Market
C. Taxation   D. Public Expenditure

603. The law relating to appropriation of payments is contained in:
A. The Negotiable Instruments Act, 1881   B. The Banking Regulation Act, 1949
C. The Contract Act, 1872   D. The Companies Act, 1956

604. Teller System has been introduced in almost all the banks. Its purpose is:
A. to create more jobs
B. to improve public relations
C. to slash down the waiting time for encashing cheques
D. to eliminate duplication of work

605. Interest on fixed (term) deposits is compounded at:
A. monthly rests
B. quarterly rests
C. half-yearly rests
D. yearly rests

606. Which is the most popular mode of advancing money by banks in India:
A. overdraft
B. cash credit
C. loan
D. purchasing/discounting bills

607. Full form of PERT is:
A. Program Entry Review Technique
B. Program Evaluation and Review Technique
C. Pre Evaluation and Review Technology
D. None of the above

608. Which of the following types of companies/organisations issue 'ULIP':
A. Insurance companies
B. Banks
C. NABARD
D. RBI

609. Which of the following is not a term related to banking/finance operations:
A. Provision Coverage Ratio
B. Securitization
C. Consolidation
D. Commodification

610. ''Account Payee'' crossing is a:
A. Restricted crossing
B. Special crossing
C. General crossing
D. None of these

611. ''Primary Deficit'' refers to:
A. Fiscal Deficit minus Interest Payments
B. Budget Deficit miuns Interest Payments
C. Monetary Deficit minus Interest Payments
D. Deficit Financing by 91-day ad hoc treasury bills

612. ''Disguised unemployment'' denotes:
A. a situation where workers are disguised
B. a situation where too many workers are doing a limited amount of work
C. a situation where workers are lazily employed
D. none of the above

613. ''Door Step Banking'' facilities to Corporate customers/Government Departments/ PSUs provide for delivery of cash at customers' place:
A. against telephonic instructions
B. against cheque deliverable at customer's place
C. against cheque delivered at the Bank
D. all of the above

614. ''Repository'' means:
A. balance held in non Currency Chest branch
B. same as Currency Chest
C. a part of Currency Chest
D. None of the above

615. A customer tenders a certain amount of money into his Savings Bank Account without mentioning his account number. Bank also could not locate the same. In such a situation the amount had to be parked in the Sundry Deposits Accounts. In this case, the relationship between the bank and the customer is that of:

A. Trustee and Beneficiary
B. Bailee and Bailor
C. Bailor and Bailee
D. Lessor and Lessee

616. Banker may reduce lending risk by:

A. ensuring that there will be no default on account of lack of liquidity and lack of willingness to pay on the part of the borrower
B. ensuring that there will be no problem of liquidity with the borrower
C. obtaining adequate security
D. all of the above

617. Bankers have to maintain secrecy of customers accounts as per the provisions of:

A. Banking Companies (Acquisition and Transfer of Undertaking) Act, 1970
B. Negotiable Instruments Act, 1881
C. Banking Regulation Act, 1949
D. None of the above

618. Banking Code & Standards Board of India (BCSBI) has been set up for providing details of banking, and to create awareness of banking. BCSBI has been set up by:

A. SBI
B. RBI
C. Ministry of Finance
D. None of these

619. Expand "FINO":

A. Fiscal Information Network Organization
B. Financial Initiative for Network Operations
C. Financial Information Network Operations Ltd
D. None of the above

620. Expand "LIBOR":

A. London Inter-bank Offered Rate
B. Legal Indian Borrowal Rate
C. FEDAI approved rates
D. ID rate for PCFC

621. Expand "NEFT":

A. National Emergency Fund For Traders
B. National Electronic Fund Transfer
C. National Emergency Fund Transfer
D. National Electronic Financial Trust

622. Expand "P.I.O" in relation to Right to Information, 2005:

A. Public Information Officer
B. Principal Information Officer
C. Press Information Officer
D. None of these

623. Foreign Trade Policy is framed by:

A. RBI
B. EXIM Bank
C. DGFT
D. Ministry of Commerce, Government of India

624. In money market, which of the following is not traded:

A. Shares and Debentures
B. Certificate of Deposit
C. Commercial Paper
D. Treasury Bills

625. In NRE account, rate of interest is linked to:
    A. LIBOR   B. Bank   C. PLR   D. RBI

626. In the Money market operations, the item widely accepted is:
    A. Inter Bank Participation Certificates   B. Certificate of Deposits
    C. Treasury Bills   D. None of the above

627. To meet a significant increase in demand for bank credit, a bank may:
    A. make use of excess reserves   B. borrow from other banks
    C. borrow from the Reserve Bank of India   D. All of the above

628. The "bank rate" is:
    A. free to fluctuate according to the forces of demand and supply
    B. set by the Reserve Bank of India
    C. set by the Reserve Bank of India as directed by the Union Ministry of Finance
    D. set by the Reserve Bank of India as directed by the Indian Banks' Association

629. The term "exchange arbitrage" is the:
    A. Arbitration of exchange disputes
    B. simultaneous buying selling of foreign exchange to make a profit because interest rates vary in different countries
    C. simultaneous purchase of a currency in one market and its sale in another market with a view to realise a profit
    D. buying of foreign currency to realise a future profit when it appreciates

630. The law regarding negotiable instruments is contained in:
    A. The Bill of Exchange Act, 1881   B. The Banking Regulation Act, 1949
    C. The Cheques Act, 1881   D. The Negotiable Instruments Act, 1881

631. The HR function in Bank primarily:
    A. limited to the training and development of the personnel
    B. the function of Personnel Management
    C. to transfers and postings of the employees
    D. takes care the comprehensive respons-ibilities of the employees development

632. Which of the following a benefit of E-Commerce:
    A. Insufficient telecommunications band width
    B. Individuals can telecommute more easily
    C. customers may be unsure of EC security
    D. EC theory and practice is constantly evolving

633. Why is B2C generally less attractive than B2B:
    A. Easier to implement   B. Less expensive to implement
    C. Larger number of organizations   D. Channel conflict

634. Which of the following is not an example of an e-payment:
    A. Smart cards   B. Cash   C. Digital checks   D. Electronic billing

635. Treasury bills are sold in India by:
    A. Reserve Bank of India   B. State Governments
    C. Commercial Banks   D. SEBI

636. Yuan is a currency of which country:
    A. Japan   B. China   C. Korea   D. Indonesia

637. Which institution acts as reinsurer:
- A. New India Insurance
- B. Life Insurance Company
- C. General Insurance Company
- D. United India Insurance

638. The 13th Finance Commission headed by Dr. Vijay Kelkar covers the period:
- A. 2008-13
- B. 2009-14
- C. 2010-15
- D. 2011-16

639. "Black Revolution" is associated with:
- A. Tea plantation
- B. Coffee plantation
- C. Rubber plantation
- D. Printing ink

640. "Blue Card" denotes:
- A. a Credit Card
- B. a Debit Card
- C. a proposition by EU to attract highly qualified professionals from other countries
- D. none of the above

641. "Channel Financing" means:
- A. financing of supply-delivery chain, i.e., dealers of identified large corporate entities financed by banks
- B. laying of agricultural canals
- C. financing through NBFCs
- D. none of the above

642. "Clause 49" is associated with:
- A. Corporate Governance
- B. Retail Trading
- C. Income Tax
- D. KYC

643. The Headquarter of Asian Development Bank (ADB) is at:
- A. Singapore
- B. Manila
- C. Hong Kong
- D. Tokyo

644. "Form 61" is associated with:
- A. persons not in receipt of taxable income
- B. persons with agricultural income
- C. both A and B
- D. None of the above

645. Which one of the following is not correctly matched?
- A. Rural Credit : NABARD
- B. Industrial Finance : SIDBI
- C. Rural poverty : SJSRY
- D. Disguised : Subsistence unemployment agriculture

646. What is the correct sequence of nationalisation of the following institutions?
1. State Bank of India
2. Bank of Baroda
3. Reserve Bank of India

Select the correct answer using the codes given below:

Codes:
- A. 3, 2, 1
- B. 3, 1, 2
- C. 2, 3, 1
- D. 2, 1, 3

647. "White Card" is a:
- A. Co-branded Credit Card without logo of the issuer
- B. Credit Card with logo of both issuer and sponsorer
- C. Litchi Card issued in Uttaranchal
- D. Card used in football by referee

648. A "Red Clause" Letter of Credit is:
A. when opening bank advises the advising bank to give advance to the exporter
B. when advising bank informs the opening bank about credit given to exporter
C. all the clauses are printed in red
D. none of the above

649. Apart from the multiple Personal Identification Number (PIN) facility, the security features available in the smart card to prevent card-related crimes and frauds are:
A. Dynamic Signature Verification
B. Voice Recognition System
C. Retinal Pattern Verification, Finger Print Verification and Vein Verification
D. Visual Recognition

650. A bank normally does not have to deal with an issue related to:
A. payments and settlement systems   B. constractual rights of creditors
C. intellectual property right   D. cases of insolvency

651. Liquid assets means:
A. Cash only
B. Cash and Debtors
C. Cash and Debtors (except bad debts)
D. Cash and Debtors (except bad debts) and Marketable Securities

652. Which of the following is the most important contributing factor affecting the profitability of banks:
A. Deteriorating productivity
B. Heavy establishment expenses
C. Huge "dead credit" in sick industries and the mounting losses on rural branches
D. Heavy losses on investment port-folio

653. For the developing countries of Asia, the international agency which provides soft loans is:
A. International Monetary Fund   B. Asian Development Bank
C. International Development Association   D. World Bank

654. No licence from RBI is required for:
A. opening a new bank branch in India
B. opening a new bank branch outside India
C. shifting an existing branch outside the city, village or town
D. shifting an existing branch within the same city, village or town

655. Commercial banks are unique among financial institutions in that they:
A. advance loans to business   B. provide insurance to depositors
C. create demand deposits   D. hold saving deposits

656. Financial year in banks is a period from:
A. January to December   B. May to June
C. April to March   D. January to April

657. "Pure Banking Nothing Else" is a slogan raised by:
A. ICICI Bank   B. HDFC Bank   C. SBI   D. UTI Bank

658. 'Smart Money' is a term used for:
A. Internal banking   B. Credit card
C. Cash with bank   D. Cash with public

659. Pledge means:
   A. advance against goods
   B. open working capital limits
   C. bailment of goods as security for payment of a debt or performance of a promise
   D. none of the above

660. What are the RBI guidelines for the development of Interest Rate Swaps (IRS):
   A. Banks can use IRS for hedging and Trading both
   B. MIFOR is a benchmark for IRS
   C. Under ISDA agreement Banks can opt for dual jurisdiction i.e., Indian as well as common law
   D. All of the above

661. SEBI is a:
   A. Statutory body   B. Advisory body
   C. Constitutional body   D. Non-statutory body

662. When was the SAARC established:
   A. On December 8, 1983   B. On January 1, 1984
   C. On December 8, 1985   D. On January 1, 1985

663. NABARD was established on the recommendation of the:
   A. Public Accounts Committee   B. Shivaraman Committee
   C. Narsimham Committee   D. All of the above

664. As per the Reserve Bank of India (RBI), the economic conditions in India are not yet suitable for full convertibility of Rupee. At present Rupee is convertible at which of the following accounts:
   A. Fully at Capital Account   B. Fully at Current Account
   C. Partially at Trade Account   D. None of the above

665. The National Stock Exchange recently launched Interest Rate Futures (IRF). IRF in fact is a:
   A. new mode of trading specifically for SME sector
   B. financial mode of trading
   C. electronic mode of transfering money from one account to another
   D. safest and fastest mode of trading at all the stock exchanges of India simultaneously

666. The Infrastructure Development Bank of India has its Headquarters in:
   A. New Delhi   B. Mumbai
   C. Bangalore (Bengluru)   D. Kolkata

667. The guarantor of a customer's account has the right:
   A. to inspect the account in the bank's books
   B. to be provided with the statement of the account
   C. to be informed only about the extent of his liability
   D. to be provided with all the information about the way the account is conducted

668. In terms of Section 59 of the Indian Contract Act, 1872, if the customer owes several distinct debts to the banker and makes payment which is not sufficient to satisfy all the debts:
   A. he has the right to request the banker to apply the payment to the discharge of some particular debt
   B. the banker has a right to appropriate the amount in satisfaction of any debt which is not time-barred, at his option
   C. the payment will be applied in discharge of the debts in chronological order notwithstanding the instructions of the customer in this regard
   D. All of the above

669. What is operational risk:
A. Risk of loss resulting from inadequate or failed internal processes
B. Failure of people and system may also cause risk
C. Operational risk may also be caused due to external events
D. All of the above

670. Financial market consists of:
A. Foreign exchange   B. Debt Instruments
C. Equities   D. All of these

671. As we all know in India currency market is regulated by the Reserve Bank of India (RBI), while "Currency futures" are jointly regulated by the RBI and which of the following other banks:
A. NABARD   B. SIDBI   C. SEBI   D. SBI

672. Which of the following is NOT a banking related term:
A. SME Finance   B. Overdraft
C. Drawing Power   D. Equinox

673. Which of the following agencies is associated with the business of Insurance sector as a regulator:
A. NPCI   B. IRDA   C. SEBI   D. AMFI

674. Which of the following is the major function of an ATM installed by banks:
A. To distribute cash by way of withdrawal from from one's account
B. To transfer money from one place to another place
C. To detect fake currency notes
D. To arrange currency notes in serial order and count them

675. Which one of the following is not an authorised means of banking transaction for the people in India:
A. On-line   B. Mobile
C. Phone   D. Video Conferencing

676. The hundred rupee currency note in India bears the signature of:
A. Finance Minister of India   B. Prime Minister of India
C. President of India   D. Governor of the RBI

677. Which of the following terms is not used in banking and finance:
A. Capital gain   B. Plan Finance   C. Market risk   D. Apartheid

678. Which of the following Rates/Ratios is not covered under the Monetary and Credit Policy of the RBI:
A. Bank Rate   B. Repo Rate
C. Cash Reserve Ratio   D. Exchange Rate of Foreign Currencies

679. Khandelwal Committee relates to study of ...... issues in Public Sector Banks:
A. Capital Adequacy Ratio   B. Human Resources
C. Branch Expansion   D. Foreign Exchange

680. The largest bank in the world in the matter of number of branch offices:
A. Banks of America NT & SA   B. State Bank of India
C. Barclays Bank   D. Citi Bank

681. Which Committee has been set up to study banking customer services by RBI:
A. Bajpai Committee   B. Melegam Committee
C. Damodaran Committee   D. Bhatt Committee

682. Six banks were nationalised because:
   A. they were grossly mismanaged
   B. the election manifest of Congress (I) contained such a commitment
   C. the Government intended to enlarge the flow of bank credit to the economically weaker sections of the society
   D. the measure was a part of restructuring the Indian banking system

683. The term "Balance of Trade" means:
   A. A point where the values of imports and exports are equal
   B. the term is used with reference to bilateral trade agreements with the countries of CIS Block
   C. the difference between the cost of the imports and exports of a country
   D. the difference between the total of transactions with foreign countries in trade, services and capital

684. The term "bank money" is used to denote:
   A. loans and advances granted by the commercial banks
   B. demand deposits used as money, i.e., deposits withdrawable by cheques
   C. loans granted by the Reserve Bank of India to the commercial banks
   D. money provided by the Reserve Bank of India to the Government

685. More number of banks' branches are located in:
   A. metropolitan areas   B. semi-urban areas
   C. urban areas   D. rural areas

686. The term "capitalisation of reserves" is used to denote:
   A. the use of reserves for the acquisition of additional capital
   B. the use of reserves for paying-off loans raised for building up fixed assets
   C. the use of reserves for issuing bonus shares to the existing shareholders
   D. the use of reserves for the replacement of depreciated assets

687. "Multi-currency basket" means:
   A. a number of international currencies to which the value of SDRs is linked
   B. selected international currencies to which the value of Asian Monetary Unit is linked
   C. number of major international currencies to which the external value of the Indian rupee is linked
   D. the name given to a group of West European currencies

688. The term "hyper-inflation" is used to denote:
   A. a situation with a moderate rise in price level
   B. an inflationary situation where the external forces are the primary contributing factors
   C. a "runway" or "galloping" inflationary situation where the monetary unit becomes almost worthless
   D. a situation where the cost of living index is rising alarmingly

689. The term "hyper-employment" means:
   A. a situation where machines are used to intensify utilisation of labour
   B. a situation where plant is used without any rest
   C. a situation where the demand for labour far exceeds its supply
   D. a situation where machines are substituted for labour

690. "Hot money" means:
   A. money earned through illegal transactions
   B. money earned through speculative transactions
   C. money used to hoard scarce commodities
   D. short-term capital movements from one country to another seeking safety or, less often, higher rate of interest

691. "Funded debt" means:
  A. all Government securities which are marketable on the stock exchange market
  B. all Government debt which is not marketable on the stock exchange market
  C. Government borrowings from the Reserve Bank of India
  D. Institutional borrowings guaranteed by the Government

692. "Free port" denotes:
  A. a port where there are no restrictions on incoming and outgoing vessels
  B. a port where no licence is required for import of goods
  C. a port which allows entry to goods without payment of import duty
  D. a port which allows free entry to goods which are to be re-exported

693. "Free trade area" denotes:
  A. a group of countries which have decided to impose no duties of any kind on their imports
  B. a group of countries which have decided to impose no duties of any kind on imports from other members of the group
  C. an area where there are no restrictions of any kind on the trading activities
  D. an area where trade is free from any kind of taxes

694. "Free zone" or "Free trade zone" denotes:
  A. an area where there are no restrictions of any kind on trading activities
  B. an area where trade is free from any kind of taxes
  C. an area near a sea-port or airport in which goods can be imported duty free, if they are to be re-exported or used in the manufacture of goods for export
  D. an area where no licence is required for import of goods

695. "Floating debt" denotes:
  A. Government securities with no definite rate of redemption, but which may be redeemed any time at the discretion of the Government
  B. that part of the public debt which consists of short term borrowings by the Government
  C. Government securities which continue changing hands
  D. Government securities whose date of maturity falls within next five years

696. "Treasury bills" means:
  A. salary bills drawn by Government officials on the treasury
  B. bills drawn by the Government contractors and other suppliers on the treasury for the dues owed to them by the Government
  C. obligations of the Government of India issued by the Reserve Bank of India and payable normally ninety-one days after issue
  D. a mode of drawings by the Treasury Officer on the Reserve Bank of India

697. "Token money" means:
  A. coins where the value of metal in them is equal to the value attached to them by law
  B. coins where the value of metal in them is less than the value attached to them by law
  C. coins where the value of metal in them is more than the value of metal attached to them by law
  D. money represented by the tokens of specified values issued by the Reserve Bank of India

698. "Bulls and Bears" are terms used in:
  A. bullion markets   B. vegetable markets
  C. stock exchange   D. commodity markets

699. The term "Paper Gold" means:
   A. paper currency fully backed by gold reserve
   B. paper currency partially backed by gold reserve
   C. international paper currency fully convertible into gold
   D. special drawing rights of the IMF

700. The previous name of State Bank of India was:
   A. National Bank of India
   B. Premier Bank of India
   C. Imperial Bank of India
   D. Royal Bank of India

701. Reserve Bank of India was nationalised in:
   A. 1945   B. 1949   C. 1950   D. 1955

702. Prior to the establishment of the Reserve Bank of India, the Government banking business was conducted by:
   A. Bank of India
   B. Central Bank of India
   C. National Bank of India
   D. Imperial Bank of India

703. Which of the following is not a general credit control measure:
   A. bank rate
   B. variable reserve ratios
   C. open market operations
   D. regulation of margin requirements on advances against agricultural commodities

704. Which of the following is not a selective credit control measure:
   A. fixation of minimum margins for lending against specific securities
   B. ceilings on the amounts of credit for certain purposes
   C. changes in the liquidity ratio
   D. discriminatory rates of interest on certain types of advances

705. Every bank wishing to commence banking business in India is required to obtain a licence from:
   A. Government of India, Ministry of Finance
   B. Government of India, Company Law Board
   C. Reserve Bank of India
   D. Registrar of Companies

706. When was the currency system in India converted into decimal system:
   A. From 1st April, 1957
   B. From 1st April, 1959
   C. From 1st April, 1961
   D. From 1st April, 1963

707. Statutory cash reserve ratio for scheduled banks is regulated by the Reserve Bank of India under powers conferred upon it by:
   A. Reserve Bank of India Act, 1934
   B. Banking Regulation Act, 1949
   C. Companies Act, 1956
   D. Union Ministry of Finance

708. Statutory cash reserve ratio for non-scheduled banks is regulated by the Reserve Bank of India under powers conferred upon it by:
   A. Reserve Bank of India Act, 1934
   B. Banking Regulation Act, 1949
   C. Companies Act, 1956
   D. Union Ministry of Finance

709. Which of the following is not the main objective of the statutory liquidity ratio (SLR):
   A. to assure solvency of commercial banks by compelling them to hold low-risk assets upto the stipulated extent

    B. to create or support a market for Government securities

    C. to allocate resources to Government for augmenting the resources of the public sector

    D. to ensure stable returns on commercial bank's funds

710. The idea that commercial banks should involve themselves increasingly in financing the requirements of the neglected sectors was first mooted in:
    A. 1955, when Imperial Bank of India was nationalised
    B. 1968, when the scheme of social control over banking was introduced
    C. 1969, when 14 major commercial banks were nationalised
    D. 1975, when internal emergency was declared

711. The definition of the priority sector was first formalised in 1972 by:
    A. Planning Commission
    B. National Development Council
    C. Reserve Bank of India
    D. Ministry of Finance, Government of India

712. Liquidity ratio is fixed by the Reserve Bank of India under the powers conferred on it by:
    A. Reserve Bank of India Act, 1934
    B. Companies Act, 1956
    C. Banking Regulation Act, 1949
    D. Special Powers given by the Union Ministry of Finance

713. The largest number of commercial banks' offices are located in:
    A. Karnataka   B. Maharashtra
    C. Tamil Nadu   D. Uttar Pradesh

714. Which of the following is not a member of the World Bank Group:
    A. International Bank for Reconstruction and Development
    B. International Development Association
    C. Bank of International Settlement
    D. International Finance Corporation

715. Dalal Street is:
    A. in Kolkata – famous for jute market
    B. in Mumbai – famous for stock exchange market
    C. in Delhi – famous for Kabari (Waste goods) market
    D. in Bangalore – famous for race course

716. The Differential Rates of Interest (DRI) Scheme is operative since:
    A. 1969   B. 1972   C. 1975   D. 1976

717. Which of the following is an apex-institution in the field of industrial finance:
    A. the Industrial Credit and Investment Corporation of India
    B. the Industrial Finance Corporation of India
    C. the Industrial Development Bank of India
    D. the Industrial Reconstruction Bank of India

718. The growth of commercial banks' advances has proportionately been less than that in deposits. This is because:
    A. the commercial banks follow a conservative credit policy
    B. the Reserve Bank of India always apply a restrictive credit policy

C. there has been a progressive increase in the statutory liquidity ratio which banks are required to maintain

D. the demand for bank credit has not increased correspondingly

719. Kisan Credit Card can be used for financing:
A. Production needs
B. Consumption needs
C. Both A and B
D. None of these

720. When was the Imperial Bank of India nationalised:
A. 1948
B. 1950
C. 1955
D. 1969

721. E-invest is for investing in:
A. IPO only
B. IPO and Mutual Funds
C. IPO, Stock Markets and Mutual Funds
D. None of the above

722. MICR is used in ...... industry:
A. Banking
B. Hospitality
C. Tourism
D. None of these

723. Who is authorised to sign 'one-rupee' note:
A. Secretary, Ministry of Finance
B. RBI Governor
C. Primer Minister
D. Finance Minister

724. Which of the following is not a development bank:
A. Industrial Finance Corporation of India
B. Industrial Development Bank of India
C. State Bank of India
D. State Financial Corporation

725. Nominee's Signature is to be obtained on:
A. Account Opening Form
B. Nomination Form
C. Specimen Signature Card
D. Need not to be obtained

726. Most banks are offering teaser rates on home loans. What does it mean:
A. The rates keep fluctuating during the period of loan with high uncertainty
B. The initial rate is offered at a rate lower than the prevailing market rate for a few months and then gradually keeps increasing
C. The initial rate is higher than the current market rate with offer of lower rates at a later date
D. Home loan borrowers of shorter duration are given preferential rate

727. Who decides on the value and volume of bank notes to be printed and on what basis:
A. Finance Ministry
B. Planning Commission
C. RBI
D. Stock Exchange

728. There are many security features which are regularly being explained and stressed to check against forged currency notes. One of them is Intaglio printing. What is it:
A. It is specialized printing of Rs. 1,000 and Rs. 500 denomination currency notes
B. It is raised printing on the currency notes of RBI seal, Ashoka Pillar emblem etc.
C. It is printing on special printing press of RBI
D. It is printing through special inks of the security features on currency notes

729. Indian Banking Regulation Act was passed in the year:
A. 1971
B. 1969
C. 1949
D. 1947

730. Audit adopted by banking company is:
A. Continuous Audit
B. Periodical Audit
C. Internal Audit
D. Balance Sheet Audit

731. Financial literacy is a serious issue for RBI, because:
   A. It would enable better understanding of banking business
   B. With better understanding more and more people would utilize the banking serfices
   C. It would mean banks can do more business
   D. It would mean the maximum number of people

732. RBI has replaced BPLR regime by Base Rate regime w.e.f.:
   A. July 1, 2010   B. July 5, 2010   C. July 11, 2010   D. July 15, 2010

733. Many a times, we read about Special Drawining Right (SDR) in newspapers. As per its definition, SDR is a monetary unit of the reserve assets of which of the following organisations/ agencies:
   A. World Bank   B. International Monetary Fund (IMF)
   C. Reserve Bank of India (RBI)   D. None of the above

734. Reserve Bank of India is:
   A. an extension wing of Ministry of Finance, Government of India
   B. a body corporate having perpetual succession and a common seal
   C. an Institution owned by Indian Banks' Association
   D. a private sector company

735. Authorised, subscribed and paid up share capital of Reserve Bank of India is:
   A. ₹ 1 crore   B. ₹ 5 crore
   C. ₹ 50 crore   D. ₹ 100 crore

736. Which Bank is the Banker to the Central Government:
   A. Central Bank of India   B. Reserve Bank of India
   C. Punjab National Bank   D. All of these

737. The term 'Ways and Means' advances refers to:
   A. the temporary advance made to the government by its Bankers to bridge the internal between expenditure and the flow of receipt of revenues
   B. the advance given by the Banks to the poorest of the society
   C. lending made under PMRY scheme
   D. all of the above

738. The Reserve Bank of India is also called the lender of the last resort to Scheduled Commercial Banks because:
   A. RBI meets directly or indirectly all the reasonable demands for financial accommodation subject to terms and conditions of the discount rate policy of RBI
   B. they are not able to get facilities from other Banks
   C. Both of the above
   D. None of the above

739. In terms of Section 19 of the Reserve Bank of India Act, 1934, the RBI has been prohibited from:
   A. making loans or advances
   B. drawing or accepting bills payable otherwise than on demand
   C. allowing interest on deposits or current accounts
   D. none of the above

740. Scheduled Banks are required to keep cash reserves with Reserve Bank of India, in terms of:
   A. Section 42(i) of the RBI Act, 1934
   B. Section 24 of the Banking Regulation Act, 1949
   C. Section 42 of the Negotiable Instruments Act, 1881
   D. None of the above

741. The cash reserve requirements for Non-schedule Banks are laid down in:
A. Section 41(i) of the Reserve Bank of India Act, 1934
B. Section 41(i) of the Negotiable Instruments Act, 1881
C. Section 41 of the Banking Regulation Act, 1881
D. None of the above

742. Cash Reserve Ratio is maintained in the form of:
A. Government Securities
B. Balance with Reserve Bank of India
C. Balance with State Bank of India
D. All of the above

743. RBI is empowered to prescribe Cash Reserve Ratio ranging between:
A. five per cent to twenty per cent of net demand and time liabilities
B. three per cent to fifteen per cent of net demand and time liabilities
C. three per cent to forty per cent of net demand and time liabilities
D. none of the above

744. The functions of Back office are:
A. It verifies and settles the deals
B. It maintains proper record of Book keeping
C. It submits financial returns of RBI
D. All of the above

745. What does LMS stand for in e-learning:
A. Learning Management System
B. Life Management System
C. Learning Management Software
D. None of the above

746. Which is not e-banking software:
A. ECS
B. IBR
C. RTGS
D. PIPS

747. Which is the feature of IBS (Integrated Banking System):
A. Multi Currency
B. Multi Entity
C. Multi Branch
D. All of these

748. What does CBS stand for IBS:
A. Centralized Banking System
B. Central Banking System
C. Currency Bank Software
D. Centralized Banking Software

749. In core banking systems:
A. Store and forward of transaction is done
B. Branch server is not required
C. Local Database is not required
D. Transaction cannot happen from a non-home branch

750. The concept of 'Carbon Credit' is associated with:
A. lending to mineral exploring companies
B. development of coal mines
C. protection of environment
D. development of uranium

751. Which of the following organisation release World Economic Outlook report:
A. World Bank
B. IMF
C. UNDP
D. WTO

752. ICRA, CRISIL and Standard and Poor's (S&P) are:
A. Credit rating agencies
B. NGOs
C. Financial Institutions
D. NBFCs

753. The Nippon Ginko is the Central Bank of:
A. South Korea
B. Japan
C. China
D. Taiwan

754. "Primary Deficit" refers to:
   A. Fiscal Deficit minus Interest Payments
   B. Budget Deficit minus Interest Payments
   C. Monetary Deficit minus Interest Payments
   D. Deficit Financing by 91 days ad hoc treasury bills

755. "Brown Projects" means:
   A. projects envisaged in metropolitan cities
   B. projects where capital infusion is of a very high order
   C. any project other than those for Agricultural activities
   D. projects aimed at modernization, diversification and expansion

756. A bank grants a temporary overdraft only for a part amount of a cheque sent through clearing. In the event of dishonour of the cheque:
   A. bank will not be a holder in due course since the bank did not part with full consideration while permitting overdraft against the dishonroured cheqe
   B. bank will be a holder in due course if it took the cheque under the circumstances as per Section 9 of the Negotiable Instruments Act, 1881
   C. bank may proceed only against its customer who was allowed the overdraft but not against drawer/endorser
   D. none of the above

757. Banks can receive deposits from customers up to a maximum period of:
   A. 10 years   B. 15 years   C. 20 years   D. 25 years

758. Certificate of Deposit (CD) is issued by a commercial bank. Which of the following is true of the same:
   A. it is issued in the form of a receipt
   B. it is issued in the form of a Bill of Exchange
   C. it is issued in the form of a Demand Promissory Note
   D. it is issued in the form of usance promissory, at a discount to the face value

759. Commercial Paper issued by an Indian Company in favour of NRIs will be on:
   A. non-repatriable and transferable basis   B. repatriable and non-transferable basis
   C. non-repatriable and non-transferable basis   D. repatriable and transferable basis

760. Credit Card related grievances can also be referred to:
   A. Consumer Forum   B. Ombudsman   C. Lok Adalat   D. All of these

761. Deposits which can be withdrawn by a customer without notice are called:
   A. Time Deposits   B. Variable Deposits
   C. Demand Deposits   D. Low Cost Deposits

762. Expand BIS:
   A. Bank for International Settlements   B. Bank for Industrial Settlements
   C. Bank for Industrial Sectors   D. Bank for International Services

763. For a foreigner temporarily residing in India, type of account to be opened is:
   A. Resident Account   B. NRO Account
   C. NRE Account   D. None of these

764. For which of the following categories of banks is "Protected Disclosure Scheme" is applicable:
   A. Co-operative Banks   B. Private Banks and Foreign Banks
   C. Public Sector Banks   D. None of the above

765. The punchline "Feel the Difference" is associated with:
A. DCB Bank
B. Deutsche Bank
C. YES Bank
D. Citibank

766. VDMS in Government transactions means:
A. Verified Date-wise Monthly Statement
B. Valuable Data Management System
C. Variable Data Matching System
D. None of the above

767. When an uncrossed bearer cheque is presented across the counter by a person not known to the bank, and the refuses to sign on the reverse of the cheque:
A. the bank can refuse payment of the cheque as the attending circumstances raise a reasonable degree of suspicion that the payment will not be a payment in due course
B. the bank would make payment, but will insist on a duly stamped receipt from the presentor of the cheque
C. the bank has to make the payment
D. endorsement on the reverse is necessary in the case of order-cheques; the bank will make payment on proper indentification of the bearer of the cheque

768. Medium-term loan will be granted:
A. to meet working capital deficit
B. for acquisition of fixed assets
C. to clear short-term debts
D. to pay public depositors

769. The term packing credit means:
A. advances against goods in packages
B. advance for import of goods
C. advance for export of goods
D. advance for financing the purchase, processing, manufacturing or packing of goods for export against a letter of credit or a confirmed order

770. The term "book debts" means:
A. all debts due to the banks by a business undertaking
B. all debts due by a business undertaking to persons/undertaking other than banks
C. debts owing to a business undertaking arising primarily out of the sale of merchandise to the customers on credit
D. moneys due on the purchase of various types of books

771. The DICGC operates the Credit Guarantee Scheme for small scale industries on behalf of the:
A. LIC
B. IBA
C. Union Government
D. None of these

772. Working capital means:
A. cash in-hand and at bank
B. current assets
C. current liabilities and provisions
D. current assets minus current liabilities

773. "Window dressing" means:
A. the modern way of decorating a branch office
B. a decorative way of presenting the Balance Sheet and Profit and Loss Account of a bank at its annual general meeting
C. manipulation of accounts with a view not to give the share holders a true and fair view
D. a pracitce of presenting final accounts of a bank with a view to exhibit a favourable position

774. The term "co-obligant" means:
   A. a person who has guaranteed the account of another person(s)
   B. a person who has executed an indemnity bond in a bank's favour
   C. a person who has assumed obligations of contract jointly with other person(s)
   D. a person/business undertaking opening a documentary letter of credit

775. The term "dormant accounts" means:
   A. accounts showing an average balance of less than ₹ 100 during a half year
   B. accounts which remains inoperative for an extended period of time
   C. accounts which have been blocked under the exchange control regulations
   D. loan/cash credit/overdraft accounts which are considered irrecoverable

776. In India, the computerization program of banks are regulated and monitored by:
   A. SBI   B. RBI   C. ET & T   D. Intell UNIV

777. The ...... Committee on computerization in year 1984 recommended introduction of mechanization at branch, RO/ZO and HO levles.
   A. Rangarajan   B. Shere
   C. Saraf   D. Second Rangarajan

778. The ...... Committee recommended for installation of Main Frame and Mini Computer system at controlling officers for processing of returns, payrolls, PF accounting and cash and investment management etc.
   A. Rangarjan   B. Second Rangarajan
   C. Shere   D. Saraf

779. Second Rangarajan Committee on computerization recommended the:
   A. None Computerized Branches   B. RO/ZO/HO Computerization
   C. Use of Networks   D. All of the above

780. Saraf Committee on Technology issues recommended:
   A. Remittance Facilities to Banks Customers
   B. Reporting of SGL Transactions in Government Securities
   C. Reporting of Currency Chest Operations & Government Transactions
   D. All of the above

781. The Saraf Committee was constituted by RBI in the year:
   A. 1973   B. 1984   C. 1994   D. 1998

782. The chair person of Shere Committee was:
   A. Mr. Rahul Shere   B. Mr. R. K. Shere
   C. Smt. K. S. Shere   D. Sri Amit Shere

783. World Investment Report is annually published by:
   A. IBRD   B. WTO   C. IMF   D. UNCTAD

784. As we know the RBI is the apex Bank of India, similarly the apex Bank of USA is called:
   A. Federal Reserve   B. The Central Bank of USA
   C. Bank of America   D. None of these

785. As a practice, all banks now deduct some amount from their pre tax income and set aside in a separate account to create a cushion for the loans which may go bad. This is called:
   A. CRR   B. SLR   C. Provisioning   D. PLR

786. Which of the following state shows the fastest growth in expanding Micro Finance business in the country:
    A. Gujarat   B. Andhra Pradesh
    C. Maharashtra   D. Karnataka

787. The regulator of Micro Finance in India is:
    A. Finance Ministry   B. Reserve Bank of India
    C. State Bank of India   D. None of these

788. Which of the following rates decided by the RBI is called "Policy Rate"?
    A. Lending Rate   B. Cash Reserve Ratio
    C. Bank Rate   D. Deposit Rate

789. Loan given by the banks to farmers/small shop owners etc. is known as ....
    A. Corporate loan   B. Business loan
    C. Priority sector loan   D. Commercial Loan

790. The Head Office of which of the following banks is in Mumbai?
    A. Punjab National Bank   B. Bank of Maharashtra
    C. UCO Bank   D. Union Bank of India

791. As per the reports, the collection of direct taxes has gone up by about 19% in last few months. Which of the following agencies releases the figures about tax collection?
    A. Central Statistical Organisation   B. Reserve Bank of India
    C. Department of Income Tax   D. Central Board of Direct Taxes

792. As we know commercial banks accept deposits from the public. What do banks do with this money?
    A. This is a type of credit creation. Bank gives this on loan.
    B. This is an income for the bank.
    C. Banks give this money directly to the govt. for developmental projects.
    D. This money is deposited with the RBI who in turn gives some interest on it to banks.

793. Which of the following is NOT a type of cheque issued by an individual?
    A. Bearer cheque   B. Order cheque
    C. Crossed cheque   D. Savings cheque

794. Which of the following terms is used in banking?
    A. Vacuum   B. Power   C. Density   D. Credit Card

795. "Sensitive Index" of Bombay Stock Exchange is called ....
    A. Forex   B. MAX   C. LIBOR   D. Sensex

796. Which of the following is the best way to get **hard cash immediately** from one's bank account at a time when banks are not working?
    A. Phone Banking   B. ATM
    C. Internet Banking   D. All of these

797. What is financial inclusion?
    A. To provide a permanent employment to the unemployed
    B. To provide a 100 days job to all those who are in need of a job
    C. To provide banking services to all those living in remote areas
    D. To ensure that all financial transactions amounting ₹ 5,000/- and above are done through banks.

798. Some major banks and financial institutions in various Western countries were to wind up their business and/or declare themselves in financial problems during last few years. This trend is technically known as:
A. Devaluation
B. Deformation
C. Global Slowdown
D. Political backdrop

799. Exporters in India get insurance cover and risk cover from which of the following organizations?
A. SIDBI
B. NABARD
C. ECGC
D. RBI

800. Which of the following places in India does not have a Stock Exchange?
A. Kolkata
B. Ahmedabad
C. Mumbai
D. Udaipur

801. Which of the following is the name of a private sector Bank in India?
A. IDBI Bank
B. Axis Bank
C. Corporation Bank
D. UCO Bank

802. The Govt. of India does not provide any direct financial assistance to which of the following schemes?
A. Mahatma Gandhi National Rural Employment Guarantee scheme
B. Rural Health Mission
C. India Aawas Yojana
D. Jeevan Sathi Yojana

803. Which of the following terms is used in banking and finance?
A. Abiotic
B. Demand Deposit
C. Fat scales
D. A diabetic

804. Names of which of the following rates/ratios cannot be seen in financial newspapers?
A. Bank Rate
B. Repo Rate
C. Cash Reserve Ratio
D. Pulse Rate

805. Which of the following is an economic term?
A. Plaintiff
B. Bunker Blaster
C. Deflation
D. Lampoon

806. Who amongst the following can take benefit of the Social Security Fund established by the Govt. of India for unorganized workers?
A. Primary school teacher
B. Employee of Sugar Factory
C. Taxtile Mazdoor
D. Rickshaw Puller

807. Who amongst the following was never a Governor of the RBI?
A. Bimal Jalan
B. Y.V. Reddy
C. Arup Roy Choudhury
D. D. Subbarao

808. Which of the following is **NOT** the name of a bank having branches in India?
A. State Bank of India
B. Naively Lignite Corporation
C. Barclays
D. HSBC

809. Banks do not provide which of the following services?
A. Issuing Bank Drafts
B. Depositing Money
C. Sale of post cards and postal stamps
D. Lockers for valueable items/documents

810. The loan given by a bank to a person to purchase house is called ....
A. Project Finance
B. Business Loan
C. Credit Loan
D. Top Up Loan

811. Which of the following is an example of cash less purchase?
1. ATM withdrawal

2. Credit Card
3. Debit Card

A. Only 1   B. Only 2   C. Only 1 and 2   D. All of these

812. Through which of the following Indians are not authorised to banking?

A. Online   B. Mobile

C. Phone   D. Vedeo Conferencing

813. Which of the following programmes the Govt. of India has launched to develop comprehensive rural infrastructure in the country?

A. Bharat Nirman   B. Indira Aawas Yojana

C. Watershed Development Programme   D. None of these

814. The name of which of the following great leaders is now associated with National Rural Employment Guarantee Scheme?

A. Indira Gandhi   B. Mahatma Gandhi

C. Jawaharlal Nehru   D. None of these

815. Which of the following is NOT the name of a multinational bank?

A. BNP Paribas   B. British Bank of Middle East

C. Standard Chartered Bank   D. Cathay Pacific

816. In order to avoid crowding of customers wanting to withdraw cash in the branches, banks have provided many delivery channels. Which of the following is one of the most popular channels of getting instant hard cash?

A. Core Banking Solution   B. Pay Orders

C. Demand Drafts   D. Automated Teller Machines

817. When someone wants to open a new savings bank account, the bank asks him/her to bring various documents. Which of the following is one of these documents?

A. Certificate of medical fitness   B. Degree Certificate

C. Proof of Residence & Identity   D. None of these

818. As we all know, when we deposit a cheque issued in our name in the bank, the bank always checks if the cheque has been crossed or not. Why is this done?

A. It ensures that the money is deposited only in the account of the person in whose name the cheque has been drawn

B. It is a process by which the person who has issued the cheque comes to know whether the cheque is encashed or not.

C. The bank insists on it only when the party wants the payment immediately and that too in cash only

D. This is the instruction of RBI that all the cheques of the amount of Rs. 10,000/- should be accepted only if they are crossed.

819. Which of the following terms is **NOT** associated with banking operations?

A. Repo Rate   B. Prime Lending Rate

C. Equator   D. Corporate Finance

820. A student has got admission to a foreign university. From where can he/she get the foreign currency?

A. From the Bank of that country only

B. From the Ministry of Foreign Affairs

C. From office of the Consulate General of that country

D. From an authorized foreign exchange dealer

821. Which of the following organizations is known as a regulator associated with the financial activities in India?

    A. ISRO   B. WHO   C. UNESCO   D. SEBI

822. Which of the following schemes was launched to promote exports of agricultural produce and their value added products in India?

    A. Vishesh Krishi and Gram Udyog Yojana

    B. Financial Inclusion Scheme

    C. Rastriya Krishi Vikas Yojana

    D. None of these

823. As per the instructions given by the RBI, now all banks are required to provide which of the following in all its branches mandatorily?

    A. Note Sorting Machines   B. Special Counters for Senior Citizens

    C. Service sector   D. All of these

824. Which of the following terms is NOT used in the field of Banking & Finance?

    A. Overdraft   B. Base Line   C. RTGS   D. GBC

825. Current Accounts can be freely opened by .... Find the **incorrect** answer.

    A. All NRIs   B. All businessmen

    C. Government department   D. HUFs

826. Which of the following apex body and regulators has asked banks to swap customer related information so that the frauds and defaults may be prevented in future?

    A. Bombay Stock Exchange (BSE)

    B. Indian Bank's Association (IBA)

    C. Securities & Exchange Board of India (SEBI)

    D. Reserve Bank of India (RBI)

827. Who amongst the following is the author of the book (released recently) "India and Global Financial Crisis : Managing Money and finance"?

    A. Dr. Bimal Jalan   B. Dr. C. Rangarajan

    C. Dr. Manmohan Singh   D. Dr. Y.V. Reddy

828. The Reserve Bank of India does not print currency notes of the denomination of ₹ ....

    A. 20/-   B. 50/-   C. 3,000/-   D. 1,000/-

829. Which of the following is considered as the financial capital of India?

    A. New Delhi   B. Kolkata   C. Ahmedabad   D. None of these

830. "Micro Credit" means:

    (1) Loans of small amounts to people in unorganized sector

    (2) Loans to Self Help Groups

    (3) Loans amounting ₹ 50 lakhs to ₹ 5 crores to Medium and Small Industries Units

    A. Only (1)   B. Only (2)   C. Only (1) and (2)   D. None of these

831. The RBI has given its permission for cash withdrawal at "POS terminals". What is the full form of "POS"?

    A. Permitted on Sale   B. Potential of Service

    C. Point of Sale   D. Permission of Sale

832. Which of the following is NOT a banking related term?
  A. SME Finance
  B. Overdraft
  C. Drawing power
  D. Equinox

833. "The Doing Business Report" is prepared by which of the following organizations every year?
  A. Asian Development Bank (ADB)
  B. World Bank
  C. International Monetary Fund (IMF)
  D. World Trade Organisation (WTO)

834. "Yen" is the currency of .....
  A. China
  B. South Korea
  C. North Korea
  D. None of these

835. Many times we read in financial newspapers/magazines about Systematic Investment Plans (SIPs). SIPs are an investment option also operated in the mode of:
  A. Mutual Funds
  B. Small Savings Schemes in Post Offices
  C. National Pension Fund
  D. National Saving Certificates

836. Who amongst the following has suggested to the banks in India to give details of fund transfers to customers via SMS/E-mails?
  A. Reserve Bank of India (RBI)
  B. India Banks' Association (IBA)
  C. Indian Institute of Banking & Finance
  D. Securities & Exchange Board of India

837. A new Foreign Bank Sarasin & Co. has launched its operations in India recently.
  This is a bank based in:
  A. USA
  B. Switzerland
  C. France
  D. None of these

838. The Head of the Reserve Bank of India is designated as the:
  A. Chief Executive Officer
  B. Managing Director
  C. Chief Banking Officer
  D. None of these

839. Whenever RBI does some Open Market Operation Transaction, actually it wishes to regulate which of the following?
  A. Inflation only
  B. Liquidity in economy
  C. Borrowing powers of the banks
  D. Flow of Foreign Direct Investments

840. In economics it is generally believed that the main objective of a Public Sector Financial Company like Bank is to:
  A. Employ more and more people
  B. Maximize total profits
  C. Maximize total production
  D. Provide financial service to the people of the nation of its origin across the country

841. In a Company the use of price sensitive corporate information by the Company—people to make gains or cover losses is known as:
  A. insider trading
  B. future trading
  C. foreign trading
  D. stock trading

842. Which of the following cannot be called as a Debt Instrument as referred in financial transactions?
  A. Certificate of Deposits
  B. Bonds
  C. Stocks
  D. Commercial Papers

843. Which of the following committees has given its recommendations on "Financial Inclusion"?
  A. Rakesh Mohan Committee
  B. Rangarajan Committee
  C. Sinha Committee
  D. None of these

844. Which of the following correctly describes what sub-prime lending is?
 1. Lending to the people with less than ideal credit status.
 2. Lending to the people who are high value customers of the banks.
 3. Lending to those who are not a regular customer of a bank.
 A. Only 1   B. Only 2   C. Only 3   D. All of these

845. The actual return of an investor is reduced sometimes as the prices of the commodities go up all of a sudden. In financial sector this type of phenomenon is known is:
 A. Probability risk   B. Market risk   C. Inflation risk   D. None of these

846. Which of the following products launched by most of the banks help farmers in getting instant credit for various agricultural purposes?
 A. Kissan Credit Card   B. Personal Loan
 C. Business Loan   D. None of these

847. Which of the following policies of the financial sectors is *basically* designed to transferring local financial assets into foreign financial asset freely and at market determined exchange rates? Policy of:
 A. Capital Accounts Convertibility   B. Financial Deficit Management
 C. Minimum Support Price   D. None of these

848. A customer wishes to purchase some US dollars in India. He/She should go to:
 A. Public Debt Division of the RBI only
 B. American Express Bank only
 C. RBI or any branch of a bank which is authorized for such business
 D. None of these

849. Which of the following products of a bank is specifically designed to provide financial help to children in their higher studies in India or in a foreign nation?
 A. Personal Loan   B. Corporate Loan
 C. Educational Loan   D. Mortgage Loan

850. A Bank/Financial Organisation these days relies heavily on e-commerce for its transaction. As a part of system security, it has introduced organisation's security awareness manual. This step of the organisation can be classified under which one of the following categories of measures for a business?
 A. Preventive   B. Compliance   C. Corrective   D. Detective

851. Which of the following is the limitation of the ATMs owing to which people are required to visit branches of the bank?
 1. It does not accept deposits.
 2. It has a limited cash disbursement capacity.
 3. Lack of human interface.
 A. Only 1   B. Only 2   C. Only 3   D. All of these

852. An industry which is fighting hard to increase its market share in existing market (with new popular products) is known as:
 A. market vendor   B. market operator
 C. market leader   D. market challenger

853. Many times we see in newpapers that some projects are launched by the government authorities on 'PPP' basis. What is the full form of 'PPP'?
 A. Preferential Payment Plan   B. Public-Private Partnership
 C. Partial Payment Project   D. Popular Private Project

854. The government of India has decided to allow Currency Futures in India. In addition to Ministry of Finance which is/are the other organisation(s) whose permission/approval is needed for such operations in India?
1. International Monetary Fund (IMF)
2. Reserve Bank of India (RBI)
3. Securities and Exchange Board of India (SEBI)
A. Only 1   B. Only 2   C. Only 3   D. Only 2 and 3

855. The Reserve Bank of India has decided to help banks, as a temporary measure, by providing additional liquidity support under LAF. What is the full form of LAF?
A. Loan Adjustment Fund   B. Liquidity Adjustment Facility
C. Long Awaited Funds   D. Loan Against Funds

856. The formal or institutional credit delivery system in rural India comprises of which of the following?
1. Cooperative Credit Institutions
2. Commercial Banks
3. Regional Rural Banks
4. Self Help Groups
A. Only 1 and 2   B. Only 3 and 4   C. Only 1, 2 and 4   D. All of these

857. The Reserve Bank of India has has issued guidelines to banks on Pillar 2 of Basel II framework. Pillar 2 deals with which of the following?
1. Better human resource management
2. Adequate capital to support risks
3. Better profitability with minimum number of employees
A. Only 1   B. Only 2   C. Only 3   D. None of these

858. Which of the following is NOT a department of the Ministry of Finance, government of India?
A. Department of Economic Affairs   B. Department of Expenditure
C. Department of Revenue   D. Department of Foreign Investments

859. The recent extraordinary global developments triggered by the bankruptcy/sellouts/restructuring of some of the world's largest financial institutions have resulted in severe disruptions of money markets and decline of stock markets across the world. What measures RBI has taken to protect Indian Markets and financial institutions from such casualties?
1. RBI has decided to keep full control on selling and purchase of foreign exchange which will be done through its offices only. Banks and other agents will not be allowed to sell/purchase the foreign exchange directly.
2. Banks are asked to lower down their prime lending rates to accommodate more and more borrowers.
3. Government of India will now sell their Security/Developments bonds only in Foreign countries through selected branches of some nationalised banks as it will attract foreign investors who are skeptical in investing in Indian Companies these days.
A. Only 1   B. Only 2   C. Only 3   D. All of these

860. Which of the following is/are different categories of inflation?
1. Open and suppressed
2. Cost push
3. Demand pull
A. Only 1   B. Both 1 and 2   C. Both 2 and 3   D. All of these

861. Which of the following services is introduced recently by the Reserve Bank of India and SEBI in India for the first time?
1. Trading of Currency futures.
2. Opening of NRI Accounts in Indian currencies.
3. Foreign Direct Investment through Participatory Notes (PNs) by the Foreign Institutional Investors.
A. Only 1 B. Only 2 C. Only 3 D. All of these

862. Many a times we read about Rural Indebtedness in various newspapers/magazines. What are the main causes of the rural indebtedness?
1. Poverty
2. Inability to repay the loans
3. Zamindari System which prevents farmers to own the land
A. Only 1 B. Only 2 C. Both 1 and 2 D. All of these

863. The process of the total valuation of the financial capital assets of a country is technically known as:
A. Market Capitalization B. Gross Domestic Product
C. Net wealth of the country D. Gross Domestic Resources

864. Which of the following is NOT the part of the organized sector of Indian Money Market?
A. Mutual Funds B. Non-Banking Financial Companies
C. Unit Trust of India D. Chit funds

865. Very often we read in newspapers/magazines about "Sovereign Wealth Funds". Which of the following is/are the correct description of the same?
1. These are the funds or the reserves of a government or central bank of a country which are invested further to earn profitable returns.
2. These are the funds, which were accumulated by some people over the years but were not put in active circulation as they retain them as Black Money for Several years.
3. The funds which are created to be used as relief funds or bailouts packages are known as sovereign funds.
A. Both 2 and 3 only B. Only 2 C. Only 3 D. Only 1

866. Very often we read about Special Economic Zones (SEZs) in newspapers. What was the purpose of promoting SEZs in India?
1. They are established to promote exports.
2. They are established to attract investments from foreign countries.
3. They are established to help poorest of the poors in India as the activities of these zones are reserved only for poors and those living below poverty line.
A. Only 1 B. Only 2 C. Only 3 D. Both 1 and 2 only

867. Which of the following banks has taken over the Centurion Bank of Punjab?
A. ICICI Bahk B. IDBI Bank C. HDFC Bank D. AXIS Bank

868. The main function of I. M. F. is to ....
A. Finance investment loans to developing countries
B. Act as a private sector lending arm of the World Bank
C. Help to solve balance of payment problems of member countries
D. Arrange international deposits from banks

869. Which of the following is not a part of the scheduled banking structure in India?
A. Money Lenders B. Public Sector Banks
C. Private Sector Banks D. Regional Rural Banks

870. The rate of interest on Savings Bank Account is stipulated by:
    A. The concerned bank   B. RBI
    C. Indian Banks Association   D. Government of India

871. Many times we read a term CBS used in banking operation. What is the full form of the letter 'C' in the term 'CBS'?
    A. Core   B. Credit   C. Continuous   D. Complete

872. At which one of the following rate, the Central Bank lends to banks against government securities?
    A. Repo Rate   B. Reverse Repo Rate   C. Bank Rate   D. SLR

873. One of the sources of income of banks is to charge fee for certain services. What are some of the services provided by the banks for which they charge fee?
    1. Issuing Demand Drafts/Pay Orders
    2. Issue of ATM/Credit/Debit Cards
    3. Electronic Transfer of Money
    A. Only 1   B. Only 2   C. Only 3   D. All of these

874. Which of the following is the full form of the term SLR as used in the banking sector?
    A. Social Lending Ratio   B. Statutory Liquidity Ratio
    C. Scheduled Liquidity Rate   D. None of these

875. As we all know, the major source of income of the banks is lending money (providing credit) and earning interest on it. In normal circumstances, the demand of the credit comes mainly from which of the following sectors?
    1. Personal Loans
    2. Priority Sector Lending & Bailout Packages
    3. Project Finance
    A. Only 1   B. Only 2   C. Only 3   D. All of these

876. "The set of directive principles issued by the Central Bank of a country or the process adopted by it to control the supply of money, availability of money, cost of money and rate of interest, etc. in order to bring stability and growth of the economy" are commonly known as:
    A. Monetary policy of the Central Bank of the country
    B. Budget of the Govt.
    C. Profit & Loss Account
    D. Business Policy of the Bank

877. Many banks have launched/fllated their subsidiaries which are fully owned by them. Banks launch subsidiaries normally for which of the following businesses?
    1. Home Loan Business
    2. To sell Insurance Policies
    3. To control Online Operations or Internet Banking business
    A. Only 1   B. Only 2   C. Only 3   D. All of these

878. When the common people of a nation start getting very high salary or wages, the consumption of the goods like eatables and white goods, also start increasing. This situation brings which of the following types of inflation in the economy?
    1. Cost push inflation
    2. Demand pull inflation
    3. Low inflation
    A. Only 1 & 3   B. Only 2   C. Only 3   D. All of these

879. The Securities & Exchange Board of India (SEBI) has asked all FIIs to divulge the structure of their offshore entities. What purpose will it serve?
1. To identify if there is any flow of funds from some questionable sources
2. To know how much money FIIs are planning to invest in India in 2010-11.
3. To forecast the possibility of any financial crisis in near future.
A. Only 1   B. Only 2   C. Only 3   D. All of these

880. Many a time we read in the newspapers that RBI has changed or revised a particular ratio/rate by a few basis points. What is basis point?
A. Ten per cent of one hundredth point   B. One hundredth of 1%
C. One hundredth of 10%   D. Ten per cent of 1000

881. Nowadays we frequently read news items about "Derivatives" as used in the world of finance and money market. Which of the following statement(s) correctly describes what a derivative is and how it affects money/finance markets?
1. Derivatives enable individuals and companies to insure themselves against financial risk.
2. Derivatives are like fixed deposits in a bank and are the safest way to invest one's idle money lying in a bank.
3. Derivatives are the financial instruments which were used in India even during the British Raj.
A. Only 3   B. Only 2   C. Only 1   D. All of these

882. For recapitalization of Public Sector Banks, the World Bank has decided to provide funds to India. These funds will be made available in the form of ....
A. Soft Loan   B. Term Loan
C. Emergency aid   D. Grants

883. Which of the following decisions taken by the RBI will promote the concept of financial inclusion in the country?
A. To appoint some additional entities as business correspondents
B. To collect reasonable service charges from the customer in a transparent manner for providing the services
C. To ask the banks to open at least 50 new accounts daily in non serviced areas
D. Only A & B

884. Which one of the following is/are implication(s) of large inflow of foreign exchange into the country?
1. It makes monetary management difficult for RBI.
2. It creates money supply, asset bubbles and inflation.
3. It weakens the competitiveness of Indian exports.
A. Only 1   B. Only 2   C. Only 3   D. All of these

885. In India, which of the following agency is responsible for announcing the Foreign Trade Policy?
A. RBI   B. EXIM-Bank
C. Foreign Ministry   D. Industry & Commerce Ministry

886. Many a time we read a term MSS in relation to banking transactions. What is the full form of MSS?
A. Money Stabilization Scheme   B. Market Stabilization Scheme
C. Maturity and Standardization Service   D. Money Stabilization Service

887. RBI's open market operation transactions are carried out with a view to regulate:
A. Liquidity in the economy   B. Prices of essential commodities
C. Inflation   D. All of the above

888. Open market operations, one of the measures taken by RBI in order to control credit expansion in the economy means:
- A. Sale or purchase of Govt. securities
- B. Issuance of different types of bonds
- C. Auction of gold
- D. None of these

889. The bank rate means:
- A. Rate of interest charged by commercial banks from borrowers
- B. Rate of interest at which commercial banks discounted bills of their borrowers
- C. Rate of interest allowed by commercial banks on their deposits
- D. Rate at which RBI purchases or rediscounts bills of exchange of commercial banks

890. What is an Indian Depository Receipt?
- A. A deposit account with a Public Sector Bank
- B. A deposit account with any of depositories in India
- C. An instrument in the form of depository receipt created by an Indian depository against underlying equity shares of the issuing company
- D. None of these

891. Fiscal deficit is:
- A. total income less Govt. borrowing
- B. total payments less total receipts
- C. total payments less capital receipts
- D. total expenditure less total receipts excluding borrowing

892. In the capital market, the term arbitrage is used with reference to:
- A. purchase of securities to cover the sale
- B. sale of securities to reduce the loss on purchase
- C. simultaneous purchase and sale of securities to make profits from price
- D. Any of the above

893. The stance of RBI monetary policy is:
- A. inflation control with adequate liquidity for growth
- B. improving credit quality of the Banks
- C. strengthening credit delivery mechanism
- D. Any of the above

894. Currency Swap is an instrument to manage:
- A. currency risk
- B. interest rate risk
- C. currency and interest rate risk
- D. cash flows in different currency

895. "Sub-prime" refers to:
- A. lending done by banks at rates below PLR
- B. funds raised by the banks at sub-Libor Rates
- C. Group of banks which are not rate as prime banks as per Banker's Almanac
- D. lending done by financing institutions including banks to customers not meeting with normally required credit appraisal standards

896. Euro Bond is an instrument:
- A. issued in the European market
- B. issued in Euro currency
- C. issued in a country other than the country of the currency of the Bond
- D. All of the above

897. Money laundering normally involves:
  A. placement of funds
  B. layering of funds
  C. integrating of funds
  D. All of these

898. The IMF and the World Bank were conceived as institutions to:
  A. Strengthening international economic co-operation and to help create a more stable and prosperous global economy
  B. IMF promotes international monetary cooperation
  C. The World Bank promotes long term economic development and poverty reduction
  D. All of these

899. Capital Market Regulator is:
  A. RBI   B. IRDA   C. NSE   D. SEBI

900. FDI refers to:
  A. Fixed Deposit Interest
  B. Fixed Deposit Investment
  C. Foreign Direct Investment
  D. Future Derivative Investment

901. Which of the following is the Regulator of the credit rating agencies in India?
  A. RBI   B. SBI   C. SIDBI   D. SEBI

902. The logo of Bank of Baroda is known as:
  A. Sun of Bank of Baroda
  B. Baroda Sun
  C. Bank of Baroda's Rays
  D. Sunlight of Bank of Baroda

903. One of the major challenges banking industries is facing these days is money laundering. Which of the following acts/norms are launched by the banks to prevent money laundering in general?
  A. Know your customer norms
  B. Banking Regulation Act
  C. Negotiable Instruments Act
  D. None of these

904. Lot of Banks in India these days are offering M-Banking Facility to their customers. What is the full form of 'M' in 'M-Banking'?
  A. Money   B. Marginal   C. Message   D. Mobile Phone

905. Which of the following is/are true about the "Sub-Prime Crisis"? (The term was very much in news recently.)
  1. It is a Mortgage Crisis referring to Credit default by the borrowers
  2. Sub-Prime borrowers were those borrowers who were rated low and were high risk borrowers
  3. This crisis originated of negligence in credit rating of the borrowers
  A. Only 1   B. Only 2   C. Only 3   D. All of these

906. Which of the following is NOT the part of the structure of the financial System in India?
  A. Industrial Finance
  B. Agricultural Finance
  C. Government Finance
  D. Personal Finance

907. Grameen Bank and Micro Credit are associated with:
  A. Manmohan Singh
  B. Bill Gates
  C. Md. Yunus
  D. Aung San Su Ki

908. As we all know Govt. of India collects tax revenue on various activities in the country. Which of the following is a part of the tax revenue of the Govt.?
1. Tax on Income
2. Tax on Expenditure
3. Tax on property or Capital Asset
4. Tax on Goods and Services

A. Both 1 and 3 only
B. Both 2 and 4 only
C. All of these
D. None of these

909. We very frequently read about Special Economic Zones (SEZs) in newspapers. These SEZs were established with which of the following objectives?
1. To attract foreign investment directly
2. To protect domestic market from direct competition from multinationals
3. To provide more capital to agriculture and allied activities

A. Only 1 B. Only 2 C. Only 3 D. All of these

910. Many times we read about Future Trading in newspapers. What is Future Trading?
1. It is nothing but a trade between any two stock exchanges where in it is decided to purchase the stocks of each other on a fixed price throughout the year
2. It is an agreement between two parties to buy and sell an underlying asset in the future at a predetermined price
3. It is agreement between Stock Exchanges that they will not trade the stocks of each other under any circumstances in future or for a given period of time

A. Only 1 B. Only 2 C. Only 3 D. All of these

911. Inflation in India is measured on which of the following indexes/indicators?

A. Cost of Living Index (COLI)
B. Consumer Price Index (CPI)
C. Gross Domestic Product (GDP)
D. Wholesale Price Index (WPI)

912. Which of the following correctly describes the concept of 'Nuclear Bank' floated by International Atomic Energy Agency?
1. It is a nuclear fuel bank to be shared by all the nations jointly.
2. It is a facility to help nations in enrichment of uranium.
3. It is an agency which will keep a close vigil on the nuclear programme of all the nations.

A. Only 1
B. Only 2
C. Both 1 and 3 only
D. Only 3

913. Which of the following schemes is not a social development Scheme?

A. Indira Awas Yojana
B. Mid Day Meal
C. Bharat Nirman Yojana
D. Sarva Shiksha Abhiyan

914. As we all know banks publish their quarterly performance to bring transparency in the system and also to give a clear picture of their performance to the public. How were results of Quarter 2 different from the results of Quarter 1 of the listed banks including giants like SBI and ICICI banks?
1. Performance was subdued in the Quarter 2.
2. Yields on advances of almost all listed banks have come down.
3. Advances grew at a slower pace when compared to deposits.

A. Only 1 is true
B. Only 2 is true
C. Only 3 is true
D. All of these

915. As per the news published in major newspapers in India Banks in India need about 12 lakh business correspondents for rural areas. What will be the role of these correspondents?
1. They will help rural people in their day-to-day banking activities.
2. They will work as a link between banks and the customers.
3. They will ascertain eligibility of rural people so that relief packages can be provided to them.
A. Only 1   B. Only 2   C. Only 3   D. All of these

916. As per the news published in a financial publication RBI is redesigning its 'ECS' to function as a Automated Clearing House (ACH) for bulk transactions. What is full form of 'ECS'?
A. Extra Closing System   B. Electronic Cheque System
C. Evening Cheque Sorter   D. Electronic Clearing Service

917. The Reserve Bank of India has asked all the banks to install 'Note Sorting Machines' in the branches. How will this help banks and the general public?
1. The machines will check for counterfeit notes and drop these from circulation.
2. This will help banks to count the notes quickly and accurately.
3. This will help in sorting out soiled notes so that they are not reissued by the banks.
A. Only 2   B. Only 1   C. Only 3   D. Only 1 and 2

918. As per the guidelines issued by the RBI, banks are preparing for a service which will allow customers to withdraw upto Rs. 1,000 using their debit cards from notified shops/stores all over the country. All such shops/stores will have 'POS' terminals for the same. What is full form of the 'POS'?
A. Payment on Sale   B. Power of Sale
C. Point of Sale   D. Payment Order Service

919. The working group set up by the RBI has suggested the launch of an Emergency Fund Facility Scheme for banks. This scheme will help which of the following types of banks?
A. Public Sector Banks   B. Small Banks
C. Urban Cooperative Banks   D. Private Banks

920. One of the major emphasis of Basel II is that banks should have:
A. adequate Capital Adequacy Ratio   B. only few branches in urban centres
C. more and more branches in rural areas   D. core banking mode of operation

921. Some world bodies/organisations/agencies are of the view that agriculture should adopt a 'Cross Disciplinary Approach', and take help of all types os sciences and studies. This approach will help in which of the following crucial problems being faced by humanity?
A. Use of Genetically Modified Crop   B. Melting of glaciers
C. Food crisis   D. None of these

922. An agreement between two nations or a group of nations which establishes unimpeded exchange and flow of goods and services between/among trade partners regardless of national boundaries is called:
A. Import Free Agreement   B. Free Trade Agreement
C. Export Free Agreement   D. None of these

923. Which of the following correctly describe what 'One Carbon Credit' is?
1. Credit permit to release one ton of carbon dioxide.
2. Providing loans to establish one new production unit which can produce carbon dioxide for industrial use.
3. Finding out one new business which can use and recycle green house gases.
A. Only 3   B. Only 2   C. Only 1   D. All of these

924. The Food and Agriculture Organisation (FAO) is a wing/agency of the:
A. World Bank
B. United Nations Organisation
C. Asian Development Bank
D. Ministry of Agriculture Govt. of India

925. At present the trade between India and China is in a state of 'Payment imbalance'. What does this mean in real terms?
1. China does not import many items from India whereas India imports more from China.
2. China does not pay India in time and a lot of delay is reported by the exporters.
3. India wants all payments to be made in US Dollars whereas China pays in its own currency.
A. Only 1
B. Only 2
C. Only 3
D. All of these

926. Which of the following terms is **not** used in Banking and Finance?
A. Bid Price
B. Jacksonian Seizure
C. Call Option
D. Bluechip

927. Which of the following terms is **not** used in Economics?
A. Exogenous
B. Depreciation
C. Deep Market
D. Zero Sum Game

928. As we know Govt. is paying much attention towards the development of watersheds and water bodies in all the areas of the country. What is/are the reasons owing to which Govt. has to take these special efforts to develop/recharge watersheds and water bodies?
1. The one single biggest problem of the agriculture in the country is inappropriate irrigation facilities and farmers' overdependence on the monsoon. Govt. wants farmers to come out of it.
2. The water table in some of the areas in the country is going down. This is a matter of great concern for all of us as this may result in severe water problem in days to come. Govt. is serious about it.
3. Around 30 to 35 per cent watersheds/water bodies in the country are not being utilized as the quality of the water in these has deteriorated over the years.
A. Only 1
B. Only 2
C. Only 3
D. All of these

929. As we know many Indian Banks are opening their branches in foreign countries these days. What in your opinion is/are the reasons owing to which these banks are willing to open branches in foreign countries?
1. India has the largest network of bank branches in the world. Hence other nations also wish to take advantage of their services.
2. Indian Banks get an opportunity to raise foreign currency funds and also the experience funding joint ventures of multinationals. This prompts them to open their branches in foreign nations.
3. As many foreign banks are functioning in India, India in turn is also required to open equal number of branches in foreign countries. Hence, Indian Banks are opening branches in these countries.
A. Only 1
B. Only 2
C. Only 3
D. Only 1 and 2

930. As a practice, all banks now deduct some amount from their pre tax income and set aside in a separate account to create a cushion for the loans which may go bad. This is called:
A. CRR
B. SLR
C. Provisioning
D. PLR

931. Which of the following norms/practices adopted by the banks is/are launched to ensure that the money from illegal activities/sources does/do not come to banks and therefore, the economic health of the nation does not get affected?
1. Know your Customer

2. Financial Inclusion

3. Branchless Banking

A. Only 1   B. Only 2   C. Only 3   D. All of these

932. Which of the following is NOT one of the recommendations of the committee setup on Financial Sector Reforms under the Chairmanship of Raghuram G. Rajan?

1. Give more freedoms to banks to setup branches and ATMS anywhere.

2. Setup an office of financial ombudsman.

3. All deposits taking institutions should be free from the supervision of the RBI.

A. Only 1   B. Only 2   C. Only 3   D. All of these

933. Federal Reserves is the Central Bank of:

A. Britain   B. U.S.A   C. Japan   D. Canada

934. The Reserve Bank of India (RBI) keeps on modifying various rates/ratios to keep the flow of liquidity in the market in a balanced situation. Which of the following rates/ratios/indexes is NOT directly controlled by the RBI?

A. Cash Reserve Ratio (CRR)   B. Repo Rate (RR)

C. Reserve Repo Rate (RRR)   D. Wholesale Price Index (WPI)

935. Many Banks have adopted/launched "Core Banking Solution (CBS)". Core Banking Solution is—

A. a marketing strategy adopted by the Banks

B. a new type of ATM useful for rural population

C. a delivery channel for quick and fast delivery

D. a new product launched to help senior citizens only as they are not able to visit branches/ATMs frequently

936. Which of the following cannot be called as a value Added service offered by a Bank?

A. Special accounts for poor sections of the society B. Accident insurance cover

C. Instant Credits of Outstation Cheques   D. Free cheques book

937. Opening the Savings Bank Account of a minor girl will be called as which of the following in Banking terminology?

A. Retail Banking   B. Merchant Banking

C. Institutional Banking   D. Social Banking

938. Which of the following is NOT a measure of the Risk Management in Banks?

A. CRR   B. RTGS   C. SLR   D. Deposit Insurance

939. As per the newspaper reports the RBI is planning to introduce 'Plastic Currency Notes'. What is/are the benefits of 'Plastic Notes'?

1. Their Shelf life will be longer.

2. It will replace plastic money or credit, debit cards which are giving birth to many fraudulent practices.

3. Printing will be cheaper.

A. Only 3   B. Only 2   C. Only 1   D. All of these

940. 'Sub Prime Lending' is a term applied to the loans made to:

A. Those borrowers who do not have a good credit history

B. Those who wish to take loan against the mortgage of tangible assets

C. Those who have a good credit history and are known to bank since 10 years

D. None of these

941. As per the reports published in various journals and newspapers the 'small borrowers' in rural areas still prefer to take informal route for their credit needs. Which of the following is the 'informal route' of credit in financial sector?

A. Credit cards

B. Loan against gold from financial institute

C. Debit cards

D. Money lender

942. What is meant by 'Underwriting' the term frequently used in financial sector?

A. Under valuation of the assets

B. The Act of taking on a risk for a fee

C. Giving a Guarantee that a loan will not become a bad loan

D. None of these

943. As we have noticed many banks of Indian origin are opening offices/branches in foreign countries. Why is this trend emerging at a very fast pace?

1. These Banks wish to provide banking facilities to foreigners as banking facilities are not plenty in many foreign countries. India wants to take an advantage of the situation.

2. These banks wish to help Indian firms to acquire funds at internationally competitiverates.

3. These banks wish to promote trade and investment between India and other countries.

A. Only 1   B. Only 2   C. Only 3   D. Only 2 and 3

944. Many economists, bankers and researchers in India often advocate that banks should equip themselves for new challenges. These challenges are in which of the following shapes/forms?

1. As Indian economy is getting increasingly integrated with the rest of the world the demand of the Corporate banking is likely to change in terms of size, composition of services and also the quality.

2. The growing foreign trade in India will have to be financed by the local banks.

3. Foreigners are habitual of the comforts provided by the technology. India has to do alot in this reference.

A. Only 1 is correct   B. Only 2 is correct   C. Only 3 is correct   D. All of these

945. Which of the following is not a banking/finance related term?

A. Credit wrap   B. EMI   C. Held to Maturity   D. Diffusion

946. Which of the following is the correct definition of the term commercial papers?

1. It is nothing but the popular name of the Judicial stamp papers used to register financial transactions.

2. It is one of the instruments through which Corporates raise debt from the market.

3. It is the name of the 'Certificate of Deposits' provided by the Banks to its retail customers.

A. Only 1   B. Only 2   C. Only 3   D. Both 1 and 2

947. Many a times we read in the newspapers a term 'Hot Money'. Which of the following is the correct definition of Hot Money?

1. This is the fund which is dumped into a country to get the advantage of a favourable interest rate and hence brings higher returns.

2. This is the fund which is provided by a bank in US $ at very short notice and at a very high rate of interest and for a longer period of repayment.

3. This is the fund which is pushed into market through Hawala or some other such illegal methods and sometimes referred also as Black Money.

A. Only 1 is correct

B. Only 1 and 2 are correct

C. Only 3 is correct

D. Both 1 and 3 are true

948. The real return to the investor sometimes gets reduced due to sudden rise in the prices of the commodities. This phenomenon in financial market is known as:

A. Market risk

B. Inflation risk

C. Credit risk

D. Diversification of funds

949. As per the reports in the leading newspapers Securities and Exchange Board of India (SEBI) has asked the Mutual Fund industry to stop 'Misselling' their schemes to investors. What is 'Misselling' of products?

1. Misselling takes place when mutual funds are sold without telling the likely returns.
2. When agents sell the products without telling investors what are the risks involved in investing in mutual funds.
3. When agents invest somebody's money in mutual funds without their knowledge, it is called misselling.

A. Only 1

B. Only 2

C. Only 3

D. All of these

950. As per newspaper reports outsourcing has become a profitable business in India and countries like China are trying to learn about it from India. What are the main factors which has/have helped India in attaining this position?

1. Availabiltiy of skilled manpower in abundance.
2. Knowledge of English language.
3. A switch over from farming to other sectors which are creating more job opportunities.

A. Only 1

B. Only 2

C. Both 1 and 2

D. All of these

951. Which of the following committees recommended the revival of Cooperative Credit institutions in states?

A. Vaidyanathan Committee

B. Rangarajan Committee

C. Sachchar Committee

D. None of these

952. Which of the following organizations/agencies has established a fund known as 'Investor protection fund'?

A. SEBI

B. NABARD

C. Bombay Stock Exchange

D. AMFI

953. India has different categories of Commercial Banks. Which of the following is NOT one such category?

A. Private Banks

B. Commodity Banks

C. Nationalized Banks

D. Co-operative Banks

954. Which of the following types of Banks are allowed to operate foreign currency accounts?

1. Foreign Banks
2. Regional Rural Banks
3. Nationalized Banks

A. Only 1

B. Only 2

C. Only 3

D. All of these

955. The money which Govt. of India spends on the development of infrastructure in country comes from which of the following sources? [Pick up the correct statement (s)]

1. Loan from World Bank/ADB etc.
2. Taxes collected from the people.
3. Loan from the RBI.

A. Only 1

B. Only 2

C. Only 3

D. All of these

956. Many times we read in financial newspapers about 'FII'. What is the full form of FII?
A. Final Investment in India
B. Foreign Investment in India
C. Formal Investment in India
D. Foreign Institutional Investment

957. Commission for Agricultural Costs and Prices (CACP) recommends:
A. Comfort Price
B. State Advised Price
C. Minimum Support Price
D. Minimum Export Price

958. The Secure Electronic Transaction (SET) specification—
A. is a notice, issued and verified by a certificate authority, that guarantees a user or Website is legitimate
B. provides private-key encryption of all data that passes between a client and server
C. allows users to choose an encryption scheme for the data that passes between a clientand a server
D. uses a public-key encryption to secure credit-card transaction systems

959. Lot of discussion is going on these days on the issue of 'Participatory Note' (P Notes) used in financial sector/money market. What is Participatory Note? [Pick up the correct statement(s)]
1. It is nothing but another name of the banking operation by which banks exchange Indian Rupee into US Dollars without depositing a single rupee in the account of the party who are NRIs. The entire operation is carried out by the banks solely on the basis of the credit and good, will of the NRI party.
2. It is an offshore derivative instrument used by overseas buyers/investors who buy shares of Indian companies listed in Indian Stock Exchange anonymously.
3. It is nothing but a type of undertaking given to the banks that they should continue investing money in stock markets on behalf of the NRIs and in case the market crashes NRI's will make the losses good without delay.
A. Only 1
B. Only 2
C. Only 3
D. All of these

960. From the given options A to D, please find out the one which is not an objective of a central Bank of a country?
A. The Central Bank of a country aims at profit
B. The Central Bank is given powers to control and regulate the working of the commercial banks
C. Central Bank generally is a organ of the government and run by government officials
D. Central Bank generally controls the credit

961. From the given options, bring out the one which is not a function/power of Reserve Bank of India:
A. To assume the responsibility of meeting directly or indirectly all reasonable demands for accommodation
B. To hold cash reserves of the commercial banks and make available financial accommodation to them
C. To enjoy monopoly of the note issue
D. To assume the responsibility of statistical analysis of data related to macro economy of India

962. Many a times we read in the newspapers about margin requirements. From the given options, find out the one which correctly indicates margin requirements:
A. Margin requirements aim at the regulation of the volume of credit as well as flow of the credit
B. Margin requirements imply that every bank has to keep certain minimum cash reserves with the Reserve Bank of India
C. Margin requirements imply that every bank has to keep certain proportion of its total deposits in the form of cash with it self
D. Margin requirements imply to a cushion against the decline in the value of the security

963. What will be the impact on the cash reserves of commercial banks if RBI conducts a sale of securities?

    A. Increase   B. Decrease

    C. Remain constant   D. Increase or decrease

964. Which among the following is a major qualitative control measure in India?

    A. Bank Rate Policy   B. Open Market Operations

    C. Reserve Ratio Requirements   D. Margin Requirements

965. Many a times we read in the financial newspapers that Reserve Bank of India is "Lender of Last Resort (LOLR)" in India. Which among the following statement gives the most correct definition of "Lender of Last Resort"?

    A. If a person or firm which is eligible to get a loan, does not get it from any commercial bank, may approach to Reserve Bank of India for loan.

    B. If the state governments are in crisis and need money for short term, they can approach RBI for this purpose.

    C. If a commercial bank is in crisis, it may place its reasonable demand for accommodation to Reserve Bank of India.

    D. A scheduled commercial bank meets all of its demands in all weathers from Reserve Bank of India

966. (The figures in this questions are imaginary). We suppose that Cash Reserve Ratio (CRR) in country's economy is 10%. The banking system wish a cash deposits of Rs. 1000 Crore, creates total deposits of Rs. 10,000 Crores. The Reserve Bank wishes that bank should create more deposits. Which among the following step will be taken by the Reserve Bank?

    A. It will lower the Cash Reserve Ratio   B. It will raise the Cash Reserve Ratio

    C. It will increase the Margin Requirements   D. It will start selling Government Securities

967. Many a times we read in the newspapers that RBI takes certain steps to curb the menace of Inflation. In this context, which among the following will not help RBI in controlling the inflation in the country?

    A. An increase in the Bank Rate

    B. An increase in the Reserve Ratio Requirements

    C. A purchase of securities in the open market

    D. Rationing of the credit

968. We suppose that Reserve Bank of India would like to increase the cash Reserves of the commercial banks. Which among the following would be most appropriate action of the RBI to achieve this aim?

    A. RBI would release gold from its reserves

    B. RBI would raise the reserve ratio

    C. RBI would buy the bonds in the open market.

    D. RBI will stop the transactions which involve the bills of exchange

969. Which among the following is a incorrect statement:

    A. The Reserve Bank of India has the special powers to control and regulate the commercial banking system

    B. A rise in the bank rate is a strong anti-deflationary monetary tool

    C. Minimum Reserve Requirements are fixed to ensure the liquidity and solvency of individual commercial banks

    D. Reserve Ratio Requirement is a quicker method than bank rate and OMO (Open Market Operations) in general credit regulations

970. Since which year, Reserve Bank of India is using the Selective Credit Control measures to control the amount of bank advances against the commodities having limited supply?
  A. 1949   B. 1956   C. 1969   D. 1973

971. The "Service area Approach" was an strategy launched to improve which of the following?
  A. Micro, Small and medium Enterprising   B. Unorganized Sector
  C. Rural Lending   D. Urban Industrial Lending

972. Which among the following bank/banks in India have set up the Financial Literacy & Credit Counselling centers?
  A. RBI   B. Scheduled Commercial Banks
  C. Foreign Banks working in India   D. Regional Rural Banks

973. Which of the following imaginary circumstances, the Reserve Bank of India will opt to sell Government securities in the open market?
  A. When the Foreign funds inflow is meek
  B. When there is enormous Foreign Funds Inflow in the Indian Economy
  C. When banks have low liquidity and need liquidity
  D. None of the above

974. Which among the following is correct full form of CAS in context with banking markets in India?
  A. Cash Authorization Scheme   B. Credit Authorization Scheme
  C. Credit Access System   D. Credit Arrangement System

975.   *List-I*   *List-II*
  1. Regulation of Capital market   (*i*) C A C P
  2. Selective credit control   (*ii*) Gadgil formula
  3. Minimum support price   (*iii*) RBI
  4. Plan transfers   (*iv*) SEBI

  Code:

	1	2	3	4
A.	(*iv*)	(*i*)	(*ii*)	(*iii*)
B.	(*iv*)	(*iii*)	(*ii*)	(*i*)
C.	(*ii*)	(*iii*)	(*iv*)	(*i*)
D.	(*iv*)	(*iii*)	(*i*)	(*ii*)

976.   *List-I*   *List-II*
  1. Reserve Bank of India   (*i*) 1968
  2. First Finance Commission   (*ii*) 1950
  3. Gadgil formula   (*iii*) 1935
  4. Planning Commission   (*iv*) 1952

  Code:

	1	2	3	4
A.	(*ii*)	(*i*)	(*iv*)	(*iii*)
B.	(*i*)	(*ii*)	(*iii*)	(*iv*)
C.	(*iii*)	(*iv*)	(*i*)	(*ii*)
D.	(*iv*)	(*iii*)	(*ii*)	(*i*)

977. Which one of the following measures is not adopted by Reserve Bank of India for controlling credit?
  A. Capital Adequacy Ratio   B. Cash Reserve Ratio
  C. Statutory Liquidity Ratio   D. Cash Deposit Ratio

978. Consider some of the following Acts to regulate industries and foreign exchange in India:
(*i*) Foreign Exchange Management Act
(*ii*) Industrial Development and Regulation Act
(*iii*)Monopolies and Restrictive Trade Practices Act
(*iv*) Foreign Exchange and Regulation Act

Arranging the above Acts in chronological order, the correct sequence is:
A. (*iii*), (*ii*), (*iv*) and (*i*)
B. (*ii*), (*iii*), (*iv*) and (*i*)
C. (*ii*), (*iv*), (*iii*) and (*i*)
D. (*i*), (*iv*), (*ii*) and (*iii*)

979. Commercial banks are the largest category of financial intermediaries; others include:
A. life-insurance companies   B. pension funds
C. savings and loan institutions   D. All of the above

980. In India national income is estimated by:
A. Finance Commission   B. Central Statistical Organisation
C. Planning Commission   D. Finance Ministry

981. High-powered money is produced by:
A. Commercial Banks   B. Co-operative Banks
C. Ministry of Finance   D. Reserve Bank of India

982. Which of the following Indian Act has been replaced by the enactment of FEMA in 1999?
A. FERA   B. Indian Copyright Act
C. Indian Patent Act   D. Both B and C

983. VAT is imposed:
A. Directly on consumer
B. On all stages between production and final stage
C. On first stage of production
D. On final stage of production

984. Increase in net RBI credit for Central Government represents:
A. Monetised Deficit   B. Fiscal Deficit   C. Revenue Deficit   D. Budgetary Deficit

985. What is 'Hawala'?
A. Illegal transactions of foreign exchange   B. Full details of a subject
C. Illegal trading of shares   D. Tax evasion

986. 'Closed Economy' is that economy in which
A. Neither export nor import takes place   B. Deficit financing takes place
C. Only export takes place   D. None of these

987. SDR is the currency of IMF which is in the form of:
A. Paper currency   B. Book-keeping entry only
C. Gold   D. None of these

988. The headquarters of SIDBI is in:
A. Lucknow   B. New Delhi   C. Mumbai   D. None of these

989. LIC of India was established in:
A. 1897   B. 1956   C. 1956   D. 1965

990. Narasimham Committee Report relates to:
  A. Insurance Sector Reform
  B. Banking Sector Reform
  C. Agricultural Sector Reform
  D. Industrial Sector Reform

991. Scheduled Bank is that bank which is:
  A. Nationalised
  B. Not Nationalised
  C. Based at foreign country
  D. Included in the second schedule of RBI

992. Which Bank is limited to the needs of agriculture and rural finance?
  A. SBI
  B. NABARD
  C. IFC
  D. RBI

993. Export credit includes:
  A. Buyers' credit only
  B. Suppliers' credit only
  C. Both A and B
  D. None of these

994. Statutory liquidity ratio (SLR) of commercial banks means:
  A. the percentage of cash that banks keep with them under rules
  B. the bank rate which is reference rate also
  C. the ratio of government and other gilt-edged securities to liquid liabilities
  D. the "reserve money"

995. If banks want to increase credit creation.
  A. they should increase interest rate to have more deposits
  B. they should reduce the rate of interest
  C. they should have high cash reserves with them
  D. they should force investors to create demand for loans

996. Monetary-base is made up of:
  A. Required reserves with the central bank and currency with the public
  B. Currency with the public and total deposits
  C. Reserves of banking system and currency with the public
  D. Borrowed reserves and non-borrowed reserves

997. As regards changes in interest rates, the most sensitive money market is the :
  A. Bill market
  B. Un-organised money market
  C. Call money market
  D. Collateral loan market

998. The Unit Banking System is very popular in
  A. England
  B. Japan
  C. India
  D. U.S.A.

999. Consider the following statements :

The success of a policy of variable reserve requirement depends on the
  1. maintenance of a fixed reserve ratio by the commercial banks
  2. maintenance of little or no excess reserves by the commercial banks
  3. presence of a developed money market of the above statements
  Codes:
  A. 2 and 3 are correct
  B. 1 and 2 are correct
  C. 3 alone is correct
  D. 1 and 3 are correct

1000. Which of the following instruments for quantitative control of credit are used by Reserve Bank of India?
1. Cash requirement ratio
2. Statutory liquidity ratio
3. Open market operations
4. Margin requirements

Select the correct answer using the following codes :

Codes:

A. 1 and 2   B. 2 and 4   C. All of these   D. None of these

1001. The objective of selective credit controls is mainly to:
A. selectively allocate credit to commercial banks
B. selectively allocate credit among borrowers
C. regulate the quantity of demand deposits created by commercial banks
D. regulate the quantity of credit created by commercial banks

1002. Grasham's law relates to :
A. money supply   B. money and prices
C. real output   D. employment

1003. 'Misery Index' represents:
A. Sum of rate of inflation and rate of unemployment
B. Product of rate of inflation and rate of unemployment
C. Proportion of very poor to poor living below the poverty line
D. Both B and C

1004. Which of the following is/are included in 'Deficit Financing' in India?
    (The term is used frequently in economic planning)
1. Borrowing from the Reserve Bank of India.
2. Issue of New Currency Notes.
3. Withdrawal of past balances/surpluses etc.
A. Only 1   B. Only 2   C. Only 3   D. All of these

1005. Which statement of the following is true for IMF?
A. It is not an agency of UNO
B. It can grant loan to any country of the world
C. It can grant loan to state Govt. of a country
D. It grants loan only to member nations

1006. The Headquarter of World Bank is situated at:
A. Manila   B. Washington D.C.
C. New York   D. Geneva

1007. Which pair is not correct?
A. EXIM Bank—Financing for export-import
B. RBI—Banker's bank
C. IDBI—Industrial finance
D. FCI—Financial assistance to commercial institutions

1008. The field given to Rangarajan Committee was:
A. Modernisation of Cloth Industry
B. To probe Share scam
C. To probe Sugar scam
D. To suggest measures for controlling BOP deficit

1009. The Headquarter of IMF is in:
A. New York
B. Washington D.C.
C. London
D. Manila

1010. According to Banking Regulation Act, RBI can fix SLR upto the ceiling of:
A. 40%
B. 50%
C. 30%
D. 45%

1011. R.N. Malhotra committee gave recommen-dations on the field of:
A. Sick Industries
B. Tax Reforms
C. Insurance Sector
D. Banking Sector

1012. IRBI—Industrial Reconstruction Bank of India was established in:
A. 1975
B. 1985
C. 1990
D. 1992

ANSWERS

1	2	3	4	5	6	7	8	9	10
A	A	B	D	A	D	C	C	A	A
11	**12**	**13**	**14**	**15**	**16**	**17**	**18**	**19**	**20**
C	C	A	B	C	B	A	A	C	B
21	**22**	**23**	**24**	**25**	**26**	**27**	**28**	**29**	**30**
C	D	B	A	D	A	B	C	D	B
31	**32**	**33**	**34**	**35**	**36**	**37**	**38**	**39**	**40**
B	C	C	D	B	C	D	A	A	D
41	**42**	**43**	**44**	**45**	**46**	**47**	**48**	**49**	**50**
A	C	A	A	B	B	C	D	C	B
51	**52**	**53**	**54**	**55**	**56**	**57**	**58**	**59**	**60**
B	A	B	D	D	C	B	C	C	B
61	**62**	**63**	**64**	**65**	**66**	**67**	**68**	**69**	**70**
D	D	D	A	A	A	A	D	B	C
71	**72**	**73**	**74**	**75**	**76**	**77**	**78**	**79**	**80**
A	C	C	A	C	B	A	C	D	D
81	**82**	**83**	**84**	**85**	**86**	**87**	**88**	**89**	**90**
D	C	A	D	A	A	C	D	B	D
91	**92**	**93**	**94**	**95**	**96**	**97**	**98**	**99**	**100**
C	A	C	C	C	A	B	B	C	C
101	**102**	**103**	**104**	**105**	**106**	**107**	**108**	**109**	**110**
C	D	C	B	C	C	B	A	C	D

111	112	113	114	115	116	117	118	119	120
C	B	B	B	B	B	C	C	C	B

121	122	123	124	125	126	127	128	129	130
C	D	C	B	D	B	B	D	C	A

131	132	133	134	135	136	137	138	139	140
D	C	B	C	C	A	C	C	B	C

141	142	143	144	145	146	147	148	149	150
B	A	B	D	B	A	C	A	B	C

151	152	153	154	155	156	157	158	159	160
C	B	B	D	C	A	C	B	D	A

161	162	163	164	165	166	167	168	169	170
B	A	C	C	A	B	A	C	D	C

171	172	173	174	175	176	177	178	179	180
C	B	A	C	C	C	C	D	D	A

181	182	183	184	185	186	187	188	189	190
B	C	C	B	D	A	C	D	D	B

191	192	193	194	195	196	197	198	199	200
B	D	A	A	B	D	A	A	B	D

201	202	203	204	205	206	207	208	209	210
D	C	B	A	D	D	D	D	D	D

211	212	213	214	215	216	217	218	219	220
C	D	D	A	D	C	C	C	A	C

221	222	223	224	225	226	227	228	229	230
A	B	A	C	A	B	B	B	B	A

231	232	233	234	235	236	237	238	239	240
D	A	D	D	C	C	C	B	C	D

241	242	243	244	245	246	247	248	249	250
C	A	A	C	A	B	C	D	C	D

251	252	253	254	255	256	257	258	259	260
B	B	C	B	C	C	C	D	B	C

261	262	263	264	265	266	267	268	269	270
C	D	D	B	A	A	C	B	A	C

271	272	273	274	275	276	277	278	279	280
B	C	D	B	B	C	C	B	D	B

281	282	283	284	285	286	287	288	289	290
D	B	C	C	D	D	C	B	C	C

291	292	293	294	295	296	297	298	299	300
D	D	C	C	C	D	B	B	A	C

301	302	303	304	305	306	307	308	309	310
A	A	D	D	B	C	C	C	B	A

311	312	313	314	315	316	317	318	319	320
D	B	D	D	C	B	B	A	D	D
321	**322**	**323**	**324**	**325**	**326**	**327**	**328**	**329**	**330**
A	A	A	B	D	D	C	A	C	A
331	**332**	**333**	**334**	**335**	**336**	**337**	**338**	**339**	**340**
C	A	B	D	D	D	A	C	A	A
341	**342**	**343**	**344**	**345**	**346**	**347**	**348**	**349**	**350**
D	A	C	A	B	A	D	A	C	B
351	**352**	**353**	**354**	**355**	**356**	**357**	**358**	**359**	**360**
B	A	B	A	B	D	A	A	D	D
361	**362**	**363**	**364**	**365**	**366**	**367**	**368**	**369**	**370**
D	B	A	D	A	D	A	A	C	D
371	**372**	**373**	**374**	**375**	**376**	**377**	**378**	**379**	**380**
D	B	D	D	C	B	D	C	D	D
381	**382**	**383**	**384**	**385**	**386**	**387**	**388**	**389**	**390**
A	B	A	A	B	C	C	D	D	C
391	**392**	**393**	**394**	**395**	**396**	**397**	**398**	**399**	**400**
C	C	B	B	B	C	B	D	B	C
401	**402**	**403**	**404**	**405**	**406**	**407**	**408**	**409**	**410**
B	B	C	C	A	B	C	B	D	C
411	**412**	**413**	**414**	**415**	**416**	**417**	**418**	**419**	**420**
B	B	A	B	A	D	B	C	B	D
421	**422**	**423**	**424**	**425**	**426**	**427**	**428**	**429**	**430**
D	B	B	C	B	D	B	C	B	C
431	**432**	**433**	**434**	**435**	**436**	**437**	**438**	**439**	**440**
B	A	A	B	B	D	D	C	D	C
441	**442**	**443**	**444**	**445**	**446**	**447**	**448**	**449**	**450**
D	C	D	C	B	B	D	D	C	A
451	**452**	**453**	**454**	**455**	**456**	**457**	**458**	**459**	**460**
D	B	D	D	D	C	C	A	C	C
461	**462**	**463**	**464**	**465**	**466**	**467**	**468**	**469**	**470**
C	B	C	B	B	A	C	B	D	D
471	**472**	**473**	**474**	**475**	**476**	**477**	**478**	**479**	**480**
A	C	D	A	A	B	D	C	B	A
481	**482**	**483**	**484**	**485**	**486**	**487**	**488**	**489**	**490**
A	C	B	B	C	B	B	B	A	D
491	**492**	**493**	**494**	**495**	**496**	**497**	**498**	**499**	**500**
A	C	D	A	A	A	C	B	B	A
501	**502**	**503**	**504**	**505**	**506**	**507**	**508**	**509**	**510**
C	C	B	C	B	B	A	B	B	B

511	512	513	514	515	516	517	518	519	520
B	D	C	C	B	A	C	A	D	C
521	522	523	524	525	526	527	528	529	530
C	D	B	D	D	C	A	D	C	A
531	532	533	534	535	536	537	538	539	540
A	A	A	C	D	B	C	B	C	C
541	542	543	544	545	546	547	548	549	550
A	B	C	D	A	C	A	A	B	A
551	552	553	554	555	556	557	558	559	560
C	A	B	D	A	D	C	A	D	A
561	562	563	564	565	566	567	568	569	570
B	A	A	D	C	A	C	A	B	B
571	572	573	574	575	576	577	578	579	580
B	A	C	D	D	B	C	A	C	D
581	582	583	584	585	586	587	588	589	590
C	B	B	B	D	A	C	C	A	C
591	592	593	594	595	596	597	598	599	600
C	D	C	A	D	C	D	C	D	C
601	602	603	604	605	606	607	608	609	610
D	B	C	C	B	B	B	A	C	C
611	612	613	614	615	616	617	618	619	620
A	B	C	C	A	A	A	B	C	A
621	622	623	624	625	626	627	628	629	630
B	A	D	A	A	C	D	B	C	D
631	632	633	634	635	636	637	638	639	640
D	B	B	B	A	B	B	C	C	C
641	642	643	644	645	646	647	648	649	650
A	A	B	B	C	B	A	A	C	C
651	652	653	654	655	656	657	658	659	660
D	C	B	D	A	C	C	B	C	D
661	662	663	664	665	666	667	668	669	670
A	C	B	B	B	D	C	A	D	D
671	672	673	674	675	676	677	678	679	680
C	D	C	A	D	D	D	D	B	B
681	682	683	684	685	686	687	688	689	690
C	C	C	B	D	C	C	C	C	D
691	692	693	694	695	696	697	698	699	700
A	D	B	C	B	C	B	C	D	C
701	702	703	704	705	706	707	708	709	710
B	D	D	C	C	A	A	B	D	B

711	712	713	714	715	716	717	718	719	720
C	C	D	C	B	B	C	C	C	C
721	722	723	724	725	726	727	728	729	730
A	A	A	C	D	B	C	B	C	A
731	732	733	734	735	736	737	738	739	740
B	A	B	B	B	B	A	A	D	A
741	742	743	744	745	746	747	748	749	750
D	B	B	D	A	D	D	A	A	C
751	752	753	754	755	756	757	758	759	760
B	A	B	A	D	B	A	D	A	B
761	762	763	764	765	766	767	768	769	770
C	A	B	B	A	A	B	B	D	C
771	772	773	774	775	776	777	778	779	780
D	D	D	C	B	B	A	A	D	D
781	782	783	784	785	786	787	788	789	790
C	C	D	A	C	B	D	B	C	D
791	792	793	794	795	796	797	798	799	800
D	A	D	D	D	B	C	C	C	D
801	802	803	804	805	806	807	808	809	810
B	D	B	D	C	D	C	B	C	D
811	812	813	814	815	816	817	818	819	820
D	D	A	B	D	D	C	A	C	A
821	822	823	824	825	826	827	828	829	830
D	A	A	B	D	D	D	C	D	D
831	832	833	834	835	836	837	838	839	840
C	D	B	D	A	A	D	D	B	D
841	842	843	844	845	846	847	848	849	850
A	C	B	A	A	A	A	C	C	A
851	852	853	854	855	856	857	858	859	860
D	D	B	D	B	C	D	D	B	C
861	862	863	864	865	866	867	868	869	870
A	D	A	D	D	D	A	C	A	B
871	872	873	874	875	876	877	878	879	880
A	A	D	B	D	A	D	B	D	B
881	882	883	884	885	886	887	888	889	890
C	C	D	D	D	B	D	A	D	C
891	892	893	894	895	896	897	898	899	900
D	C	D	D	D	C	D	D	D	C
901	902	903	904	905	906	907	908	909	910
D	B	D	D	D	D	C	C	A	B

911	912	913	914	915	916	917	918	919	920
D	B	C	B	A	D	D	C	C	A
921	922	923	924	925	926	927	928	929	930
C	B	D	B	C	B	A	A	B	D
931	932	933	934	935	936	937	938	939	940
A	A	B	D	C	D	A	B	C	A
941	942	943	944	945	946	947	948	949	950
D	A	D	A	D	B	A	B	B	C
951	952	953	954	955	956	957	958	959	960
A	C	B	C	D	D	C	D	B	A
961	962	963	964	965	966	967	968	969	970
D	D	B	D	C	A	C	C	B	B
971	972	973	974	975	976	977	978	979	980
C	B	B	B	D	C	D	B	D	B
981	982	983	984	985	986	987	988	989	990
D	A	B	A	A	A	B	A	B	B
991	992	993	994	995	996	997	998	999	1000
D	B	B	C	A	B	C	D	D	C
1001	1002	1003	1004	1005	1006	1007	1008	1009	1010
B	A	B	A	D	B	D	D	B	A
1011	1012								
C	B								

✩✩✩✩✩✩